PAGAN ROME
AND THE
EARLY
CHRISTIANS

PAGAN ROME
AND THE
EARLY
CHRISTIANS

Stephen Benko

B. T. BATSFORD LTD.
LONDON

To
Stephen Ernest Benko, Ph.D.

Contents

PREFACE ix
ABBREVIATIONS xi

i. The Name and Its Implications	1
ii. Portrait of an Early Christian	30
iii. The Charges of Immorality and Cannibalism	54
iv. The Kiss	79
v. Magic and Early Christianity	103
vi. Pagan Criticism of Christian Theology and Ethics	140

SUMMARY 163
BIBLIOGRAPHY 164
INDEX 177

PREFACE

The task of looking at the history of early Christianity from where the non-Christian Romans and Greeks stood is a fascinating and challenging one. One way of doing this is to study what the pagans said about Christians. There are no pagan references to Christianity in the first century of the empire and very few in the second. These have been collected and are easily accessible to students; many of them, moreover, were subject to detailed and precise scholarly analyses. I myself contributed to this effort with an article entitled, "Pagan Criticism of Christianity During the First Centuries A.D." (*Aufstieg und Niedergang der römischen Welt* II. 23/2 pp. 1055–1118). In that essay I collected and translated into English most passages from the works of Latin and Greek authors which mention Christians. It was this study that suggested to me to take one further step and ask the question why the pagans looked at Christians the way they did. To understand the pagan mentality, to find the clues that would shed light on their reaction, to search for their motives means to step out of our own preconceptions and to try to place ourselves into their history and milieu. My objective in this study is to interpret the material available to us from pagan authors in their own context and to avoid retrojecting into the second century the value judgments of the twentieth century.

This is necessary because the early church fathers' rejection of pagan charges against Christianity tends to slant the view against the pagans as if all anti-Christian authors had been victims of vicious misinformation and even guilty of malicious ill will. Pagan works are, therefore, sometimes treated with condescension and scorn, and the general tone of the scholarship of these works is that the pagans needed to be enlightened because what they thought and said about Christians was false. The premise of this book is to give the pagans the benefit of doubt and to assume that they have been right. The question then is, of course, to analyze within what context and what limitations their charges were true and how the church dealt with those problems.

Each chapter deals with a particular topic. First, we will investigate the fact that the name Christian alone caused many pagans to condemn Christianity. Second, we will follow the life story of an early Christian, Peregrinus, who returned to paganism. His story holds valuable insights concerning pagan-Christian relations. In the third chapter we analyze the pagan charges of cannibalism and immorality, and in the fourth we deal with the problems that may have been caused by the practice of the "holy kiss". The fifth chapter raises the question of whether the Christians were practicing magic, and if so, in what form and to what extent. Finally, we examine the scholarly criticism of Christian theology and ethics as they appeared to Galen and Celsus toward the end of the second century. Each of these chapters is complete in itself and the connecting link between them is the common vantage point: each sheds some light on a certain aspect of Christianity from the pagan side.

The basic material assembled in my article in the *ANRW* was enlarged here with new research especially in the area of Greco-Roman magical practices and Christianity for which California State University, Fresno, granted me a sabbatical during the winter session of 1981. I should like to express my gratitude for this generosity. My indebtedness to many scholarly works done in this area of historical research is obvious; the extensive footnotes and bibliographies give credit to those who traveled this path before me. This book has been written with the general reader in mind and thus technical terms and the use of foreign languages was avoided. The expert in the field and the student who wishes to learn more is advised to turn to the works listed in the bibliographies.

I should like to thank those colleagues of mine in the USA and in Europe who read portions of this manuscript and offered their friendly and constructive criticism. The library staff of California State University, Fresno, was helpful beyond the call of duty.

ABBREVIATIONS

ANF	Ante Nicene Fathers. Reprint by Eerdmans, 1951.
ANRW	Aufstieg und Niedergang der römischen Welt. Edited by A. Temporini and W. Haase. Berlin, de Gruyter. (Volumes still being published)
CSEL	*Corpus Scriptorum Ecclesiasticorum Latinorum,* 1866 ff.
GCS	Die griechischen christlichen Schriftsteller der ersten drei Jahrhunderte.
LCL	Loeb Classical Library
MPG	Migne, *Patrologia Series Graeca*
MPL	Migne, *Patrologia Series Latina*
NPNF	Nicene and Post Nicene Fathers. Reprint by Eerdmans, 1951.
RAC	Reallexikon für Antike und Christentum 1941 ff.
RGG³	Die Religion in Geschichte und Gegenwart, 3rd edition.
SHA	*Scriptores Historiae Augustae*
Theol. Realenc.	Theologische Realencyclopaedie

The Name and Its Implications

S OMETIME DURING THE reign of Emperor Antoninus Pius (86-161), a married woman became a Christian, although her husband did not. Later, irreconcilable differences arose between the two, and the woman divorced her husband. She did this simply by giving him a *repudium*, i.e., a letter of divorce. The embittered husband then denounced his former wife to the authorities on the charge of being a Christian. She was immediately arrested, but then granted a temporary release by the emperor so that she might put her affairs in order before reporting to the court to answer the accusation. The husband now denounced the woman's instructor in the Christian faith, a man by the name of Ptolemaeus, who was also arrested, put in chains, and carried off to prison, where he endured a long period of harsh treatment. Finally the day of his trial arrived, and he was led before the judge, Urbicus. Urbicus asked only one question of Ptolemaeus: "Are you a Christian?" When he replied in the affirmative, Ptolemaeus was sentenced to death and, since death sentences in Rome were carried out immediately, led away to execution. A certain Lucius, having witnessed the proceeding, rose in indignation and cried out to the judge: "Why did you pass such a sentence? Was this man convicted of a crime? Is he an adulterer, a murderer, a robber? All he did was confess that he was a Christian!" To this Urbicus replied: "It seems that you are a Christian too!" "Yes," said Lucius, "I am!" Urbicus promptly had him executed as well. A third Christian now came forward and received the same sentence. Justin, the philosopher and later Christian martyr (ca. 100-ca. 165), heard about this incident and in protest wrote a letter to the emperor, which has survived under the name of *The Second Apology* of Justin Martyr.[1]

The judge did not act capriciously; he based his sentences on judicial precedents and on universal imperial policy. Nor was the case of the three martyrs an isolated one. Second-century Christian apologists often complained that although other defendants were tried in court on the basis of specific charges that were properly investigated by the magistrates, Christians received the death sentence simply because of their name. Justin himself, in his *First Apology*, addressed to Emperor Antoninus Pius, begged for nothing more than that specific charges be presented against the Christians and that only if the charges were substantiated should the persons involved be punished as they deserved. But, he argued, if no one could bring proof of criminal activities then their punishment simply for being Christian was a gross violation of reason and justice. "By the mere application of a name, nothing is decided, either good or evil, apart from the actions implied in the name; and indeed, so far at least as one may judge from the name we are accused of, we are a most excellent people."[2]

In the second part of this sentence Justin referred to the occasional spelling of the name "Christian" as *Chrestianus* in Latin, and the coincidence that in the Greek language the word *Chrēstos* means "good." So, in the same chapter he wrote: "For we are accused of being Christians (*Chrestiani*) but to hate what is good (*Chrēstos*) is unjust." This is, of course, merely a play on words, more bitter than sarcastic.[3] Nevertheless, serious circumstances had brought forth his plea: innocent people were being punished by death simply because of their name. To be sure, Justin admitted that some Christians were indeed guilty of criminal activities. Justin, therefore, asked that criminals be punished as criminals and not as Christians and that the innocent be permitted to go free. Later, he quoted the words of Jesus: "By their works you shall know them . . . ," and added: "We ask, therefore, that you should punish those who are not living according to his teachings and are Christians only in name."[4] Tatian, a pupil of Justin's, who later went to the eastern part of the empire and founded a gnostic-encratitic sect, also wrote an apology called *Address to the Greeks*, in which he argued in much the same way as his master: "Is it not unreasonable that, while the robber is not to be punished for the name he bears, but only when the truth about him has been clearly ascertained, yet we are to be assailed with abuse on a judgment formed without examination."[5]

Some twenty years later, Athenagoras, "The Athenian philosopher and Christian," as he is identified in the title of his essay, wrote *A Plea for the Christians*, addressing it to Marcus Aurelius and his son Commodus (ca. 177). Athenagoras started with the same complaint:

Matt 7 16

"Why is a mere name odious to you? Names are not deserving of hatred; it is the unjust act that calls for penalty and punishment." Yet, he said, the Christians were harassed and made to suffer unjustly, contrary to all law and reason. Athenagoras did not try to excuse Christians from punishment if they were convicted of a crime, "but if the accusation relates merely to our name" then, he argued, this spiteful treatment should end. In the case of the Christians their mere name carried more weight than the evidence. "No name in and by itself is reckoned either good or bad; names appear bad or good according as the actions underlying them are bad or good."[6] Equal justice should be applied to all, Athenagoras argued, and he refuted the charges and rumors leveled against Christians.

Tertullian, the Carthaginian lawyer and Christian (160-220), also discussed the Romans' treatment of the Christians. He wrote two treatises in refutation of false rumors that associated Christians with evil practices: the *Ad nationes* and the *Apologeticum*, both written in 197. From his writings it is clear that twenty years after Athenagoras's plea (and thirty years after Justin's death) the situation had not changed at all. "No name of a crime stands against us, but only the crime of a name," Tertullian cried in *Ad nationes*. "What crime, what offence, what fault is there in a name?" He went on to explain, as Justin had done before him, that since *Chrēstos* means good, the name should not be punished. In the *Apologeticum* Tertullian again protested the discrimination against Christians in judicial proceedings.

> If it is certain that we are the most wicked of men, why do you treat us so differently from all fellows, that is, from other criminals, it being only fair that the same crime should get the same treatment? When the charges made against us are made against others, they are permitted to make use both of their own lips and of hired pleaders to show their innocence. They have full opportunity of answer and debate; in fact, it is against the law to condemn anybody undefended and unheard. Christians alone are forbidden to say anything in exculpation of themselves, in defence of the truth, to help the judge to a righteous decision; all that is cared about is having what the public hatred demands—the confession of the name, not examination of the charge.

Then Tertullian tried to demonstrate that the magistrates acted illogically in their treatment of the Christians: he argued that when criminals denied the charges brought against them, nobody readily believed them, but when a Christian denied what he was, everybody was immediately satisfied. But when a Christian admitted what he was, the magistrate then wanted to hear him deny it![7]

These complaints, echoed by many other early Christian apologists, were dramatically substantiated by a description of the martyrdom of Polycarp, bishop of Smyrna. At the time of his arrest the magistrate urged Polycarp to save his life by performing the required sacrifices. He refused. Then he was brought into the stadium of the city of Smyrna, where the proconsul tried with no greater success to persuade him to change his mind. When it became clear that all appeals were for nought, the proconsul "sent his herald to proclaim in the midst of the stadium thrice 'Polycarp has confessed that he is a Christian.'" The multitude then demanded the execution of the eighty-six-year-old bishop. He was burned at the stake, probably on February 22, 156. Now, if that were the end of the story we could perhaps accept the claim that the Greco-Roman population had an unfounded and illogical bias against the Christians. But the account of Polycarp's martyrdom continues. We read that as soon as the pronouncement was made, "the whole multitude both of the heathen and Jews, who dwelt at Smyrna, cried out with uncontrollable fury, and in a loud voice, 'This is the teacher of Asia, the father of the Christians, and the overthrower of our gods, he who has been teaching many not to sacrifice, or to worship the gods.'"[8] It appears that the second-century Christian apologists oversimplified matters when they asserted that the people associated nothing bad with the Christian name. Polycarp's case brings to surface the real accusation: He was an overthrower of the gods, and he encouraged many people not to sacrifice or to worship the gods. This, then, is the real reason why he was executed; the multitude assumed that by professing to being a Christian he had confessed to luring the people away from their ancient gods, thus upsetting the prevailing social order.

The Letters of Pliny and Trajan

Fortunately, there exists a non-Christian document that deals with the Christian problem, which permits us to see it from the perspective of the pagans.[9] The document is the famous correspondence of the governor of Bithynia-and-Pontus, Pliny the Younger, with Emperor Trajan. Gais Plinius Caecilius Secundus (61 or 62–ca. 113), was the son of a landowner, was raised by his uncle, the author Pliny the Elder. Like most Roman citizens of his class, he studied rhetoric (under Quintilian) and then entered the civil service. He moved upward through the ranks, becoming consul in 100, after having held other important positions, notably those of prefect of the military treasury, *praefectus aerari militaris*, established by Octavian Augustus for military expenditures, and prefect of the old republican treasury, *aerarium Saturni*, the traditional treasury that administered all income from the provinces. He was a member of Trajan's advisory council, *consilum principis*, and thus part of the "high society" of his times.

Pliny's letter to Trajan is an important source on early Christianity. Because of his legal training and experience in government, Trajan chose Pliny as governor of the province of Bithynia-and-Pontus, where he served from September 111 until his death in 113. The province was in a state of disorder, and Trajan gave Pliny considerable freedom to do whatever was needed to restore law and order. As a loyal civil servant Pliny knew the limits of his authority and frequently consulted the emperor when matters of importance came to his attention. Trajan then would send a reply informing Pliny of his decisions. Pliny saved copies of his letters together with Trajan's replies and later published them. The correspondence has survived, and it is one of these exchanges of letters, dated 111, that deals with the Christians.

But before we turn to the letters it is important to know a little more about Trajan. Born in Spain of a Roman father and a Spanish mother, he rose rapidly in the administration and was governor of Upper Germany when the aged Emperor Nerva adopted him and made him his legal heir. Trajan was emperor from 98 to 117, and on his death the Senate bestowed on him the honorary title "Best Emperor," *Optimis Princeps*. He richly deserved this title not only because of his military conquests but also because of his enlightened and progressive policies at home. His family background probably made him particularly sensitive to the problems of the provinces, and his letters to Pliny reveal a paternalistic interest in everything that was happening in Bithynia-and-Pontus, especially matters affecting the welfare of its inhabitants and the financial health of its communities. The letters of these two Romans, giving us the first report of the pagan encounter with Christianity, are worth quoting in full.

   It is a rule, Sir, which I inviolably observe, to refer to you in all my
   doubts; for who is more capable of guiding my uncertainty or inform-

ing my ignorance? Having never been present at any trials of the Christians, I am unacquainted with the method and limits to be observed either in examining or punishing them. Whether any difference is to be made on account of age, or no distinction allowed between the youngest and the adult; whether repentance admits to a pardon, or if a man has been once a Christian it avails him nothing to recant; whether the mere profession Christianity, albeit without crimes, or only the crimes associated therewith are punishable—in all these points I am greatly doubtful.

In the meanwhile, the method I have observed towards those who have been denounced to me as Christians is this: I interrogated them whether they were Christians; if they confessed it, I repeated the question twice again, adding the threat of capital punishment; if they still persevered, I ordered them to be executed. For whatever the nature of their creed might be, I could at least feel no doubt that contumacy and inflexible obstinancy deserved chastisement. There were others also possessed with the same infatuation, but being citizens of Rome, I directed them be carried thither.

These accusations spread (as is usually the case) from the mere fact of the matter being investigated and several forms of the mischief came to light. A placard was put up, without any signature, accusing a large number of persons by name. Those who denied they were, or had ever been, Christians, who repeated after me an invocation to the gods, and offered adoration, with wine and frankincense, to your image, which I had ordered to be brought for that purpose, together with those of the gods, and who finally cursed Christ—none of which acts, it is said, those who are really Christians can be forced into performing—these I thought it proper to discharge. Others who were named by that informer at first confessed themselves Christians, and then denied it; true, they had been of the persuasion but they had quitted it, some three years ago. They all worshipped your statute and the images of the gods, and cursed Christ.

They affirmed, however, the whole of their guilt, or their error, was, that they were in the habit of meeting on a certain fixed day before it was light, when they sang in alternate verses a hymn to Christ, as to a god, and bound themselves by a solemn oath, not to commit any wicked deeds, fraud, theft or adultery, never to falsify their word, nor deny a trust when they should be called upon to deliver it up; after which it was their custom to separate, and then reassemble to partake of food—but food of an ordinary and innocent kind. Even this practice, however, they had abandoned after the publication of my edict, by which, according to your orders, I had forbidden political associations. I judged it so much the more necessary to extract the real truth, with the assistance of torture, from two female slaves, who were styled deaconesses: but I could discover nothing more than depraved and excessive superstition.

I therefore adjourned the proceedings, and betook myself at once to your counsel. For the matter seemed to me well worth referring to you,—especially considering the numbers endangered. Persons of all ranks and ages, and of both sexes are, and will be, involved in the prosecution. For this contagious superstition is not confined to the cities only, but had spread through the villages and rural districts; it seems possible, however, to check and cure it. 'Tis certain at least that the temples, which had been almost deserted, begin now to be frequented; and the sacred festivals, after a long intermission, are again revived; while there is a general demand for sacrificial animals, which for some time past have met with but few purchasers. From hence it is easy to imagine what multitudes may be reclaimed from this error, if a door be left open to repentance. [Pliny's letter to Trajan, 10.96]

The method you have pursued, my dear Pliny, in sifting the cases of those denounced to you as Christians is extremely proper. It is not possible to lay down any general rule which can be applied as the fixed standard in all cases of this nature. No search should be made for these people; when they are denounced and found guilty they must be punished; with the restriction, however, that when the party denies himself to be a Christian, and shall give proof that he is not (that is, by adoring our gods) he shall be pardoned on the ground of repentance, even though he may have formerly incurred suspicion. Informations without the accuser's name subscribed must not be admitted in evidence against anyone, as it is introducing a very dangerous precedent, and by no means agreeable to the spirit of the age." [Trajan's reply, 10.97][10]

Pliny wrote to the emperor due to the many controversial issues that arose whenever charges were leveled against Christians and to ask his advice. Because he had never attended a legal investigation of Christians, he was unfamiliar with the procedures to be followed. This may mean that such investigations, trials, had already taken place and Pliny knew about them, although he himself had never been involved in any. Then there were other problems: as a judge should he make a distinction between children and adults, should he pardon and release a Christian who denounced his faith, and, perhaps most important, should he regard the mere profession of Christianity (the name alone) as sufficient ground for sentencing, or should he look for an actual crime committed by the accused and possibly dismiss the case if the accuser could not specify any charges besides "the name"?

We have seen that the prosecution of Christians began with their denunciation by individuals exercising a legal right to act as informers for the state. Pliny made it clear that this was also the case in Bithynia-and-Pontus but he did not give any hint as to who the informers were, and so we must resort to hypothesis in order to identify a particular group of people with an interest in hurting the Christians. According to Acts 19:23 ff., a silversmith by the name of Demetrius stirred up the people against the Christians because of his fear that, if Paul was permitted to continue making converts, demand for sacrificial items would decline and those engaged in the business would suffer financial loss. Could this have been the case in Bithynia-and-Pontus? Perhaps so. At the end of his letters Pliny mentioned that temples were nearly deserted and the trade in the meat of sacrificial victims had declined—until he began to crack down on the Christians. But again in Acts 18:12 ff., the Jews are mentioned as the ones who denounced Paul to the proconsul Gallio with arguments that could have been used elsewhere and that remind us of the charges against Polycarp: "This man is persuading men to worship God contrary to the law." Gallio, a brother of Seneca and proconsul in Achaea around 51–53, refused to hear the case with these words: "If it were a matter of wrong-doing or vicious crime, I should have reason to bear with you, O Jews; but since it is a matter of questions about *words and names* and your own law, see to it yourself; I refuse to be a judge of these things." Gallio, in other words refused to try a case based on "the name" alone and which lacked specific charges. The resemblance to Pliny's situation is very close, although we must remember that Pliny faced the problem some sixty years later, by which time Christians had become a much more noticeable minority in some areas. Thus, although Gallio treated the problem as an internal affair of the Jews (which it was then), Pliny could no longer afford to take this stand.

Whoever the informers may have been, the information that they related to Pliny was simply that they knew certain people to be "Christians." They mentioned no crimes, a fact that did not seem to disturb the governor, at least in the first few cases. He proceeded with the trials as if the charge had been murder or adultery or something else specifically forbidden by law. He asked the accused whether the charge was true or not, just as a judge today asks the accused "How do you plead? Guilty or not guilty?" The difference, of course, lay in the question that Pliny asked: "Are you a Christian?" If the prisoner acknowledged that he was, Pliny repeated the question twice more, explaining the nature of the punishment that a guilty verdict would bring. Then, if the answer remained the same, he pronounced the death sentence, and the condemned was led away for immediate execution, unless he was a Roman citizen, in which case he was sent to Rome.[11] A lengthy trial and the calling of witnesses was only necessary if the person denied the charge, as the next part of Pliny's letter makes clear. Before we go any further we must ask why Pliny, a well-trained lawyer and experienced civil servant, acted in such a way. Why did he not summarily dismiss the case, as Gallio had done? It appears from Tertullian, although he was unclear on this point, that Nero issued a law against the Christians, the so-called *institutum Neronianum*, the only law of Nero's that was not abolished after his death.[12] If this was indeed the case, Pliny could have had a legal justification. But, if Nero did indeed pass an *institutum Neronianum* against the Christians, it is very doubtful that it was maintained after his death, when all other laws passed by him were invalidated. In all likelihood, no anti-Christian law existed; thus Tertullian meant only that the persecution of Christians began with Nero and, alone among his practices, seems to have survived him. Moreover, if a law had existed, Pliny would not have had to write to Trajan for instructions.[13] Therefore, we must look elsewhere for an answer.

One clue is provided by a small incident related by the elder Pliny. The emperor Claudius once received a Roman knight for an audience, in the course of which it was noticed that the knight wore a Druidic talisman on his breast. For this he was immediately sentenced to death.[14] Druidism constituted the main rallying point for forces in Gaul that resisted Romanization of the province, so that sympathy with Druidism could be interpreted as anti-Romanism and as a crime against the state. Its adherents were also known to perform human sacrifices, a practice abhorrent to Romans. Such were the negative connotations attached to the name "Druid" that without any further investigation the Romans presumed criminal behavior. So it must have been with Pliny; he identified the Christians so closely with certain antisocial and criminal activities (rightly and wrongly is not now the point) as to regard an affirmative answer to his question as an admission of criminal guilt.

After the first few executions Pliny, being a man of integrity, began to have second thoughts. Of course, it was too late to do anything about those who had already been killed, so he justified his actions to the emperor (and possibly first of all to himself) with the statement that "whatever the nature of their creed might be, I could at least feel no doubt that contumacy and inflexible obstinacy deserved chastisement." What "contumacy"? Admitting three times that they were

Christians? And what "inflexible obstinacy"? Denying the governor's authority, contemptuous behavior, arrogance? Neither of these normally merited capital punishment, and his explanation sounds like a lame excuse. But Pliny resolved to be more careful in the future. The trials set off a torrent of denunciations. These he investigated thoroughly—although he was mildly reprimanded by the emperor for accepting anonymous accusations, in violation of the Roman concept of justice that required the accuser to face the accused. The governor found that some accusations were without merit because the accused denied that they had ever been Christians. Others admitted that they had been Christians at one time, but were no longer. In both cases Pliny administered a simple test consisting of three parts. First, the accused worshipped the Roman gods, repeating after Pliny a simple invocation to the gods; second, they made a sacrifice, offering frankincense and wine before the images of the gods and the emperor; third, they cursed Christ. We do not know the origin of this last custom, the cursing of Christ. Nor do we know how Pliny thought of using this device to force the accused to demonstrate publicly that they never had been, or were no longer, Christians. The cursing of Christ is mentioned in 1. Cor. 12:3, indicating that the Romans used it as early as the time of Paul. "No one speaking of the Spirit of God ever says 'Jesus be cursed' and no one can say 'Jesus the Lord' except by the Holy Spirit." Several allusions to it also exist in the early Christian literature of the second century, after Pliny's time. For example, the governor of the province of Asia urged the aged Bishop Polycarp to blaspheme Christ in order to gain his freedom, by saying "Jesus be cursed" or "Christ be cursed."[15] Pliny undoubtedly knew that a real Christian would never agree to do this, nor to the other two parts of the test.

Once exonerated, the former Christians furnished Pliny with a description of Christian practices that so aroused his suspicions that he ordered the torture of two female Christian slaves to uncover the whole truth. To his great relief, he found nothing more than a "depraved and excessive supersition." But what had troubled him in the accounts by the former Christians, causing him to undertake further investigation?

First, the Christians came together "before daylight," and that suggested some sort of conspiracy under cover of the darkness of night. That Christians gathered at daybreak in commemoration of the resurrection did not occur to Pliny (how could it?), but he may well have remembered that in Roman history conspiracies against the government and nightly meetings often went hand in hand, for example in 63 B.C., when Cataline had tried to overthrow the government. This event was well known even in Pliny's time because of the published speeches by Cicero[16] and the account by Sallust.[17] Indeed, even Plutarch (ca. 46-120), a contemporary of Pliny's, mentioned it in his biography of Cicero,[18] and the satirist Juvenal (ca. 60-140), another contemporary of Pliny's, referred to it in one of his poems.[19] The venerated Twelve Tables, the very foundation of Roman law, forbade nightly meetings,[20] and thus Pliny's suspicions were understandably aroused. And Pliny was not alone in his apprehension of this Christian custom. The general public associated nightly meetings with secrecy, and secrecy meant that the Christians had something to hide. Minucius Felix (*floruit* 200-240), probably drawing on the anti-Christian rhetoric of Marcus Cornelius Fronto (ca. 100-166), criticized the Christians in his book *Octavius* as, among other things an "unlawful and desperate faction . . . which is leagued together by nightly meetings . . . a people skulking and shunning the light. . . ." Then he added the ominous sentence: "Certainly suspicion is applicable to secret and nocturnal rites!"[21] And as late as the early third century, Bishop Cyprian was accused of being a member of a "nefarious conspiracy."[22] Of course, as we shall presently see, the public associated secrecy and nightly meetings with harmful magic, which only added to Pliny's problem.

Livy's description of the suppression of the Bacchanalia in 186 B.C. may also have colored Pliny's and other educated Romans' view of Christianity. Although this event took place almost three hundred years before Pliny's time, the tremendous popularity of Livy's history of Rome made the story available and well known to the reading public, which may have drawn parallels between the Bacchanalia and the Christian problem. Whether it did we cannot know for sure (no Roman author likens Christianity to the Bacchanalian conspiracy), but a brief look at Livy 39.8-19 shows that a close comparison was indeed feasible. According to Livy, the two consuls in the year 186 investigated secret conspiracies, among them the Bacchanalia, which had been introduced to Etruria by a Greek acting as, in Livy's words, a "priest of secret rites performed by night." "Like the contagion of pestilence," the Bacchanalia spread to Rome, where devotees including people of high rank, engaged in illegal activities. The secrets of the Bacchanalia were betrayed to one of the consuls, who reported his

findings to the Senate. "Great panic seized the Fathers, both on the
public account, lest these conspiracies and gatherings by night might
produce something of hidden treachery or danger, and privately each
for himself, lest anyone might be involved in the mischief." The
Senate passed an ordinance forbidding Bacchic assemblies throughout Italy, and in Rome guards were placed everywhere to see that no
night meetings were held and that provisions were made against fire.
After these precautionary measures the consuls called a meeting of
the people and addressed them from the *Rostra* of the Forum. A
prayer was said, and one of the consuls explained that a false and
foreign religion (*prava et externo religio*) was driving men to crime
and lust. "Of what sort, do you think, are first, gatherings held by
night, second, meetings of men and women in common?" The security of the state seemed, therefore, threatened by a foreign ritual. The
consuls promised to take strong measures. Many thousands were
arrested, and the Bacchanalia were forbidden except for the traditional local observances of the rites of Bacchus. Livy's account ends
at this point.[23] It shows that secret nightly gatherings of all kinds, but
especially those in which men and women met promiscuously for a
religious observance of foreign origin, had been suspect for a very long
time. Any upright Roman administrator would have recognized the
possibility of treason, arson, or magic in the Christians' night meetings, as Pliny had done. In Roman eyes the Christians could be up to
no good if they had to hide what they were doing. This conclusion
was inevitable for anyone who lacked further information. Here
again we sense, that, as with Polycarp, the Christians did not receive
the treatment they did from the Romans simply because of their
name. Instead their treatment stemmed from the Roman suspicion
and fear of serious crime against the established order.

Furthermore, other aspects of the Christians' meetings disturbed
Pliny. They sang a hymn (*carmen*) to Christ as to a god, they took an
oath (*sacramentum*) not to commit major crimes, and they had a
common meal—all potentially dangerous signs. A *carmen* was not
necessarily a harmless raising of voices; it could also signify an
"incantation," the casting of a magical spell. It is in this latter sense
that the word is used in the Twelve Tables.[24] But of course, the term
could also mean just a solemn saying in rhythmical form, such as the
Carmen Arvale, the ritual hymn of the Arval brethren, or the *Carmen
Saliare*, the ritual hymn of the Saliar priests. The word *sacramentum*
could be equally ambiguous. It could simply mean the oath of alle-

giance of a soldier or, more sinisterly, the initiation into a mystery in which the candidate took an oath of secrecy and allegiance to the principles of the cult. And such a mystery-oath was not necessarily innocent and harmless, as the case of the Bacchanalia had shown.[25] In the Catilinian conspiracy the participants had also taken an oath that they reinforced by murder and the communal eating of human flesh.[26] Was the eating together and the oath taking by the Christians also part of some strange magical practice? What did these Christians eat during their nightly meeting? Pliny was pleased to report to the emperor that his investigation had revealed that the Christians ate food "of an ordinary and innocent kind" and that they had even stopped their communal meals when Trajan forbade the formation of clubs (*collegia*). Furthermore, the *carmen* was not a magical spell but an innocent hymn. Nor was there any sign of a conspiracy with political overtones; the Christians simply took an oath to observe the law.[27]

Pliny was now satisfied that the name was not identical with crime. He reversed his original strict stand and adopted an attitude of leniency toward the Christians. He suspended any further trials, and he recommended to the emperor to leave the way open for repentance. Christianity, he said, should be treated as a curable disease. If it was so treated a multitude of people could be restored to spiritual health.

Trajan did not address the major issue of whether the name alone or the crimes connected with the name should be punished in his short reply to Pliny. Instead Trajan laid down certain principles covering the trial of Christians that remained in force for the next several generations. Trajan's fundamental concern was that the trials conform to accepted standards. Thus, those standing trial must be openly accused and convicted before being punished. Accused of what, and punished for what? All indications are that for Trajan the name alone (*nomen ipsum*) constituted the crime. It appears that he tacitly assumed that Christianity automatically and inevitably led to wrongdoing, at least in the sense that refusal to worship the Roman gods harmed the tranquility of the state. Therefore, Trajan stipulated, those who worshipped the gods, regardless of whether they were falsely accused or apostatized during the trial, should be permitted to go free. Anonymous denunciations were not to be accepted because they were contrary to "the spirit of the age." Here Trajan contrasted his own enlightened rule with that of previous emperors, who had terrorized people with spies and had threatened the lives of their citizens. In short, Trajan's rescript accepted the name alone as still sufficient to bring punishment to a Christian, but it made trials more difficult and orderly and at least temporarily restrained violent mob actions. Significantly, it embodied no legislation against Christians. Trajan ordered no general persecution and, indeed, expressly forbade the hunting down of Christians. His rescript thus effected some slight improvement in the lot of the Christian community, but, in spite of Pliny's noble effort, the odium of the name remained.

Tacitus and Suetonius

The works of two historians, both contemporaries of Pliny, namely Tacitus (ca. 55–ca. 117) and Suetonius (ca. 70–ca. 160), shed further light on Roman treatment of Christians. Tacitus's political career began under Vespasian (69-79) and continued under his two sons, Titus (79-81) and Domitian (89-96). During the reign of Trajan, Tacitus reached the zenith of his senatorial career when he was appointed governor of the province of Asia, which embraced the western part of Asia Minor, southwest of Bithynia-and-Pontus, where Pliny was governor. Tacitus probably served as governor during 112-113, just after Pliny had written his report on the Christians. Like Pliny, Tacitus also belonged to the upper class, and this is reflected in his historical perspectives and analyses. He turned to the writing of history in middle age, producing several magnificent books that are still considered veritable gems among the historical works of ancient times. Gaius Suetonius Tranquillus, probably born during the first year of Vespasian's rule, was younger than Tacitus and Pliny. Little is known of his life, except that he was a lawyer and a close friend of Pliny. Suetonius must have been a polished and prolific writer (the tenth-century lexicon *Suda* mentions eighteen titles by him) but only one of his works survives, the *Lives of the Twelve Caesars*, a series of biographies of the emperors beginning with Julius Caesar and ending with Domitian. Although these histories do not compare favorably with the searching and often tortured analytical accounts by Tacitus, they are invaluable sources for the human side of the emperors' lives. A painstaking researcher, interested in minute details, he wrote with brevity and candor, making his subjects come alive.

Suetonius and Tacitus mention Christianity only once each in their surviving works. First, let us deal with the passage by Tacitus in the *Annals*, published in 117. Originally the *Annals* included the time span from the death of Augustus to the death of Nero; large parts of it are lost, however, and the account that has come down to us ends in the year 66. In the following passage Tacitus describes the fire in Rome in 66 during Nero's reign.

> So far, the precautions taken were suggested by human prudence: now means were sought for appeasing deity, and application was made to the Sibylline books; at the injunction of which public prayers were offered to Vulcan, Ceres, and Proserpine, while Juno was propitiated by the matrons, first in the Capitol, then at the nearest point of the sea-shore, where water was drawn for sprinkling the temple and image of the goddess. Ritual banquets and all-night vigils were celebrated by women in the married state. But neither human help, nor imperial munificence, nor all the modes of placating Heaven, could stifle scandal or dispel the belief that the fire had taken place by order. Therefore to scotch the rumour, Nero substituted as culprits, and punished with the utmost refinements of cruelty, a class of men, loathed for their vices, whom the crowd styled Christians.[28] Christus, the founder of the name, had undergone the death penalty in the reign of Tiberius, by sentence of the procurator Pontius Pilatus, and the pernicious superstition was checked for a moment, only to break out once more, not merely in Judaea, the home of the disease, but in the capital itself, where all things horrible or shameful in the world collect and find a vogue. First, then, the confessed members of the sect were arrested; next, on their disclosures, vast numbers were convicted, not so much on the count of arson as for hatred of the human race. And derision accompanied their end: they were covered with wild beasts' skins and torn to death by dogs; or they were fastened on crosses, and, when daylight failed were burned to serve as lamps by night. Nero had offered his gardens for the spectacle, and gave an exhibition in his circus, mixing with the crowd in the habit of a charioteer, or mounted on his car. Hence, in spite of a guilt which had earned the most exemplary punishment, there arose a sentiment of pity, due to the impression that they were being sacrificed not for the welfare of the state but to the ferocity of a single man. [15.44][29]

Despite the fact that Tacitus's purpose in this passage was not the same as Pliny's—Tacitus did not seek to deal with the problem of Christianity but rather to illustrate the depravity of Nero—we can still uncover much of his view of this, for him new, Christian phenomenon. Clearly, he was familiar with Christianity. As governor of Asia he could hardly have been ignorant of Trajan's rescript, and his province must have had just as many if not more Christians than Pliny's had. Furthermore, Tacitus was in Rome in 95, when Emperor

Domitian's niece Domitilla and her husband, Favius Clemens, were "accused of atheism, for which offense a number of others also, who had been carried away into Jewish customs, were condemned, some to death, others to confiscation of property."[30] Domitilla was exiled and Clemens was executed, although embracing Jewish customs was not a crime, since Judaism was a recognized religion. Thus it is possible that Judaism here really means Christianity and that Tacitus knew about the existence of Christian groups in Rome even before he came to Asia. He was too good a historian not to look into the origin of the cult, and he even discovered that its founder was one "Christus,"[31] executed during the reign of Tiberius by order of Pontius Pilatus. Tacitus saw Christianity as a "superstition" of Jewish origin, and he disliked the Jews as a people. He characterized Jewish customs as "perverse and disgusting" and the Jews themselves as a people who are true only to each other, for "the rest of mankind they hate and view as enemies."[32] He also charged the Christians with a "hatred of the human race." It seems that he drew no distinction between Jews and Christians, in spite of the fact that by the time he wrote the *Annals* important differences did exist between the two groups, as further investigation would have made clear.

But the burning of Rome happened more than fifty years before Tacitus wrote, when Jews and Christians had not yet completely parted company. Tacitus regarded Nero's action as aimed against a particularly dangerous Jewish sect, and he fully approved of it. The Christians were a people "who were hated because of their crimes"; they were "guilty and deserved exemplary punishment." What was their guilt? What crimes did they commit? Tacitus did not say. Perhaps he simply associated some of the rumors that he himself had picked up about the Christians, and that were by the second century indelibly attached to the name, with Nero's time. Whether he believed that Christians indeed started the fire is difficult to determine. He said that the Christians confessed, but we do not know whether they confessed to starting the fire or, as in Pliny's initial investigation, simply to being Christians. To be sure, it was not uncommon for arsonists to be condemned to die by burning or by being torn to pieces by animals.[33] But Tacitus quickly dropped the charge of arson and talked instead of the Christians' "hatred of the human race." Suetonius, in his biography of Nero, treated both the fire and the persecution of the Christians, but in two different places and as unrelated events. Later Christian writers, in describing the Neronian persecutions, made no reference to the charge of arson either. Some scholars have proposed that Christians did indeed start the fire in an attempt to hasten the coming of the eschatological flames; however, this cannot be considered as more than conjecture.[34]

Destructive fires sometimes did break out in Rome, and the fear of such conflagrations is a recurring theme in Roman literature. In both the suppression of the Bacchanalia and the Catalinian conspiracy, the accused were suspected of seeking to set the city on fire. Josephus, in his description of the plight of the Jews in Antioch before and after the capture of Jerusalem, also mentions a problem with arsonists. At the beginning of hostilities between Romans and Jews, a renegade Jew, Antiochus, in an effort to convince the Greeks that he had totally given up Judaism, denounced the Jews in the theater and accused them of a conspiracy to burn down the whole city in a single night. He also named persons supposedly involved in the plot, and they were immediately arrested and burned to death in the theater itself. A pogrom broke out against the Jews during which, on Antiochus's advice, the Jews were forced to sacrifice according to Greek customs, on pain of execution. Now, after the capture of Jerusalem, a fire did break out in Antioch, destroying large parts of the city. Antiochus put the blame on the Jews, and the magistrates had difficulty restraining the mob. Eventually the real culprits for the fire were identified as a group of people who could not pay their debts and thought that by burning down the hall of records they might avoid being called on to do so. None of them was Jewish.[35]

The great fire at Rome in 64, described by Tacitus, may also have been deliberately set; Tacitus reported that people were seen openly hurling brands, and that after five days, when the flames had finally begun to die down, they suddenly flared up again.[36] But who started the fire? The popular suspicion that Nero started it because he had grandiose plans to rebuild the city is hardly tenable since his own house was devoured by the flames, and even Tacitus admitted that the emperor went to great lengths to relieve the sufferings of the population.

What, then, can we conclude about this tragic fire and, most of all, about the involvement of Christians in it? The Jews, of course, could have been an easy target because they were regarded as misanthropes, not by Tacitus alone, but by the vast majority of Romans, and they had a long history of conflict with the authorities in Rome. In 139 B.C. the city authorities had expelled them for "attempting to corrupt

Roman morals by the cult of Jupiter Sabazius."[37] Tiberius expelled them again in A.D. 19 because they "had flocked to Rome in great numbers and were converting many of the natives to their ways."[38] Josephus attributes this expulsion to a charge that four Jews had stolen an offering from a Roman matron.[39] In this expulsion Tiberius had several Jews executed and four thousand sent to Sardinia. In A.D. 41 Claudius took action against them. Dio wrote, "As for the Jews, who had again increased so greatly that by reason of their multitude it would have been hard without raising a tumult to bar them from the city, he did not drive them out, but ordered them, while continuing their traditional mode of life not to hold meetings."[40] Eight years later, in 49, Claudius did expel the Jews from Rome. In this last expulsion, according to Acts 18:2, Aquila and Priscilla, who may already have been converted to Christianity, had to leave Rome and moved to Corinth, where they became companions of Paul's.

Suetonius briefly recorded Claudius's edict of 49: "Since the Jews constantly made disturbance at the instigation of Chrestus, he expelled them from Rome."[41] Once again we see the colloquial Latin spelling of *Christus* as *Chrestus*, which Christian apologists used to compare with the similar sounding Greek word *Chrēstos*, meaning "good." Some scholars believe that Suetonius referred here to Jesus Christ, and that the disturbances occurred in the synagogues between Jews who accepted Jesus Christ as the Messiah and those who did not.[42] Acts 13:44ff., and 17:1ff., shows that these messianic controversies did not necessarily remain within the walls of the synagogue or the boundaries of the congregation. Sometimes the contending factions became so volatile as to carry their demonstrations into the streets, thus calling forth the intervention of the magistrates, among them Gallio, whom we discussed above.[43] This could have happened in Rome at the relatively early date of 49, but in this case we must assume that Suetonius confused the founder of the Christian religion with somebody who lived in Rome around this time, an unlikely possibility. In another passage (quoted below) he does spell the name "Christian" with an "i," just as Tacitus does; so he, too, must have understood that the name "Christian" derived from the name of the founder of the movement, Christus. In point of fact, the name Chrestus was very common in Rome.[44] We may, therefore, with some justification assume that Suetonius was indeed referring to a person by the name of Chrestus. If such is the case, then it remains only to ask what was the nature of the disturbances caused by this Chrestus.

Demonstrations, street fights, and clashes of all kinds involving Jews were not unusual during this time. The *Antiquities*, by Josephus, reports several of them. When the newly appointed Jewish king, Agrippa I, visited Alexandria in 38 serious riots occurred in which the Jews suffered grievously. When Agrippa died in 44 riots broke out in Caesarea and Sebaste, and when Fadus became governor the Jews rioted in Jerusalem. To these must be added a series of Jewish out-bursts led by radical religious and political enthusiasts, such as the disturbances instigated in Philadelphia in 45 or 46, first by a certain Annibas and then by Theudas and Tholomaeus. In 46 the Roman proconsul Tiberius Alexander (himself of Jewish origin), crucified the two sons of Judas of Galilee for leading a popular revolt. Finally in 48 the Jews attacked Samaria.[45] Widespread resentment among the Jews against Roman rule eventually led to the disastrous war that broke out in 66. No sharp line divided political zeal and religious enthu-siasm, and their resentment was not restricted to the occupied terri-tories of Judea and Jerusalem.[46] Jews living in other areas of the empire felt great sympathy for their compatriots in the "mother country," and the spirit of resistance and revolution spread as far as Rome. Paul, when he wrote his letter to the Romans around 58 or 59, may have had Jewish troublemakers in mind when he warned: "You who boast in the law, do you dishonor God by breaking the law? For as it is written, 'The name of God is blasphemed among the Gentiles because of you.'" And again toward the end of his letter: "Let every-one be subject to the governing authorities . . . he who resists the authorities resists what God has appointed. . . . Pay all of them their dues, taxes to whom taxes are due, revenue to whom revenue is due . . . let us conduct ourselves becoming as in the day . . . not in quarreling and jealousy . . ."[47]

The abolition of the Jewish state by Claudius in 44 goaded the Jews to new heights of rage. Did Claudius issue his decree because he assumed that Chrestus was such a Jewish radical who incited mem-bers of the synagogue in Rome to riotous activities? This is a hypoth-esis only, as is the notion that fifteen years later, in 64 (by which time the Jews had returned to the city again), Jewish anarchists set the fire described by Tacitus. We know that by this time the situation in Judea had deteriorated to the point of no return; indeed, war broke out only two years later. From this perspective we can understand why the Romans identified the Christians as the incendiaries. But, in fact, it was not Nero who shifted the blame to the Christians (Nero had no idea that Christians existed), but rather the leaders of the Jewish synagogue, who were alarmed by official investigations that blamed Jewish fanatics and so placed the entire Jewish community in danger. In 64 Christians were still known as Jews, and the Roman authorities failed to distinguish peaceful Jews from rebellious Jews, and Jews from Christians. Both moderate and radical elements of the synagogue disliked the Christians, and they thus made easy scapegoats. As a matter of fact, Jewish hostility toward Christians was so well known that even Tertullian referred to the synagogues as the "fountains of persecution."[48] And the Jews had a good connection through which to gain the ear of Nero, namely his wife Poppaea, who, according to Josephus, was sympathetic to the Jewish religion and pleaded with her husband on behalf of the Jews.[49] So we come full circle back to Tacitus. The arsonists were Jews, people whose "hatred of the human race" was well known to all, and more specifically a particular group of Jews called Christians.[50]

The only clear reference by Suetonius to the Christians is in the following passage:

> During his reign many abuses were severely punished and put down, and no fewer new laws were made: a limit was set on expenditures: the public banquets were confined to a distribution of food; the sale of any kind of cooked viands in the taverns was forbidden, with the exception of pulse and vegetables, whereas before every sort of dainty was exposed for sale. Punishment was inflicted on the Christians, a class of men given to a new and mischievous superstition. He put an end to the diversions of the chariot drivers, who from immunity of long standing claimed the right of ranging at large and amusing themselves by cheating and robbing the people. The pantomimic actors and their partisans were banished from the city. [Nero 16.2][51]

Suetonius called Christianity a "new and mischievous superstition" (*superstitio nova et malefica*), very clearly echoing the judgments of Tacitus and Pliny.[52] Although Suetonius said no more than this his contempt is clear in the way he automatically relegated Christians to the lowest rank of society by mentioning them in the same breath with chariot drivers and pantomimic actors. Suetonius used the word "*malefica*" in his account of the Christians. Perhaps because he, too, associated the name "Christian" with heinous offenses against the law without further examining the true character of the movement. But the word *malefica*, like the English word "malefic," may also carry connotations of magical practices and sorcery. It is in this sense that Morton Smith understands the passage that he translates as follows: "Penalties were imposed on the Christians, a kind of men holding a new superstition that involved the practice of magic."[53] Moreover, Smith believes that the basic reason behind the earliest persecution of the Christians was the suspicion, shared by the authorities and the general public, that Christianity was "an organization for the practice of magic." It was this same suspicion that Pliny investigated when he heard that the Christians were eating a meal together and chanting a *carmen*. Pliny, of course, concluded that such practices were harmless—but only after torturing two deaconesses. It appears that the Roman mind tended in some ill-defined way to link the name "Christian" with magic.

Summary

Let us now return to our original question: "What is in a name?" The three Roman historians whose writings we have investigated were all contemporaries, and all reflected the aristocratic, well-bred Roman's judgment that Christianity was one of a multitude of degraded foreign cults—"atrocious and shameful things," as Tacitus put it—that infested Rome. Most of them came from the eastern provinces, prompting the satirist Juvenal to complain bitterly that the "Syrian Orontes flows into the Tiber."[54] Romans of higher social classes believed that these oriental superstitions polluted Roman life and that they attacked the very fiber of society like a debilitating disease. All three historians had firmly ingrained antipathies that, brought together and attached to the name Christian, gave rise to the summary judgment that Christianity was a disruptive social phenomenon and a danger to the security of the state. Therefore, Christians deserved their punishment.

Romans associated a number of negative characteristics with the Christian name. As a *new* superstition, Christianity could not claim the sanction of antiquity. The Romans had an exceptionally fine sense of time, which was deeply rooted in their religion. While the Jews, according to Tacitus, had "only a mental conception of one God," the Romans believed in a panoply of gods who were no mere "beings," abstract and remote, but were vivid, distinctive personali-

ties who intervened frequently in the lives of the people.[55] Hence, the
Romans looked back on an unbroken chain of divine interventions in
their history. This history, as it unfolded in space and time, was the
realization of a divinely preordained plan. Roman religion placed
heavy emphasis on learning the divine will and assisting the divine
fatum toward its process of fulfillment.[56] In this way a harmonious
relationship could be maintained between the divine and human
spheres; new and unproven religious practices, on the other hand
could only disturb this harmony and thus endanger the security of
the state. Especially dangerous were religious practices not native to
Rome. It was for this reason that the Romans had suppressed the
Bacchanalia; they were *prava et externa religio* (a false and foreign
religion). Still, with characteristic consistency, the Senate excepted
from the general prohibition of Bacchic worship a few cases "where
an ancient altar or image had been consecrated."[57] Even Tacitus, who
had nothing but contempt for the "perverse and disgusting" customs
of the Jews, reluctantly admitted that "Jewish worship is vindicated
by its antiquity."[58] Christianity, however, could not claim the
approval of antiquity, because as an outgrowth of Judaism it was of
recent origin, and Tacitus knew the exact time when the movement
started—a mere twenty-five years or so before he was born.

Furthermore, the Romans saw Christianity as a superstition rather
than as a legitimate religion, such as their own state cult or others
that had been authorized.[59] The Romans used the word superstition
mainly in connection with foreign cults, including Judaism, which
Cicero called "a barbarous superstition"[60] and which Tacitus equally
detested, as we have seen above. As an offshoot of Judaism, Christianity shared the opprobrium heaped on the parent religion. Our three
authors go further, however, in condemning Christianity. Judaism
was "perverse, disgusting and barbarous," but Christianity, besides
having all of these defects in full measure, was also "depraved, excessive, foreign and new," and therefore much worse than Judaism. In
the early second century Romans thought that believers in these
superstitions of Eastern origin generally indulged in strange processions, unusual music, the beating of drums, perhaps incantations and
enchantments, and sometimes sexual deviations. In the *Golden Ass*,
Apuleius (ca. 127-171) described such a sect. A wandering group of
emasculated male worshippers of the Great Goddess of Syria went
from town to town and accompanied their rites with the playing of
cymbals, tambourines, castanets, and horns. When the group reached

a village they started an ecstatic dance during which they bit and slashed themselves and one of them fell into a frenzy and began to confess his guilts, yelling loudly in prophetic tones. Then he whipped himself until blood oozed from his wounds. The group also included one physically normal man whom they used for acts of sexual perversion. Apuleius characterized them with terms like "scum," "odious creatures," "disgusting creatures"; he thought that they looked absolutely hideous when they painted their faces and eyelids and put on their garish clothing and went out to perform their dances.[61] Unfortunately, because of its Eastern origin, the Romans may have associated Christianity with such behavior. Some of the liturgical practices of Christians, notably glossolalia, confessions of sins, prophecies, sacraments, and the sexual aberrations of fringe groups, may have contributed to a distorted picture of this "oriental superstition."[62]

The Jewish origin of Christianity counted against it in the eyes of Tacitus and, more especially, of Pliny. In fact, much of the aristocratic Roman hostility toward Christianity derived from recent experience with the Jews as enemies of Rome. The memory of the great Jewish war, which finally ended in 73, probably remained vivid for all Romans, and those Romans in the eastern provinces, like Pliny and Tacitus, must have heard rumors that a Jewish rebellion was again brewing around the Mediterranean. Messianic expectations still smoldered among the Jews, and books such as the Apocalypse of Baruch (or, 2 Baruch) and the Apocalypse of Ezra (or, 2 Esdras)[63] kept alive the hope of the destruction of Rome and the dominion of the Messiah. Although it is unlikely that either Pliny, Tacitus, or Suetonius read such Jewish literature, they certainly heard about the clashes between Jews and Greeks in Alexandria in 110, as a result of which two delegations went to Rome to present their rival cases to Trajan. In the same year the Parthian king provoked Trajan by deposing the reigning king of Armenia; a war between Rome and Parthia was in the air, and Jews looked to the Parthians as their future liberators. At about the same time a Jewish revolt broke out in Cyrenaica, during which Jews massacred thousands of Gentiles in a desperate attempt to establish a national Jewish state. Later, when the Roman armies were away fighting in Parthia, a Jewish uprising broke out in Egypt (115) and spread to Cyprus. In time, of course, the Romans ruthlessly and thoroughly subdued all these outbursts.[64] Nevertheless, it is understandable that Romans familiar with Jewish

sentiments or knowledgeable about the state of Jewish affairs suspected a Jewish conspiracy. In particular, Pliny's actions seem
justifiable after he had received reports about certain Jewish sectarians who held nightly meetings, ate together, chanted *carmina*, and
took an oath. And it is proof of Pliny's enlightened mentality that
after his initial repressive reaction he was willing and able to seek out
the truth.

We must conclude, therefore, that the Christian complaint that the
Romans persecuted them simply on account of their name (*nomen
ipsum*) is somewhat exaggerated and only partly true. In fact, the
Romans associated the name with so many real or imagined, questionable, illegal, and perhaps even criminal activities that not even
the most neutral Roman observer could see clearly the true intentions and convictions of the Christians—whatever their name may
have meant. For the name could have designated a Jewish splinter
group, Gnostic sectarians (they, too, went under the name Christian),
or mainstream Christians of diverse theologies that included radicals
and those who favored accommodation with the state. The above
analysis of three Roman historians shows their confusion about the
Christians and the associations that came into the minds of these
refined aristocrats when they heard their name: radical Jews conspir-
ing against the state, perhaps planning another revolt; secretive magicians casting spells at nightly meetings; members of a superstition
originating in Syria involved in typical, shameful practices. The
Christian apologists admitted some justification for these charges,
and after they had vented their anger over the alleged injustice they
quietly settled down to refute specific charges, among which the
most important were atheism, cannibalism, and sexual libertinism.
Atheism, that is refusal to worship the Greco-Roman gods and to
sacrifice before the image of the emperor, was a relatively straightfor-
ward charge that they easily answered, unlike the charges of cannibalism and libertinism.

NOTES

1. Justin Martyr *ii Apol.*; E.T., *ANF* 1.188ff.
2. *Apol.* 1.3-4; *ANF* 1.163ff.
3. For a collection of passages from the writings of the early Christian

fathers concerning this play on words, see Stephen Benko, "Pagan Criticism of Christianity," *Aufstieg und Niedergang der römischen Welt*. II. 32/2 (Berlin: Walter de Gruyter, 1980), p. 105.

4. *Apol.* 1.16; and Matt. 7.16; 22.17ff.

5. *Oratio* 27.1; *ANF* 2.76.

6. Athenagoras, *A Plea for the Christians*, chaps. 1 and 2; *ANF* 2.129-130.

7. *Ad nationes* 6, *ANF* 3.111; *Apologeticum* 1, *ANF* 3.18-19.

8. *The Martyrdom of Polycarp* 12.2, *ANF* 1.41.

9. The word is not used in a derogatory sense but rather as a general term for all members of the Roman empire who were not Christians. They may have been devotees of Greek and Roman state cults, initiates of mystery religions, followers of philosophical schools that demanded a certain conduct of life, or even people having a particular interest in spiritual matters. But most of them were not "pagans" in the modern sense of the word as St. Paul sharply observed standing in the middle of the Areopagus: "Men of Athens, I perceive that in every way you are very religious." (*Acts* 17.22).

10. William Melmath, *Pliny: Letters*, Loeb (London: William Heinemann, 1935), pp. 401–7.

11. As was Paul, according to Acts 25:11–12, 25; 26:32.

12. *Ad nationes* 1.7; *ANF* 3.114; and *Apologeticum* 5. It reads as follows: "This name of ours . . . was ruthlessly condemned under Nero, and you may weigh its worth and character even from the person of its persecutor. If that prince was a pious man, then the Christians are impious; if he was just, if he was pure, then the Christians are unjust and impure; if he was not a public enemy, we are enemies of our country: what sort of men we are, our persecutor himself shows, since he of course punished what produced hostility to himself. Now, although every other institution which existed under Nero has been destroyed, yet this of ours has firmly remained. . . ."

13. On this problem see A. Bourgery, "Le probléme de l'Institutum Neronianum," *Latomus* 2 (1938):106-11; J. W. P. Borleffs, "Institutum Neronianum," *Vigiliae Christianae* 6 (1952): 129-45; Ch. Samuagne, "Tertullian et l'Institutum Neronianum," *Theologische Zeitschrift* 17 (1961): 334-35; J. Zeiller, "Institutum Neronianum," *Revue d'histoire ecclésiastique* 55 (1955): 393-400.

14. *Naturalis Historia* 29.54 quoted by R. Freudenberger, *Das Verhalten der Römischen Behörden gegen die Christen im 2. Jahrhundert dargestellt am Brief des Plinius an Trajan und der Reskripten Trajans und Hadrians* (Munich: Beck, 1969), p. 87.

15. *Martyrdom of Polycarp* 9.3. See also Ignatius *Smyrnaeans* 5.2; Hermas *Sim.* 6.2.3; 8.6.4; 8.8.2; etc.

16. Cicero *Catiline* 1.1.7, E.T., C. D. Younge (London: H. G. Bohn, 1852). The following verses are particularly relevant: "Do you not see that your conspiracy is already arrested and rendered powerless by the knowledge which everyone here possesses of it? What is there that you did last night, what the night before, where is it that you were, who was there that you summoned to meet you, what design was there which was adapted by you. . . ." 3.6.3: "For what is there, O Catiline, that you can still expect, if night is not able to veil your nefarious meetings in darkness, and if private houses cannot conceal the voice of your conspiracy within their walls; if everything is seen and displayed?" 4.8.3: "Listen while I speak of the night before . . . I say that you came the night before (I will say nothing obscurely) into the Scythe dealer's street, to the house of Marcus Lecca; that many of

your accomplices in the same insanity and wickedness came there too."
4.9.7: "You were, then Catiline, at Lecca's that night; you divided Italy into
sections. . . ."

17. *De Catilinae Coniuratione* 43.2.

18. Plutarch *Cicero* 18.2.1, E.T., B. Perrin, Loeb (London: W. Heinemann
1958) "A night had also been fixed for the attempt, a night of the Saturnalia
and swords, tow and brimstone had been carried to the house of Cathegus and
hidden there."

19. "You [Catiline] plot a night attact, you propose to give our houses and
temples to the flames . . ." *Sat.* 8.231ff.

20. *Twelve Tables* 8.26: "No person shall hold meetings by night in the
city."

21. See *Octavius* 8 and 9.

22. *Acta Cypr.* 4

23. Several scholars have analyzed the many similarities between Livy's
report and Pliny's letter. R. M. Grant, "Pliny and the Christians" *Harvard
Theological Review* 41 (1948), 273ff., even suggested that Livy's account
served as a model for Pliny. A. D. Nock, *Conversion* (1933; reprint ed.,
Oxford: Oxford University Press, 1952), p. 71ff., points out that Livy's reference to the great number of initiates as "almost a second people" "is very
reminiscent of Christianity." This observation was made first by Edward
Gibbon, *History of the Decline and Fall of the Roman Empire*, ed. J. B. Bury,
vol. 2 (London: Methuen, 1909), p. 65. Albert Henrichs, *Die Phoinikika des
Lollianos* (Bonn: Rudolf Habelt Verlag, 1972), p. 44ff, examined the passage
carefully and concluded that the most important ritual elements of the
Bacchanalia can be discovered in the novel by Lollianos; both were based on
identical mythical conceptions (p. 47). For bibliography on the suppression of
the Bacchanalia see Henrichs, *Phoinikika*; and M. P. Nilsson in the *Oxford
Classical Dictionary* 2d ed., p. 158.

24. Lucan, *Pharsalia* 6.706-7. "*Carmina cano*" means "I chant these
spells."

25. On this problem see F. J. Dölger, "*Sacramentum Militiae*, "*Antike und
Christentum* 2 (1930): 268ff.; "*Sacramentum infanticidii*," ibid., 4 (1934):
188ff. For bibliography on the Christian usage of the word *sacramentum* see
A. Henrichs, *Phoinikika*, p. 39, fn. 8.

26. See Sallust *Bellum Catilinae* 22; Plutarch *Cicero* 10.31.1; Dio Cassius
37.30.4

27. The way Pliny mentioned Christians in the same breath with *collegia*
makes it appear that he put Christians in the same category as private clubs,
such as the firemen's company mentioned by him in Ep. 10.33-34. These
were legal according to the Twelve Tables, in the opinion of Gaius *Digest of
Justinian* 47.22.4: "'*Sodales sunt qui eiusdem collegii sunt quam Graeci
ἑταίραν vocant*' = Associates are persons who belong to the same collegium
for which the Greeks use the term ἑταίρα. These are granted by a law (of the
Twelve Tables) the right to pass any binding rule they like for themselves,
provided that they cause no violation of public law. . . ." E. H. Warmington,
Remains of Old Latin, Loeb (Cambridge: Harvard University Press, 1961),
3:493. Ever since the Bacchanalian crisis, however, clubs were under suspicion. Julius Caesar forbade them, excepting only those of ancient origin
(Suetonius *Caesar* 42), Augustus placed them under strict control and made
them carry a license (Suetonius *Augustus* 32; Dio 53.36). Illicit clubs could be

prosecuted and their members regarded as taking part in a riot, for which the punishment was death (*Digest* 47.22.3 [Marcian]; 47.22.2, 48.4.1 [Ulpian]; Paulus *Sentences* 5.29) Characteristically, Trajan did not allow the firemen's brigade to be formed—clubs could do more damage than fires. Tacitus *Annals* 14.17 also reports that after a riot between the inhabitants of Nuceria and Pompeii, all associations formed in Pompeii "in defiance of the laws" were dissolved. See on this topic R. Wilken, "Collegia, Philosophical Schools, and Theology." in *The Catacombs and the Colosseum*, ed., S. Benko and J. O'Rourke (Valley Forge, Pa.: Judson Press, 1971), pp. 268–94; and Samuel Dill, *Roman Society from Nero to Marcus Aurelius* (Cleveland: World Publishing Co., 1964), pp. 251–86.

28. Concerning the spelling of the name here see R. Syme, *Tacitus* (Oxford: Oxford University Press, 1958), 2:469.

29. John Jackson, *Tacitus: The Annals* (London: William Heinemann, 1962), pp. 283–85.

30. Dio *Roman History* 67.14.2.

31. And not Chrestus; see above Syme, *Tacitus*, 1958.

32. *Histories* 5.5 (written prior to the *Annals*). Cf. Menahem Stern, *Greek and Latin Authors on Jews and Judaism* (Leiden: E. J. Brill, 1980) 2:39. (For comments on *Annales* 15.44 see pp. 88–93; compare this with Diodorus Siculus *Bibliotheca* 34.1-3; Philostratus *Life* 5.33; and as a defense, Josephus *Contra Apionem* 2.15.

33. The Roman legislation on arson in the *Codex Justinianus* is as follows, *Digest* 47.9.9: Gaius, on the Law of the 12 Tables, Bk. IV. "Anyone who sets fire to a house, or a pile of grain near a house shall be chained, scourged, and put to death by fire, provided he committed the act knowingly and deliberately. If, however, it occurred by accident, that is to say, through negligence, he shall be ordered to make good the damage; or if he is insolvent, he shall receive a light chastisement. Every kind of building is included in the term house." 47.9.12: Ulpianus, On the Duty of Proconsuls, Bk. VIII.: "(1) Persons of low rank who designedly cause a fire in a town shall be thrown to wild beasts and those of superior station shall suffer death, or else be banished to some island." E.T.: S. P. Scott, *Corpus Juris Civilis. The Civil Law*, vol. 5 (1932; reprint ed. New York: AMS Press, 1973).

34. This view has been put forward most recently by John Bishop, *Nero, the Man, and the Legend* (London: R. Hale, 1964), pp. 79–89. Prior to Bishop, other scholars made similar suggestions. A good review of the various hypotheses is found in Jean Beaujeu, "L'incendie de Rome en 64 et les Chrétiens," *Latomus* 19 (1960): 65-80, 291-311; See also L. Hermann, "Quels Chrétiens ont incendié Rome?" *Revue Belge de Philologie*, 27 (1949): 633-51; A. Kurfess, "Der Brand und die Christenverfolgung im Jahre 64 N. Chr.," *Mnemosyne* 6 (1938):261ff.; Gunther Scheda, "Nero und der Brand Roms," *Historia* 16 (1967):111-15. On Nero see B. W. Henderson, *Life and Principate of the Emperor Nero* (London: Methuen 1903); G. Charles-Picard, *Auguste et Neron: Le Secret de l'empire*, E.T.; Ortzen Len, *Augustus and Nero* (New York: Apollo, 1966); M. P. Charlesworth, *Documents Illustrating the Reigns of Claudius and Nero* (New York: Cambridge University Press, 1951); B. H. Warmington, *Nero: Reality and Legend* (New York: Norton, 1969); G. Walter, *Nero* (London: Allen and Unwin, 1957); A. Momigliano, "Nero," *Cambridge Ancient History* (Cambridge: Cambridge University Press, 1963); pp. 702–42. The standard reference works, such as *The Cambridge Ancient*

History Series and August F. Pauly, Georg Wissowa, and Wilhem Kroll, *Pauly's Realencyclopädie der Classichen Altertumswissenschaft* (Stuttgart: Druckenmuller Verlag, 1893–1978) are always safe sources.

35. *The Jewish War* 7.3.3.
36. *Annals* 15.38-40.
37. Valerius Maximus *Facta et dicta memorabilia* 1.3.3.
38. Dio 57.18.5
39. *Antiquities* 18.8.3; see also Suetonius *Lives of the Twelve Caesars*, *Tiberius* 36.
40. Dio 60.6.6.
41. J. C. Rolfe, *Suetonius*, Loeb (New York: Macmillan, 1914), p. 53. Compare with Dio *History* 60.6.6 and Orosius *Historia adversus paganos* 7.6.15-16.
42. F. F. Bruce, *New Testament History* (New York: Doubleday, 1972), pp. 297ff. H. W. Montefiore, "Josephus and the New Testament," *Novum Testamentum* 4 (1960):139; F. V. Filson, *A New Testament History* (Philadelphia: Westminster, 1964), p. 66 in particular. Also see W. H. C. Frend, *Martyrdom and Persecution in the Early Church* (New York: Doubleday, 1967), p. 122; A. Hilgenfeld, *Historisch-Kritische Einleitung in das Neue Testament* (Leipzig: Fues's Verlag, 1875), p. 303, fn. 4.
43. Acts 18:12.
44. Many examples exist in the *Thesaurus Linguae Latinae: Onomastikon*, vol. 2 (Leipzig: Teubner, 1907-1913); and *A Dictionary of Christian Biography*, ed. W. Smith and H. Wace (London: Smith-Wace, 1877).
45. Josephus *Antiquities* 18.310 ff.; 19.354 ff.; 20.6 ff.; 20.3-4; 20.97f.; 20.100-102; 20.105-7. Also Philo *Legatio ad Gaium* and *In Flaccum*.
46. The words "zealots" and "sicarii" are usually attached to these revolutionary Jews who in common parlance are called "the Zealots" or the "Zealot party." Much has been written about this aspect of Jewish history. Best known are the works of S. Brandon, *Jesus and the Zealots* (Manchester: Manchester University Press, 1967); M. Hengel, *Die Zeloten* (Leiden: E. J. Brill, 1961); O. Cullmann, "Die Bedeutung der Zeloten-bewegung für das Neue Testament," *Vorträge und Aufsätze*, ed. K. Fröhlich (Zürich: Zwingli Verlag), 1966, pp. 292ff.; O. Cullmann, *Jesus and the Revolutionaries* (New York: Harper and Row, 1970); Morton Smith, "Zealots and Sicarii: Their Origins and Relation," *Harvard Theological Review* 64 (1971): pp. 1–19 has shown how complex the problem is and how easy it is to make incorrect statements about "the Zealots." In the same essay, with his usual ἀκριβεία Smith reviewed and criticized many articles and books written on this topic.
47. Rom. 2:23f., 13:1ff.
48. "*Synagogas Judaeorum fontes persecutionum*" *Scorpiace* 10.
49. A "God-fearer" or "*theosebes*" *Antiquities* 20.195.
50. See Stephen Benko, "The Edict of Claudius of A.D. 49," *Theologische Zeitschrift* 25 (1969):406-18. This hypothesis assumes, of course, that the fire did not break out by accident, although, in fact, that could indeed have happened. But in this case, too, we must account for those who, according to Tacitus (15.38), "forbade the extinguishing of the flames" and "openly hurled brands." These people also claimed that "there was one who gave them authority." (Bishop, *Nero*, p. 88 interprets this as meaning that the Christians' "orders were the Lords.") Tacitus also says that after five days the fire was put out and then started again "and to this conflagration there attached

the greater infamy . . ." (15.40). The role of arsonists, therefore, cannot be excluded.

51. J. C. Rolfe, *Suetonius, Nero*, p. 111.

52. "destructive superstition", *exitiabilis superstio*; and "depraved and excessive superstition," *superstitio prava, immodica*.

53. Smith, *Jesus the Magician* (New York: Harper and Row, 1978), pp. 50ff.

54. *Sat.* 3.2.

55. *Histories* 5.5.

56. On the Roman concept of time see Stephen Benko, "Virgil's Fourth Eclogue in Christian Interpretation," *ANRW* II. Principat, 31/1 (Berlin: Walter de Gruyter, 1980), pp. 688ff.; also W. Pötscher, "Numen and Numen Augusti," *ANRW* II. 16/1, pp. 355-92; W. Pötscher, "Das Römische Fatum— Begriff und Verwendung." *ANRW* II 16/1, pp. 393–424.

57. Livy 39.18.7.

58. *Histories* 5.5.

59. Cicero *De legibus* 2.8.

60. *Pro Flacco* 66.

61. Or, *Metamorphoses* 8.27–28.

62. Plutarch (A.D. 50-120) eloquently expressed how an intellectual of the early second century viewed superstition in his essay *De superstitione* (Loeb, *Moralia*, 2:452-95): Plutarch thought that superstition was worse then atheism because it produces fear, for the superstitious man believes there are gods "but that they are the cause of pain and injury." On superstition in general see Dill, *Roman Society from Nero to Marcus Aurelius*, pp. 443–83. Virgil (70-19) put these words in the mouth of King Evander: "No idle superstition (*vana superstitio*) that knows not the gods of old has ordered these our solemn rites," *Aeneid* 8.187 Did the knowledge of some eastern superstitions prompt Virgil to make such a statement?

63. Both were composed around A.D. 100. For a brief introduction and bibliography see Robert H. Pfeiffer, *History of New Testament Times With an Introduction to the Apocrypha* (New York: Harper and Brothers, 1949), pp. 81ff.

64. See Dio Cassius 68.32.1 ff. Michael Grant, *The Jews in the Roman World* (New York: Scribners, 1973), pp. 231ff. presents a brief survey of the situation. Grant also has an excellent bibliography on Jewish-Roman relations at the end of his book. The standard reference is now Menahem Stern, *Greek and Latin Authors on Jews and Judaism*, vol. 1, *From Herodotus to Plutarch*, vol. 2 *From Tacitus to Simplicius* (Leiden: E. J. Brill, 1974, 1980).

II

Portrait of an Early Christian

THE STRANGE CAREER OF Peregrinus Proteus, who lived in the second century, gives us a valuable insight into the lives of Christian congregations and the mentality of individual Christians. In his biography of Peregrinus, Lucian of Samosata, although an unsympathetic observer, included many details concerning Christianity.[1] Peregrinus himself was not a typical Christian of the day, but his switching in and out of the church was probably not an isolated phenomenon,[2] and his later life shows a faint resemblance to the Christian ascetics of the second century on, and to the Christian monks who appeared in the eastern Mediterranean about a hundred years later.

Peregrinus (110-165) was born in Parium in Mysia in the northwest corner of Asia Minor to a fairly well-to-do family. We know very little about his early life except that later, when he was already famous, he was accused of having committed adultery as a teen-ager, for which he was duly punished. It was also said that he had homosexual experiences, and the parents of one of the boys whom he corrupted wanted to sue him, but Peregrinus paid them off with a large cash present, and so they never filed charges with the governor. His father died at about the age of sixty, and Peregrinus was suspected of being responsible for his death. It was even rumored that he strangled his father in order to come into the possession of his inheritance. The case was, however, never tried and Peregrinus went into voluntary exile.

From Asia Minor Peregrinus eventually arrived in Palestine, and it was here that his life took a decisive turn. He became acquainted with Christian people who instructed him in their religion, which was new to him, and in a short time Peregrinus became a prominent member of the Christian community in Palestine. By nature he was an intelligent man, inclined to philosophy, and his expounding of the

Scriptures was received with great admiration. He soon rose to a position of leadership in the congregation, wrote several books, and came to be regarded by many as a prophet. In fact, he was so well known that someone eventually filed formal charges against him for being a Christian. Peregrinus was arrested in accordance with the imperial rescript of Trajan and sent to jail. Trajan had ordered that Christians should not be hounded, but, if they were formally accused of being Christian, regular legal proceedings could be started against them.

The congregation immediately took action to have Peregrinus released. When that failed they went out of their way to make prison life as pleasant as possible for him. In their eyes Peregrinus now belonged to the category of apostles who had suffered imprisonment because of their belief in Christ.[3] No doubt the congregation remembered the words of Jesus: "Come, O blessed of my Father, inherit the kingdom prepared for you from the foundations of the world. . . . for I was in prison and you came to me."[4] They also knew of the saying by the apostle Paul, that imprisonment placed a Christian somewhat above other believers: "Are they servants of Christ? I am a better one. . . . with far greater labors, far more imprisonments, with countless beatings, and often near death. . . ."[5] The Scriptures thus encouraged a sympathetic attitude toward prisoners of conscience, and members of the congregation, old and young alike, came to visit Peregrinus.[6] They looked on him as a martyr. They read the Bible to him, provided him with food, kept him company, and in some cases they even bribed the prison guards to let them spend the night with him. The news of his martyrdom spread to other Christian communities, and, from as far away as Asia Minor, congregations sent committees to visit him, paying all expenses from the church treasury. Many sent cash donations, possibly to defray the legal expenses of his defense.

The concern that Christians nurtured toward each other must have impressed many pagans.[7] But if, as sometimes happened, such concern reached excessive proportions then the efforts of the congregation could become counterproductive. People accused Peregrinus of enriching himself with the money that Christians sent him, they also criticized the amount and quality of the food prepared for him. And the pagans were not alone in such criticism. Tertullian, a Christian apologist, warned that Christians often overdid their concern for prisoners, setting up cookshops in the prisons to serve untrustworthy martyrs! He cited the example of one such prisoner who overindulged in eating and drinking and enjoyed the conveniences of life, including the bath, to such a degree that at the end he was reluctant to be executed as a martyr.[8] Nevertheless, the practice of lavishly helping Christian prisoners continued until Constantine the Great (285-337) became sole ruler and all persecutions stopped. But just before this happened his coemperor and rival, Licinius (312-334), decided to withdraw his favor from the Christians, and new persecutions flared up in his part of the empire around 320. Licinius published a law that forbade anyone to visit Christian prisoners, to bring them food, or to show any sort of mercy or kindness toward them; persons who violated the law were to share the fate of the prisoners visited and were to be jailed immediately.[9]

Peregrinus never actually reached the stage of martyrdom. The governor ordered his release from prison, perhaps because he did not wish to create a martyr, perhaps because the accuser no longer wished to press the charge. Even the customary flogging was omitted and Peregrinus was set free. He went back to Parium to take possession of his inheritance, but he discovered that most of it was gone. Only the farmland remained. Still, this had considerable cash value, and Peregrinus could have used it to establish himself in the world. Instead he decided on a life of poverty. His enemies claimed that the murder of his father was still fresh in the minds of the townspeople, and this made it impossible for him to live in Parium. Whatever his motives, he called a meeting of the people and appeared before them with an old coat covering his body, a sack on his shoulder, his hair grown long, and a staff in his hand. He announced his wish to donate his entire property to Parium and then walked away.

No Christian in good standing needed to worry about what to eat, drink, or where to sleep. The hospitality of the congregations took care of the needs of the brethren on the roads, and Peregrinus was now well known in Christian circles as someone who had endured suffering for his faith. He sustained his life by these means for some time until something happened that turned the Christians against him. He may have eaten meat that was consecrated to pagan gods, an act forbidden to Christians.[10] In any event, the church excommunicated him. Now he would have gladly taken possession of his father's farm, but, because he had given it away of his own free will, he no longer had any claim to it. He wandered on and reached Egypt where he became the pupil of the philosopher Agathobolus. He shaved his head and underwent various humiliations, including public flogging, until well trained in the art of contempt for the world.

The way of life that Peregrinus now adopted placed him within a group commonly known as "Cynics" after their founder, Diogenes of Sinope (400-324), who was nicknamed κύων or "dog," by his contemporaries.[11] Diogenes taught that a man should fulfill his natural needs in the simplest possible way, because nothing that was natural was indecent. He argued that only convention made some natural things dishonorable, and so he taught his followers to avoid convention, to suppress their sense of shame, and to do everything that was natural in public. It is mainly for this reason that he was called a dog. Diogenes' many followers transformed his original principles into practical ways of life. Some emphasized renunciation of worldly possessions; others preached asceticism, simplicity, and independence. Cynic philosophers wandered around the Hellenistic world teaching, with only a cane in their hands and a knapsack on their backs. In the first and second centuries A.D., they became the main social critics of their day against the overweening ways of the emperors.[12] Roman historians report that time and again Cynic beggers flooded into Rome, and that their obnoxious arrogance often irritated the ruling class. Roman public opinion, however, was extremely tolerant of all philosophical and religious movements, and the authorities put up with the antics of the Cynics until they began to advocate anarchy and the overthrow of the government. Emperor Vespasian (69-79), for example, only banished Demetrius the Cynic from Rome when his attacks became excessively vituperative. In the words of Dio Cassius:[13] "Inasmuch as many others, too, including Demetrius the cynic, actuated by the Stoic principles, were taking advantage of the name of philosophy to teach publicly many doctrines inappropriate to the times, and in this way were subtly corrupting some of their hearers, Mucianus. . . . persuaded Vespasian to expel such persons from the city." This same Mucianus described these undesirable elements to Vespasian in the following terms:

> They are full of empty boasting, and if one of them lets his beard grow long, elevates his eyebrows, wears his coarse mantle thrown back over his shoulder and goes barefooted, he straightaway lays claim to wisdom, bravery and righteousness and gives himself great airs, even though he may not know either his letters or how to swim, as the saying goes. They look down upon everybody and call a man of good

family a mollycoddle, the low-born slender-witted, a handsome person licentious, an ugly person a simpleton, the rich man greedy, and
the poor man servile.[14]

When Demetrius did not immediately obey the order to leave Italy,
Vespasian sent the following message to him: "You are doing everything to force me to kill you, but I do not slay a barking dog."[15] The
words "barking dog" are, of course, a pun on the meaning of the word
"Cynic," but, beyond the witticism, we must admire the patience of
Vespasian and his wisdom in not creating an unworthy martyr. Two
other Cynics who engaged in similar antics fared much worse. One of
them, Diogenes, publicly criticized Titus for entertaining the
thought of marrying the Jewish princess Berenice. For this insult
Titus had Diogenes flogged. "And after him Heras, expecting no
harsher punishment, gave vent to many senseless yelpings in true
Cynic fashion, and for this he was beheaded."[16] The Christian Tatian
described these philosophers in the following terms:

> They leave uncovered one of their shoulders; they let their hair grow
> long; they cultivate their beards; their nails are like the claws of wild
> beasts. Though they say they want nothing, yet, like Proteus, they
> need a currier for their wallet, and a weaver for their mantle, and a
> woodcutter for their staff, and the rich, and a cook also for their
> gluttony.[17] O man competing with the dog, you know not God, and so
> have turned to the imitation of an irrational animal. You cry out in
> public with an assumption of authority, and take upon you to avenge
> your own self; and if you receive nothing, you indulge in abuse, and
> philosophy is with you the art of getting money.[18]

Peregrinus followed in the steps of his Cynic predecessors and
sailed to Italy. As soon as he arrived in Rome, he began to criticize
everybody and everything, in particular Emperor Antoninus Pius
(137-165), who was one of the mildest and most beneficent rulers the
empire had ever had. True to his general philosophy of tolerance, the
emperor took no measures to silence Peregrinus who became bolder
and bolder in his public criticism of outstanding Roman citizens.
Finally the city prefect told him to leave Rome. He went to Greece
and acted in a similar manner there. He encouraged the Greeks to
rebel against Rome,[19] picked on prominent individuals, and criticized
towns. Like political radicals of all ages who use the liberties provided by the government to demand the overthrow of that very same
government and system, Peregrinus attacked the wealthy Herodes

Atticus for building a water system in Olympia while at the same time drinking the water. After this particular speech he was attacked by the crowd, and he saved his life only by escaping to the temple of Zeus.

Peregrinus was not always so outrageous and provocative. In Athens he gave regular lectures to students of philosophy, including Aulus Gellius (130-180), who later wrote the book *Attic Nights*,[20] in which he included many references to his student days and experiences. In his book Gellius remembered Peregrinus as a "man of fortitude and dignity [*Virum Graven et Constantem*]," and he described an incident when one day Peregrinus noticed a Roman knight yawning during a speech and severely rebuked him, showing no deference to his social status. As a true Cynic, Peregrinus lived in a hut outside the city where Gellius used to visit him. During their conversations Peregrinus discussed many noble thoughts. A wise man, he said, should avoid sin for the sake of honesty and justice and not merely for fear that someone might find out. But he must always remember that nothing will remain hidden forever, and thus, if he is too weak to avoid temptations, at least the thought of being discovered in the future ought to hold him back from doing wrong.[21]

By this time, a strange new obsession occupied Peregrinus. He was going to demonstrate in a dramatic, unique way how to have inner strength in the face of adversity and how to defy death. This would be his ultimate lesson to his followers and students, an example that they would never forget. At the Olympic games he announced that four years later at the conclusion of the next games he would burn himself to death. The announcement stirred up a great deal of interest among the Greeks. Some, especially his followers led by Theagenes, his most successful pupil, praised his fortitude and compared him to the Brahmans of India. They even claimed that the Sybil had uttered an oracle about the forthcoming self-immolation of Peregrinus, and they declared that this would assure him of a place on Olympus, next to Heracles and Hephaestus. Others made jokes about him, and they said that he would probably back out at the last minute claiming that Olympia was sacred ground dedicated to Zeus who did not want it desecrated by death. Still others said that it would be just fine if there were one Cynic less, and better yet if he took a few of his disciples with him into the flames.

A number of precedents for suicide by self-immolation existed. Everyone in the ancient world knew the story of Calanus, an Indian ascetic in the camp of Alexander the Great. According to the story, when Alexander reached India he became interested in the ascetics, who lived in the forests and spent their days in meditation. He visited them, and they told him that conquering the world meant nothing for he possessed no more than they did, namely as much ground as he could stand on. One of these ascetics, Calanus, attached himself to Alexander's army and became a teacher of the Macedonian general Lysimachus. When the army reached Susa, Calanus became ill and announced that he no longer wished to live and had a pyre built in the middle of the camp. Calanus said farewell to the generals but not to Alexander; to him he simply said "We shall meet again at Babylon," thus prophesying his death. Then Calanus laid down on the pyre, covered his face, and remained motionless until the flames devoured him, while the elephants gave the royal salute and the trumpets sounded.[22] The legend of Empedocles was equally well known. It told the story of a fifth century B.C. philosopher who threw himself into the fiery crater of Mount Aetna.[23] Closer to the memory of the Greeks was the self-immolation of another Indian in Athens in 20 B.C., whose motives, according to Dio Cassius, were unknown; he may have done it because of his old age, because of philosophical reasons, or because he just wanted to provide a spectacle for the benefit of Augustus who was in Athens at the time.[24]

The year of the Olympic games arrived, and as usual huge crowds came to watch the contests. This year (165), however, the prospect of the public suicide of Peregrinus added to the excitement. In the great temple of Zeus people argued about Peregrinus, and at one point he himself came with a large crowd and made a speech. He reviewed his life and the difficulties and dangers he had endured. Now the time had come for him to crown his life with a death like that of Heracles and thus to give all men an example of how to defy death. The reaction of the crowd was divided: some were moved to pity and asked Peregrinus to save himself, while others yelled at him to finish what he had begun. When the athletic contests had finished Peregrinus announced the place and time of the immolation: it was to be around midnight, about two miles east of Olympia. The pyre was set in the ground about six feet deep, and a large crowd waited around it. When the moon came up, Peregrinus arrived with other Cynics in a solemn procession, all holding torches in their hands. They lit the fire at different points. Peregrinus stepped forward to the edge of the flaming pit, put down his club, and took off his sack and coat. There he stood for a moment, a sixty-five-year-old man clad only in a dirty undershirt—a pitiful sight, indeed. Casting incense on the fire he cried out: "Be gracious to me, gods of my father and my mother!" Then he jumped into the flames and disappeared.[25] Soon the odor of burning flesh began to fill the air.

The Cynics stayed for awhile looking sadly into the flames and then dispersed. In due course souvenir hunters came to pick through the ashes, and the event was relegated in most men's minds to the status of a weird curiosity. But followers and admirers of Peregrinus were deeply moved by his death. Some claimed they had seen a vulture flying from the flames to Olympus at the moment Peregrinus had jumped into the pit; others claimed Peregrinus had appeared dressed in white, walking happily with a crown of ivy on his head. His memory lingered on. According to the Christian apologist Athenagoras, his native city of Parium erected a statue to Peregrinus that uttered prophecies.[26] In spite of the fact that the Christians had excommunicated Peregrinus, Tertullian mentioned him as an example to would-be martyrs.[27]

Not all Christians wrote so appreciatively of Peregrinus. One of his contemporaries, the Christian Tatian, used him as an example that nobody could be perfectly self-sufficient, not even a Cynic, because even he has need of the services of others to make his cloak, his wallet, and his staff.[28] Another of his contemporaries, who claimed to have witnessed his death, Lucian of Samosata (ca. 120–ca. 180), composed a vituperative satire soon after the event called *On the Death of Peregrinus*.[29] In it he recorded everything detrimental that he could dig up about the life of this old Cynic, including such trivial revelations as that once on a ship Peregrinus was frightened by a storm, and that on another occasion he ate too much and vomited. According to Lucian, Peregrinus fully deserved to die in the flames; he was merely a lunatic driven by hunger for publicity. He no more deserved to be admired than did the notorious Herostratus, who, unable to excel in anything in the world, had in 356 B.C. burnt down the temple of Artemis in Ephesus, one of the seven wonders of the world. To be sure, Peregrinus got the publicity that he so avidly desired; when he announced his decision in Olympia, a huge crowd had followed him. But Lucian asked if Peregrinus did not remember that even larger multitudes accompanied criminals led away for execution. Lucian argued that suicide in itself was bad, a man should not run away from life; but if someone had to die, they should do it quietly, in a dignified way, without saying a word to anyone, somewhere in seclusion. Peregrinus had to do it in Olympia, of all places, when the greatest number of people were present, on consecrated ground, in a theatrical fashion.

Lucian also criticized Peregrinus in another satire called *The Runaways*.[30] In this satire Lucian tried to further discredit Peregrinus as well as his followers, who were already building up a cult of their new saint. From the beginning to end, this satire is a savage attack on the Cynics, who are presented as a worthless rabble and as false philosophers. The scene opens on Olympus as Apollo and Zeus discuss the fiery death of Peregrinus. Instead of praising his death as a heroic act, Zeus refers to it as an annoyance that should never have happened; he finds the horrid stench of the burning body almost unbearable. At this point, Philosophia enters and, at the request of Zeus, states how a group of so-called philosophers brought disgrace upon her by their "abominable way of living, full of ignorance, impudence, and wantonness."[31] She relates that after Zeus sent her to earth she first went to India and made disciples of the Brahmans. They now live according to the tenets of philosophy and die "a marvelous kind of death." Zeus interrupts her by saying that a similar type of self-immolation has occurred recently in Olympia, and asks whether Philosophia was there. No, she replies, she did not go to Olympia to see the death of Peregrinus because so many detestable people were there, filling the temple with their howlings. So Lucian made the point that "philosophy" was absent when Peregrinus committed suicide.

Philosophia then goes on to describe the Cynics in a lengthy speech. They are mostly slaves, she contends, who as children had no time to learn philosophy because they always had to do manual work. But when they grew up and saw how philosophers were respected by the multitude, they wanted to become philosophers also. Since, however, they were not equipped to be philosophers, they could only put on the appearance of philosophy, like the jackass in Aesop's tale who donned a lion's skin and claimed to be a lion. These men put on a cloak, carry a wallet and staff, and make a lot of noise. As they go from house to house they are fed and even given money by people who take them for true philosophers. This, of course, they are not. For one thing, "they do not even tolerate investigation," and whenever they are questioned on any point they begin to shout abuses. The cities are filled with them, especially with those who call on the names of Diogenes, Antisthenes, and Crates (well-known Greek Cynics). But the later Cynics do not even imitate what is good in the nature of dogs, such as guarding the house and staying at home, but instead imitate only the dogs' barking and thievishness. Philosophia now asks what this will result in. If the fraud is permitted to go on, all working men will leave their jobs to become Cynics and, instead of toiling from morning to evening, will live off other people. To make matters worse, she goes on, these Cynics are morally deficient in their private lives. They are drunkards, liars, and seducers of women, and, when they have collected enough money, they throw aside the philosopher's garb and live like rich men. By the time Philosophia ends her tirade, Zeus decides that he must take action to wipe out this disease, and he sends Hercules to accomplish the task. Lucian thus implied that Peregrinus was the same kind of counterfeit philosopher.[32]

In Lucian's opinion, Peregrinus had been no more sincere during the Christian phase of his life. He took advantage of the credulous nature of the Christians, whom Lucian characterized with the following words:

> The poor souls have convinced themselves that they all will be immortal and will live forever, on account of which they think lightly of death and most of them surrender to it voluntarily. Furthermore, their first lawgiver convinced them that they are all each other's brothers once they deny the Greek gods, by which they break the laws and worship that crucified sophist and live according to his rules. They despise all things and consider them common property, accepting such doctrines by faith alone. So if a cheater who is able to make a profit from the situation comes to them, he quickly becomes rich, laughing at the simple people.[33]

Of course, the Christians of Palestine were not such simpletons; in fact, they kept a very sharp eye out for would-be swindlers. The *Didache* advised congregations to welcome persons who came to them in the name of Jesus Christ and to help travelers. But if a traveler stayed and took advantage of the hospitality of the congregation for longer than two or three days without working, the *Didache* warned, he was a false Christian: "Beware of such men!"[34] And, in fact, the Christians in Palestine unceremoniously excommunicated Peregrinus from the church, despite his prior imprisonment, once it became apparent that he would not comply with Christian standards.

Lucian's criticism of Christians touched on another serious point, namely, the Christians' contempt of death. It is unclear from his satires whether Lucian connected Peregrinus's contempt for death with his Christian past or his later Cynic convictions. At any rate, this aspect of Christian life was so well known that Epictetus (ca. 50–ca. 130), the Stoic philosopher who lived a generation or two before Peregrinus and Lucian, knew about it and commented favorably on it. At one point, Epictetus discussed the problem of fear. Why do people fear a tyrant? Children have no fear of swords, guards, or anything else that surround a tyrant. And if a man desires to die, and comes before a tyrant, that man is not afraid either, because the sword, which for others is an object of fear, is something that he himself wishes. Again, if a man cares nothing for life or material possession, for him death holds no fear either. "Therefore," Epictetus continued, "if madness can produce this attitude of mind toward the things which have just been mentioned, and also habit, as with the Galilaeans, cannot reason and demonstration teach a man that God has made all things in the universe, and the whole universe itself to be free from hindrance and to contain its end in itself, and the parts of it to serve the needs of the whole?"[35] Epictetus, a former slave, taught first in Rome and then in Nicopolis, Epirus. Both cities had a Christian congregation at a very early date, and, according to Titus 3:12, the apostle Paul spent a whole winter in Nicopolis. Epictetus, therefore, had a good opportunity to learn something about the Christians, whom he called Galilaeans, and he seems to have been particularly impressed by their lack of fear before the authorities. He attributed this attitude to habit, and he argued that philosophy should be able to create a similar frame of mind in any man.

The famous medical doctor Galen (ca. 129-199) had a similar opinion. He thought that the Jews and Christians were a simple people, below the level of philosophers. Since demonstrative arguments were too much for them, they based their faith on parables and miracles, and yet some Christians acted in the same way as philosophers, "for their contempt of death is patent to us every day. . . ."[36]

Not all pagans, however, shared the benign views of Epictetus and Galen. Many of them adopted exactly the same position as Lucian had concerning Peregrinus, and they bade the Christians to "Go, all of you and kill yourselves and go to your God and leave us in peace."[37] Tertullian reported that when Arrius Antonius harassed Christians in Asia, Christians from the whole province presented themselves before his judgment seat in one group. He ordered some to be led away to execution, and to the rest he said: "O miserable men, if you wish to die, you have precipices or halters."[38]

Tertullian angrily rejected these pagan attacks and defended the virtue of the Christians' contempt of death. "This is the attitude in which we conquer!" he wrote. "It is our victory robe, it is for us a sort of triumphal car. Naturally enough, therefore, we do not please the vanquished; on account of this, indeed, we are counted a desperate reckless race. But the very desperation and recklessness you object to in us, among yourselves lift high the standard of virtue in the cause of glory and of fame." Tertullian pointed out that the pagans had their own heroes who had become famous and venerated by all because of their contempt of death. Gaius Mucius Scaevola, for example, a legendary hero from Rome's mythical past, had slipped into the camp of Porsenna, king of Etruscan Clusium, when he besieged Rome. Mucius tried to kill Porsenna, but he was discovered and taken before the king. When threatened with death he calmly placed his right hand on the fire in a nearby brazier. This defiance so impressed Porsenna that he immediately set Mucius free. The Romans admired the "sublimity of mind" of Mucius and the "mental resolution" of another Roman hero Empedocles, yet they dismissed the Christians' contempt of death as "obstinacy" and "reckless foolhardiness." Nonetheless, if the pagans could do such things for human reasons, certainly the Christians could do them for God.[39]

Origen defended the Christian attitude toward suffering and death in a similar manner against attacks by the Roman Celsus. Origen argued that when Christians exposed their bodies to torture, they helped to prevent the work of evil demons, and so their sacrifice was not in vain. He wrote: "Indeed we think it both reasonable in itself and well pleasing to God, to suffer pain for the sake of virtue, to undergo torture for the sake of piety, and even to suffer death for the sake of holiness . . . and we maintain that to overcome the love of life is to enjoy a great good."[40]

Marcus Aurelius (161-180), the philosopher-emperor, has left us a brief but interesting note on Christians, which, if nothing else, at least shows how an emperor, and probably many aristocratic Romans, viewed the new religion and, in particular, the Christian attitude toward death. The note appears in *Meditations*, a collection of Stoic aphorisms that he composed while fighting Rome's enemies on the Danube frontier.

What an admirable soul is that which is ready and willing if the time has come to be released from the body, whether that release means

> extinction, dispersal, or survival. This readiness must be the result of
> a specific decision; not as with the Christians, of obstinate opposi-
> tion, but of a reasoned and dignified decision, and without dramatics
> if it is to convince anyone else.[41]

The message in the passage is obvious. Although Christians do not
fear death, they make a show of their martyrdom. To a true philosopher, Marcus Aurelius argued, this was nothing but repulsive theat-
rics. Man should be ready to give up his soul in a simple, dignified
manner. From his note it is clear that Marcus Aurelius was quite
familiar with the phenomenon of Christian martyrdom. How did he
learn about it, and what specific instances did he have in mind when
he wrote this note? We know that the Christian apologists Justin
Martyr (ca. 114-165), Miltiades (dates unknown), Apollinaris (around
172), Melito (bishop of Sardis in Lydia, ca. 190), and Athenagoras
(around 177) addressed some of their writings explaining Christianity
to Marcus Aurelius, but whether the emperor actually read any of
them is more than questionable. The pagans did not usually read
Christian literature, and Tertullian scornfully remarked: "No one
comes for guidance to our writings unless he is already a Christian."[42]
It is, therefore, unlikely that Aurelius got his information on the
Christians from such writers. Another possibility is that the emperor
had heard of the torture and execution of several Christians in Lyons
and Vienne in 177. In this year a local but violent persecution broke
out in southern Gaul, and the Christians in the area prepared a
written report on their sufferings. Eusebius (263-339), in turn, included this report in his *Church History*.[43]

But how much did Marcus Aurelius know about the persecution in
Gaul? And what was his position concerning persecutions in
general?[44] There are reasons to believe that Marcus Aurelius actually
made it possible for the authorities to persecute Christians. He certainly does not seem to have intervened in the events of 177 at Lyons
and Vienne. Furthermore, Melito wrote that certain decrees of the
emperor opened new persecutions. "What never before happened, the
race of the pious is now persecuted, driven about in Asia, by new and
strange decrees. For the shameless informers, and those that crave the
property of others, taking occasion from the edicts of the emperor,
openly perpetrate robbery; night and day plundering those who are
guilty of no crime."[45] The exact nature of the "new and strange
decrees," referred to by Melito, is unclear. We do know that Marcus
Aurelius issued a decree providing the death penalty for those who

"create superstitious fear of a divine being in credulous people."[46] It could be that this decree was used to justify measures taken against Christians, although Marcus Aurelius probably had soothsayers and astrologers, not Christians, in mind when he issued it.

Soothsayers, astrologers, and magicians were plentiful in the second century, and their numbers increased still further after the plague of 167 and the Germanic invasions of about the same time. The Christians also attracted many new followers during this period of crisis because they cared for the sick and their philosophy helped make life meaningful in a time of sudden death.[47] It is not impossible that the magistrates lumped the Christians together with sooth-sayers and superstitious people. These magistrates probably did not differentiate between a soothsayer and a prophet, and most pagans already classified Christianity as a superstition. The emperor also probably knew about the spectacular suicide of Peregrinus Proteus. If so, he would have seen it as a disgusting spectacle because of its theatrical form. But it is unlikely that he could have known anything of Peregrinus's early Christian experimentation. Nevertheless, such a dramatic suicide, whether in southern Gaul or in southern Greece, would not have filled him with admiration.

Clearly, the Romans did not generally applaud the Christians' contempt for death. Where then did Peregrinus get the idea of a voluntary and public death? No doubt he knew that many Cynics committed suicide when they became old, so to an extent he fol-lowed Cynic customs. But the manner of his death was peculiar, and in choosing it he may have been influenced by many examples such as those of Calanus, the Brahmans, Empedocles, or perhaps even the Christian martyrs, such as Bishop Polycarp, who suffered martyrdom by burning in 156.[48] And Peregrinus probably had heard of Polycarp. These examples may have played some role in the crystallization of his idea, for Peregrinus was a restless soul who was always searching and always knocking at different doors. He lived in an age when people were especially sensitive to the problems of life and death, and they spent much time and energy trying to save their souls.[49]

Lucian's criticism of Peregrinus—that he lacked sincerity and only committed suicide to gain notoriety—is certainly unjustified and cruel. After all, Peregrinus did give away his inheritance and did live a life of poverty, teaching and preaching his philosophy. He did not find spiritual satisfaction in the organized church, and so he searched for it in wayward directions. Lucian, however, saw all non-Roman phi-

losophies, including Christianity, as senseless and useless. He
thought that belief in the supernatural was ridiculous, and he preferred to live as an "ordinary man, without fantastic and vain
hopes."[50] This Lucian did, and he sneered at anyone who tried to find
a deeper meaning to human existence and a fulfillment that was
higher than the ordinary. Peregrinus and Lucian, therefore, offer an
interesting contrast in this respect: one renounced his life in search of
spiritual gains, while the other decided to keep his life and forfeit
everything else.

Nowhere in our meager resources concerning Peregrinus do we
find any hint of what happened to his Christian faith after he was
excommunicated from the church. Did he give up Christianity completely, or did he live a Christian life outside the bounds of the
organized church? We have already seen that Lucian's harsh judgment of him was probably unjustified. Doubtless, many Cynics exactly fitted Lucian's description and were skeptical, nihilistic,
fraudulent freeloaders.[51] But the little we know of the teachings of
Peregrinus, aside from the hostile remarks by Lucian, indicates that
he was a deeply religious man and a mystic. He was also an ascetic
and died a poor man. Was he, then, an early example of the Christian
ascetics? Perhaps in a limited sense, for Peregrinus displayed many
qualities that were also characteristic of the very early church and
those Christians who lived a "truly self-sacrificing life."[52] His association with the organized church ended with his excommunication,
but it seems that the sheer weight of his radicalism forced him to
deviate from orthodox standards. His training in Alexandria under a
Cynic master further molded his personality, and the Peregrinus we
meet in Rome and Greece is a strange mixture of Greek and Christian
ideals. It is obvious, however, from Lucian's account, that in his later
life his religion expressed itself more in pagan than in Christian
terms. In the second century, an age of syncretism, it was still possible to cross from one religious community to another, especially if
both had many common ideals.[53]

It is not difficult to find many similarities between the life of
Peregrinus and the Christian ideal represented in the New Testament. Jesus taught his followers to separate themselves completely
from the world and even from their own families. They renounced
worldly treasures because these tied a person's heart to the world. He
advised rich young men to give away their wealth because it is hard
for a rich man to enter the kingdom of God. Jesus himself did not have

a place of his own to lay down his head to sleep, and he wandered "through cities and villages, preaching" and accepting the donations of those "who provided for him out of their means." He sent out his twelve disciples in strict independence from worldly needs; he allowed them to take only one piece of clothing, no bag, no staff, not even sandals. Thus, we find the early Christian missionaries walking the highways and preaching. Philip, for example, ran along the desert road to Gaza beside the chariot of the Ethiopian eunuch until he was invited to "come up and sit with him." The Apostle Paul in his traveling ministry was so completely "free of all men" that he even preferred to pay for his own expenses, although he acknowledged the right of other missionaries to be taken care of by those whose spiritual needs they served.[54]

Soon the Roman world was full of such wandering Christian missionaries who "have set out [on their journey] for his sake and have accepted nothing from the heathen."[55] What distinguished them from wandering Cynic philosophers? Outwardly, probably nothing, which may be the main reason why the *Didache* is so anxious to warn against false teachers. "If a teacher teaches another doctrine. . . . do not listen to him"; "if he stays three days, he is a false prophet"; "if he asks for money, he is a false prophet."[56] It is tempting to see in these false teachers, who tried to take advantage of their hosts, Cynics of the same breed that Lucian so despised. The point is, however, that not only was a Cynic's way of life compatible with Christian faith, but that the Christians may have adopted Cynic ways, in particular Christian missionaries. It was possible for Peregrinus to retain his Christian faith—or at least some elements of it—and to live as a Cynic wandering apostle, outside of the church. We must remember too that Peregrinus adopted the Cynic garb some time before his excommunication, and thus, at least for a time, he was a *bona fide* Christian while he lived as a Cynic; unless Lucian's chronology is incorrect. Even in later years, particularly just before his death, his behavior was in at least one striking respect reminiscent of apostolic practices. He sent letters to cities in the form of testaments, exhortations, and ordinances. The Greek words here are "diathekas," "paraineseis," and "nomous," all of which are strongly rooted in the Judeo-Christian tradition. These letters were carried by ambassadors, called "messengers from the dead," again words that closely resemble those used by Ignatius of Antioch in the letters that he wrote on his way to execution in Rome around 110.[57]

If Peregrinus indeed combined Christian principles and philosophy, he was not alone. During this same period, Justin Martyr in Rome preached Christianity in a philosopher's garb. Justin's most vocal opponent was a Cynic by the name of Crescens, who may also have been Christian at one time but now did his best to avoid such suspicions.[58] Tatian, a pupil of Justin's, became a Christian extremist, and around 172 moved away from Rome and back to his native East where he founded a sect, called the "Encratites," or "Abstinents." This sect embraced strict rules of self-discipline, rejected the use of meat and wine, and condemned marriage as adultery. The church father Hippolytus (ca. 170-235) called Tatian "very Cynic,"[59] and the mainstream church treated him as a heretic. The Greek rhetorician Aelius Aristides (ca. 128-181) compared Cynics and Christians in a speech written in defense of the great heroes of the Golden Age of Greece. He wrote:

> Who on earth could tolerate these enemies who lash out more solecism than words? . . . When they steal, they say that they 'share.' They call their envy 'philosophy' and their mendicity 'disdain of wordly goods.' They frequent the doorways, talking more often to the doorkeepers than to the masters, making up for their lowly conditions by using impudence. They deceive like flatterers, handle insults like superior men, combining the two most opposite and repugnant vices: vileness and insolence. Their behavior is very similar to those blasphemous people in Palestine. They, too, manifest their impiety by the obvious signs that they do not recognize those who are above them, and they separated themselves from the Greeks and from everything good. They are incapable as far as they are concerned of contributing in any matter whatsoever toward any common good, but when it comes to undermining home life, bringing trouble and discord into families and claiming to be leaders of all things, they are the most skillful men.[60]

The "blasphemous people in Palestine" may have been the Christians, but the rest of the passage fits very well the general conception of the Cynics, and if this is what Aristides meant then his comparison touched on an interesting similarity between the two movements. In the charges that he leveled at Cynics and Palestinians one can almost recognize the voice of that great opponent of Christianity, Celsus, who charged that Christians contributed nothing to the common welfare of the empire and undermined home life. This view was widespread and popular.

Indeed, as the case of Peregrinus shows, a strange empathy existed between serious Christians and serious Cynics. To begin with they were both radicals who refused to accept halfway applications of their philosophies. A major characteristic of Cynicism was its "insistence on the practical aspect of philosophy,"[61] and it is a well-known fact that Christianity likewise appealed to people more as a distinct way of life than as a set of doctrines. Writers of early Christian literature continually admonished Christians to do certain things and to avoid doing others, for example, some Christians sold their property.[62] Occasionally we also meet people like Origen (ca. 185-253), who interpreted Matt. 19:12 literally and castrated himself for the Kingdom of Heaven; or, like Tertullian (ca. 160–ca. 220) who set the most rigorous standards concerning what occupation a Christian might or might not enter.[63] The most eminent radicals, of course, were the martyrs who willingly accepted the ultimate for their faith.

In *The Runaways* Lucian depicted the Cynics as people who exchanged their daily chores for an easy life, which they saw as the "Age of Kronos," or the "Golden Age." Celsus accused Christianity of encouraging the same irresponsible conduct, because it held out to the believers the promise of Paradise and the eschatological hope of the Kingdom of God. The Christians' withdrawal from many daily activities of pagan life (such as the festivals, the theater, and the circus), as well as their refusal to assume certain political offices were held against them as it alienated them from society. If everybody acted the way the Christians did, the empire would fall apart, Celsus wrote.[64] An element of escapism, whereby the harsh realities of life could either be avoided or at least be made tolerable by hope, existed in both movements. No wonder then that both attracted large numbers of slaves and persons from the lower stratum of society. Peregrinus, too, had followers, as Lucian said *"para goun tois idiotais,"* i.e., among the uneducated.[65] Interestingly enough, critics of Christianity like Celsus, used exactly the same phrase to depict the membership of the church. They argued that the Christian Church attracted converts from the untrained and uneducated mass. The church freely admitted this fact, and we have many references to it in early Christian literature. This element of escapism was fully developed in the anchorite movement, the voluntary withdrawal of Christian ascetics from society.[66] The roots of anchoritism and monasticism are manifold (escape for religious, political, or economic reasons was possible), but the actual event was always the same. A man disposed of his material belongings and left his village and his relatives as Peregrinus did. He then moved to the desert away from civilization and settled in the neighborhood of an older hermit to receive his training in self-denial, much in the manner of the Cynics.

Both movements had a strong element of asceticism. Cynic philosophy stressed self-sufficiency, shamelessness, and "Askesis." The Cynic led a life of austerity, possessing only one cloak, a wallet, and a club and avoiding all luxuries of life. The word "Askesis" means "training" and mostly refers to the training of athletes. The Cynic had to go through a period of strenuous training (as Peregrinus had done in Alexandria) to kill worldly ambitions, to endure physical pain, and to liberate one's self from desires. Likewise, the Christian was constantly admonished not to satisfy the desires of the flesh but rather to be like a "master athlete," "God's athlete," and a "great athlete" who for God's sake suffers blows to conquer. "The greater the toil, the greater the gain!" and the prize was immortality and eternal life![67] The later monks of the Egyptian desert followed this same principle: they were the *athletae Dei*, training themselves in continence, curbing human passion, anger, and desire, and renouncing the world.

Thus, in addition to the fact that both Cynics and Christians, if they were honest in their convictions, preferred to practice what they preached, there ran through the two movements a number of other common strands among which the most obvious were radicalism, escapism, and asceticism. To these we may add a detached view of the world, contempt of death, and strict monotheism. Later, when Christianity emerged as the victor in the Roman world, the church welcomed the Cynics. By the end of the fourth century a bishop in Constantinople, Maximus, even confessed himself to be a Cynic philosopher, and he wore the mantle and staff of the Cynics in public. As pagan Cynicism declined, Christian monasticism increased, and by the sixth century Cynicism as a pagan philosophy had disappeared. Obviously, those who would have been attracted to the Cynic way of life found their place in monasticism. Yet, as D. R. Dudley has shown, many features of the original movement can be recognized in later Western civilization, for example, in the image of St. Francis of Assisi and the various ascetic movements of the Middle Ages.[68] Even the nicknames of the Dominicans, *Domini-canes*, meaning "dogs of the Lord," can be understood either as referring to bloodhounds who seek out the enemies of God (soon after its foundation in the thirteenth century the order became closely linked with

the Inquisition), or as the "Cynics of the Lord" totally dedicated to
his service and for that purpose give up all their personal interests.
The history of Christianity is full of such examples. Ignaz Parham-
mer, the man who commissioned Mozart to compose the *Wai-
senhaus Mass* (K. 139), "dressed as a pilgrim with beard, staff, and
cloak," i.e., as a typical Cynic, or wandering apostle, or pilgrim,
whichever name one chooses as most appropriate.[69]

More than anything else, Cynicism was a state of mind, and as such
it appears even in more recent times. Think of someone like Tolstoy,
who like Peregrinus was well read in religious and philosophical
literature but refused to settle down on his family estate preferring to
put into practice his beliefs. He gave up his fortune, renounced
royalties to his writings, wore simple peasant clothing, and adopted
an ascetic life. His aim was self-sufficiency; he even made his own
boots. He preached the gospel of love as the only way to make society
better. Finally, he even decided to find perfect freedom by leaving
home and wandering, but he was already 82 years old and died a few
days later in a small railway station. Like Peregrinus, the church also
excommunicated Tolstoy, and he was therefore buried at his estate
without ecclesiastical rites.

Still, to return to our point of departure once more, it would be
far-fetched to call Peregrinus a *Christian* monastic. Perhaps he, like
so many others, did renounce the Christian faith. It is, however,
difficult to see how someone who was so totally committed as he was
in his early life could do so. It is equally difficult to believe that
someone who interpreted the Scriptures and published several books
on the subject could become wholly unaffected by Christianity.
Perhaps it is best to classify him as a dedicated Cynic permeated with
Christian ideals. He lived like a Cynic but in some ways he gives the
appearance of an early Christian ascetic. Although he did not withdraw to the desert—in the middle of the second century there was no
reason to do that—he did withdraw from society into a hut outside of
the city where he talked about sin, the wisdom of avoiding it, and
other similar matters. His death bears a faint resemblance to the
death of St. Anthony, the father of Christian monasticism, in that
they both died in a circle of their disciples having no other worldly
possessions than the meager clothing they wore. Peregrinus, we read,
had nothing but a shirt, a cloak, a wallet, and a Hercules-club, and
even these he laid aside, keeping nothing but a filthy shirt to cover his
nakedness, before he jumped into the fire. St. Anthony, according to

Athanasius, died in 356, attended by two of his disciples to whom he gave his last will regarding the disposition of his possessions. "The sheepskin and the old cloak I am lying on," he said "give to Athanasius the bishop; he brought it to me new. Let Serapion the bishop have the other skeepskin; do you take my haircloth, and farewell, ye that are my heartstrings, for Anthony is going, and will not be with you in this world anymore."[70]

NOTES

1. The following story of Peregrinus is based on Lucian's *De Morte Peregrini*, for which I used the Loeb edition by A. M. Harmon (Cambridge: Harvard University Press, 1969); the few remarks by Aulus Gellius in *Attic Nights*, E.T., J. C. Rolfe, Loeb (1927; reprint ed., London: Heinemann, 1952); and some references by the church fathers that are identified in the text.

2. It is not profitable to overemphasize the steadfastness of Christians by restricting our views to the martyrs only. There were many nominal Christians and borderline cases as is amply proven by the huge numbers who fell away during times of persecution. During the third and early fourth centuries the *libellati* (those who received certificates that they performed the required state sacrifices) and the *traditores* (those who willingly gave up sacred books to the authorities) became serious problems for the church when they desired to re-enter the church. Not all Christians were lifelong members and not all of them chose the way of martyrdom.

3. Acts 16:23.

4. Matt. 25:34-36.

5. 2 Cor. 11:23.

6. See also Heb. 10:34.

7. See for example, *Passio Peretuae* 3.5; 51; Ignatius, *Smyrn.* 6.2; Tertullian, *Ad Martyres* 1.

8. *De jejunio* 12. Tertullian wrote this treatise during the Montanist period of his life, and it reflects his extremely rigoristic attitude.

9. Eusebius, *Church History* 10.8.

10. Acts 15:29. Lucian does not clearly explain why the Christians turned against Peregrinus. See *De Morte Peregrini* chap. 16.

11. See Diogenes Laertius 6.20-81.

12. The impact of Cynic philosophy on Roman society during the first and second centuries A.D. is eloquently analyzed by Samuel Dill, *Roman Society from Nero to Marcus Aurelius* (1904; reprint ed., Cleveland: Meridian, 1964), pp. 334-383.

13. Dio Cassius *Roman History* 65.13, Loeb, E. T., E. Cary.

14. Ibid., 65.12.2.

15. Ibid., 65.13.3.

16. Ibid., 65.15.5.

17. No doubt Tatian meant here that the Cynics received their food from the tables of rich men; without the rich they could not survive.

18. *Oratio ad Graecos* 25, *ANF* 2.75. See also Dio Chrysostom's (40-112) criticism in *Or.* 32.9-10 in Dill, *Roman Society*, p. 349–50.; and A. D. Nock, *Conversion* (Oxford: Oxford University Press, 1965), pp. 168ff.

19. According to the *Historia Augusta, Antoninus Pius 5* there was a rebellion in Achaia during the reign of Antoninus Pius.

20. So titled because Gellius collected much of the material for it during the winter nights he spent in Athens.

21. *Attic Nights* 12.11; 8.3; 11.1–7.

22. Arrian *Anabasis* 7.3; Plutarch *Parallel Lives, Alexander* 65, 69-70, and many other ancient authors preserved the Calanus story. See Pauly, Wissowa, and Kroll, *Realencylopädie*, 10 (1919), 1544–45; W. W. Tarn, *Alexander the Great* (1948; reprint ed., Boston: Beacon Press, 1956), p. 110; and Moses Hadas, *Hellenistic Culture* (1959; reprint ed., New York: W. W. Norton, 1972), pp. 178f., who examined the interest of Hellenistic authors "in virtuous men who encountered death in some memorable way"; Roger Pack, "The 'Volatilization' of Peregrinus Proteus," *American Journal of Philosophy* 67 (1946): 334-45 also mentions the names of Sardanopalus, Semiramis, Hamilcar, and Croesus as examples of death by fire.

23. See Diogenes Laertius *Lives* 8.15-77. Lucian *Icaromenippus* 13 repeats the legend when he sarcastically says that Empedocles was carried upward by the smoke from Aetna; see also *De Morte Peregrini* 1.

24. Dio 54.9.10. See also Plutarch *Alexander* 65, 69; and Strabo *Geography* 15.1.68.

25. Lucian criticized Peregrinus for this. With reference to the Indian Calanus, he said that the Indians "do not leap into the fire . . . but when they have built their pyre, they stand close beside it motionless and endure being toasted; then, mounting upon it, they cremate themselves decorously . . ."; *De morte Peregrini* 25. See also *Fugitivi* 7: "[The holy men of India] ascend a very lofty pyre and endure cremation without any change in their outward appearance or their sitting position."

26. *Legatio* 26. Cf. The report of Lucian in *Adv. Indoctum* (*The Ignorant Book Collector*) 14: "Only a day or two ago another man paid a talent for the staff which Proteus the Cynic laid aside before leaping into the fire; and he keeps this treasure and displays it . . . Yet the original owner of this marvelous possession surpassed even you yourself in ignorance and indecency . . . ," E.T., A. M. Harmon, Loeb, vol. 3 (Cambridge: Harvard University Press, 1969), p. 193.

27. *Ad Martyres* 4.

28. *Oratio Ad Graecos* 25.

29. *De Morte Peregrini*.

30. *Fugitivi*, E. T., A. M. Harmon, Loeb, vol. 5 (Cambridge: Harvard University Press, 1972), pp. 59-61.

31. Ibid., 4.

32. For a criticism of Lucian's "cold merciless spirit" see Dill, *Roman Society*, pp. 353ff.

33. *De Morte Peregini* 13. Lucian also referred to the Christians in his treatise on *Alexander the False Prophet*, Loeb, E.T., A. M. Harmon, 4:299, 255. Lucian was not primarily concerned with Christianity as such. In *De Morte Peregrini* he wanted to ridicule Peregrinus's vainglorious thirst for fame, and in *Alexander* he wanted to expose the hand of a trickster. In his own mind he may have put Alexander and Jesus in the same class; both were imposters who misled their followers and made them do unreasonable

things. H. D. Betz, "Lukian von Samosata und das Christentum," *Novum Testamentum* 3 (1958):233, argues that Lucian saw Jesus as the founder of a new mystery religion. Also see Chapter 5 below.

34. *Didache* 12.

35. Epictetus *Discourses* 4.7.1-6, Loeb, E.T., W. A. Oldfather, 2:361-63.

36. R. Walzer, *Galen on Jews and Christians* (London: Oxford University Press, 1949), pp. 14-15. Celsus also approved Christians' willingness to die for their faith; see Origen *Contra Celsum* 1.8.

37. Justin Martyr *Apology* 2.4. Compare this with Celsus: "If they [the Christians] refuse to render due service to the gods, and to respect those who are set over this service, let them not come to manhood, or marry wives, or have children, or indeed take any share in the affairs of life; but let them depart hence with all speed, and leave no posterity behind them, that such a race may become extinct from the face of the earth." Origen *Contra Celsum* 8. 55.

38. *To Scapula* 5.

39. *Apology* 50, *ANF* 3.54-55; also *Ad Nationes* 18, *ANF* 3.126.

40. Origen *Contra Celsum* 8.54.

41. *Meditations* 11.3. G. M. A. Grube, *The Meditations* (New York: Bobbs-Merrill, 1963), p. 111. See also the comments of Edward Meyer, *Ursprung and Anfänge des Christentums* (Stuttgart: Cotta, 1923), 1:530ff.

42. *Testimony of the Soul* 1.

43. *Church History* 5.1.

44. It would be interesting to know to what degree the emperor was influenced by his advisor Fronto whose violent anti-Christian attitude was well known. Junius Rusticus, a judge and another counselor of Marcus Aurelius, had condemned Justin to Martyrdom in 165. These relationships must have influenced the decisions made by the emperor.

45. Eusebius *Church History* 4.26.5.

46. *Digest* 48.19.30.

47. William H. McNeill, *Plagues and Peoples* (New York: Doubleday, 1976), pp. 121ff.

48. *The Martyrdom of Polycarp* 12.3ff. About the date of Peregrinus' death see also H. Nissen "Die Abfassungszeit von Arrian's Anabasis," *Rheinisches Museum* 43 (1888):254. W. R. Halliday, *The Pagan Background of Early Christianity* (Liverpool: University Press of Liverpool, 1925), p. 190 sees in the death of Peregrinus "a passion for martyrdom in itself, like that which becomes characteristic of certain phases of Early Christianity." Cf. A. D. Nock, *Conversion*, p. 201 characterizes it "as a way of apotheosis" and mentions it after the statement that for the men of the ancient world "the prospect of being forgotten was . . . very terrible, and to avoid that a man would do and suffer much."

49. See T. R. Glover, *The Conflict of Religions in the Early Roman Empire* (Boston: Beacon Press, 1960).

50. *Hermotimus* 84.

51. See Dill *Roman Society*, 351ff.

52. See O. Chadwick, *Western Monasticism*, Library of Christian Classics, vol. 12 (Philadelphia: Westminster Press, 1958), pp. 13ff., 361. The similarities between Cynics and Christians did not escape the attention of scholars. Emperor Julian (361-363) made such a comparison in his *Or.* 7.224A and B, where he equated the Christian monks with the Cynics of the pagan world. See Ch. N. Cochrane, *Christianity and Classical Culture* (Oxford:

Oxford University Press, 1957), pp. 209–10, 339–40. Also P. Wendland, *Die Hellenistisch-Römische Kultur in Ihren Beziehungen zu Judentum und Christentum* (Tübingen: Mohr, 1912), pp. 92-93, 226-27; W. R. Halliday, *Pagan Background*, pp. 126–27, 169–70, 201–2; Edwin Hatch, *The Influence of Greek Ideas on Christianity* (New York: Harper, 1957), p. 166ff., cf. the scathing remarks on monasticism in Gibbon, *Decline and Fall*, ch. 37; W. H. C. Frend, *Martyrdom and Persecution in the Early Church* (New York: Doubleday, 1957), p. 204.

53. See Dill, *Roman Society*, p. 355.

54. Luke 14:26, 12:32-23, 8:1-3; Matt. 6:19-21, 8:20, 10:5-10; Mark 10:17-25; Acts 8:26-31; 1. Cor. 9:19; 9:1ff.

55. John 7.

56. 11.2; 5-6.

57. Smyrn. 11 and *Polyc.* 7.

58. Justin *Apology* 2.3. Frend, *Martyrdom and Persecution*, p. 203 suggests that behind the denunciation of Justin by Crescens may have been "the professional jealousy of a rival but less successful preacher of reform."

59. *Refutation* 14.

60. *Huper Tōn Tettarōn* 2.394ff. Author's translation.

61. D. R. Dudley, *A History of Cynicism* (London: Methuen, 1937), pp. 127, 188.

62. Acts 2.45.

63. See for example, *de Idololatria* and other similar treatises.

64. Origen *Contra Celsum* 8.48.

65. *De Morte Peregrini* 18.

66. From the Greek *anachōreo*, meaning withdraw, retire, take refuge.

67. Ignatius *To Polycarp* 1.3; 2.3; 3.1.

68. *A History of Cynicism*, pp. 209ff.

69. A Hutchings, *Mozart, The Musician* (New York: Macmillan, 1976), p. 10.

70. Athanasius *Vita S. Antonii* 92. E. T., *Nicene and Post Nicene Fathers*, Series 2, 4:196-231. This quotation is taken from H. Waddel, *The Desert Fathers* (Ann Arbor: University of Michigan Press, 1957), p. 1.

III

The Charges of Immorality and Cannibalism

S OMETIME AROUND THE year 200 a Christian lawyer by the name of Minucius Felix wrote a dialogue in remembrance of his deceased friend Octavius.[1] The dialogue consists of an exchange of speeches between a pagan (Q. Caecilius Natalis) and a Christian (Octavius Januarius) with Minucius Felix serving as a kind of moderator. They discuss the major Roman grievances against the Christians, and many of the arguments used by the pagan are probably based on a now lost, anti-Christian oration by Marcus Cornelius Fronto (ca. 100-166), a famous orator and the teacher of the future emperors Marcus Aurelius and Lucius Verus. Although few of his writings survive, we know, through the references of other authors, of Fronto's intense hatred of the Christians.[2]

Minucius Felix cast his dialogue in the form of a personal reminiscence. Octavius comes to Rome for a visit, and he goes with Minucius and Caecilius to Ostia for a stroll along the seashore. Along the way they come across a statue of the god Serapis. Immediately Caecilius kisses his hand and places it on the statue, a widespread custom of the time. Although an enlightened pagan would never identify a statue with the god whom it depicted, he would respect the statue as a representation of that god and very likely would kiss it. Some statues were worn smooth by much kissing, just as one foot of the statue of St. Peter in Rome is worn smooth because of the caressing and kissing over many centuries by pious visitors and pilgrims.

Seeing the pagan sign, Octavius urges Minucius not to permit Caecilius to continue in such ignorance. They go on and enjoy the sights, but at length Caecilius, disturbed by Octavius's remark, proposes to debate the matter with him. So they sit down, Minucius in the middle and the two adversaries on either side. Caecilius starts the debate by asking whether the world is ruled by providence. He argues that man will never have a sure answer to this question because the human mind cannot encompass the divine. It is only with colossal arrogance that some uneducated and ignorant people make categorical statements about the universe that is, in fact, beyond their comprehension. Caecilius argues, therefore, that it is much better to adhere to a religion that has been sanctified by antiquity and has proven its value. History has shown, for example, how the Roman ancestral religion has benefited the Roman people. Indeed the Roman religion is so ancient and so salutary that nobody should be permitted to attack it.

Caecilius now makes his attack upon the Christians more explicit.

> Why is it not a thing to be lamented, that men (for you will bear with my making use pretty freely of the force of the plea that I have undertaken)—that men, I say, of a reprobate, unlawful, and desperate faction, should rage against the gods? Who, having gathered together from the lowest dregs the more unskilled, and women, credulous and, by the facility of their sex, yielding, establish a herd of a profane conspiracy, which is leagued together by nightly meetings, and solemn fasts, and unhuman meats—not by any sacred rite, but by that which requires expiation—a people skulking and shunning the light, silent in public, but garrulous in corners. They despise the temples as dead-houses, they reject the gods, they laugh at sacred things; wretched, they pity, if they are allowed, the priests; half naked themselves, they despise honours and purple robes. Oh, wondrous folly and incredible audacity! They despise present torments, although they fear those which are uncertain and future; and while they fear to die after death, they do not fear to die or the present: so does a deceitful hope sooth their fear with the solace of a revival.
>
> And now, as wickeder things advance more fruitfully, and abandoned manners creep on day by day, those abominable shrines of an impious assembly are maturing themselves throughout the whole world. Assuredly this confederacy ought to be rooted out and execrated. They know one another by secret marks and insignia, and they love one another almost before they know one another. Everywhere also there is mingled among them a certain religion of lust, and they call one another promiscuously brothers and sisters, that even a not unusual debauchery may by the intervention of that sacred name become incestuous: it is thus that their vain and senseless superstition glories in crimes. Nor, concerning these things, would intelligent report speak of things so great and various, and requiring to be prefaced by an apology, unless truth were at the bottom of it. I hear that they adore the head of an ass, that basest of creatures, consecrated by I

know not what silly persuasion—worthy and appropriate religion for such manners. Some say that they worship the virilia of their pontiff and priest, and adore the nature, as it were, of their common parent. I know not whether these things are false; certainly suspicion is applicable to secret and nocturnal rites; and he who explains their ceremonies by reference to a man punished by extreme suffering for his wickedness, and to the deadly wood of the cross, appropriates fitting altars for reprobate and wicked men, that they may worship what they deserve. Now the story about the initiation of young novices is as much to be detested as it is well known. An infant covered over with meal, that it may deceive the unwary, is placed before him who is to be stained with their rites; this infant is slain by the young pupil, who has been urged on as if to harmless blows on the surface of the meal, with dark and secret wounds. Thirstily—O horror! they lick up its blood; eagerly they divide its limbs. By this victim they are pledged together; with their consciousness of wickedness they are covenanted to mutual silence. Such sacred rites as these are more foul than any sacrileges. And of their banqueting it is well known all men speak of it everywhere; even the speech of our Cirtensian testifies to it. On a solemn day they assemble at the feast, with all their children, sisters, mothers, people of every sex and every age. There, after much feasting, when the fellowship has grown warm, and the fervour of incestuous lust has grown hot with drunkenness, a dog that has been tied to the chandelier is provoked, by throwing a small piece of offal beyond the length of a line by which he is bound, to rush and spring; and thus the conscious light being overturned and extinguished in the shameless darkness, the connection of abominable lust involve them in the uncertainty of fate. Although not all in fact, yet in consciousness all are alike incestuous, since by the desire of all of them everything is sought for which can happen in the act of each individual.[3]

Caecilius uses the familiar argument that the fact that the Christians practiced their perverted religion under the cloak of secrecy demonstrated the validity of nearly all his charges. Why conceal something that is good? Only crimes need to be kept secret. Why do the Christians not have altars, temples, images, just as everybody else? Why do they conduct their services in secret? Why do they not proclaim their teachings publicly? And who is this unique, solitary god of theirs? Only one other nation worships a single god, namely those miserable Jews, and they at least do so openly. Besides, Caecilius argues, the Jewish god has amply revealed that he has no power, for he could not save his people from Roman subjugation and defeat. The Christian god is worse according to Caecilius: he is a restless, nosy person going from one place to another, mixing himself in everybody's business. Caecilius refers here to the Christian belief in an omnipresent and omniscient god.

Caecilius argues that the Christian belief about the end of the world and life after death is as absurd as the rest of their religion. They say that the whole universe, including the sky and the stars, will go up in flames—as if divine laws of nature could be thus replaced by chaos! Then they add to their lunacy by claiming that after their bodies have turned to ashes, they will rise again. In short, first they say that the universe will perish, and then they say that they will live again. Because of their belief in the resurrection they reject crema-tion, as if it would make a difference by what means a corpse were reduced to ashes. And when they rise again, what bodies will they have? The same as before, or new ones, or no bodies at all? If there is no body there can be no intelligence, no soul, no life. A person cannot receive the same body, because it will already have decomposed, but given another body he will not be the same man, but a new one. So it is clear that resurrection is nothing but a figment of a morbid imagination.

Caecilius depicts Christians as gullible fools who are unable to draw any conclusions from their present situation. Most of them are poor people, he says, suffering from hunger and cold, and their god not only permits them to live in that way, but wants them to. Caecilius asks what kind of god is he, weak or wicked? Also, why does he not help when Christians are persecuted and threatened with tortures. How is it that this god can bring the dead to life but cannot help those who live? The Romans have done much better without this god: they created an empire, they rule the whole world including the Christians.

Caecilius goes on to discuss the social life of Christians, which he sees as similarly foolish. They look toward the future with fear but at the same time deny themselves simple pleasures of life. They do not go to shows, public banquets, or sacred games; they do not eat meat or drink wine used in a religious ritual; they do not participate in processions. It seems that they are afraid of the gods whose very existence they deny. They do not adorn their heads with flowers, do not use perfumes or ointments on their bodies, and do not even decorate the tombs with garlands. They deny themselves enjoyment in the present life in anticipation of a new life that they will never have. How can a group of such neurotic, boorish people have the audacity to discuss matters pertaining to heaven? They would do better to pay attention to the here and now, and at least try to understand their civic duties. Caecilius adds finally that if a person cannot resist meddling in philosophy, he should seek to imitate Socrates, who advised that we not concern ourselves with things that are above us. But Caecilius cautions that in addition to Socrates, many other great minds have struggled unsuccessfully with these issues. Therefore, we should not presume to be able to resolve them with any finality. After a brief interlude, Octavius speaks, and one by one he refutes the pagan arguments put forward by Caecilius.[4]

Many of the charges mentioned by Caecilius against the Christians are based on hearsay, and he reports them as such. "I hear that they adore the head of an ass . . . ," "Some say that they worship the genitals of their priests . . . ," and "I know not whether these things are false. . . ." Caecilius maintains, however, that such rumors would not persist unless there were some truth behind them, and suspicion is justified when things are done secretly under cover of darkness. Nevertheless, despite his criticism of the Christians, Caecilius does tacitly accept that the Christians have a right to their religion. Except for infanticide, which would have been considered a grave crime by the authorities, Caecilius treats all the beliefs and the practices that he imputes to the Christians as matters for them to decide freely for themselves, however foolish and depraved they may be. The almost unbelievable religious tolerance of the Romans is well demonstrated here. The tone of his speech is such that we can virtually see and hear Fronto raising his right arm and shouting at his listeners the rhetorical question: "Why do the authorities permit such behavior?" His very question shows that the authorities do, in fact, permit it.

The real objection against Christianity for the pagans was not that the Christians were monotheists, or that they worshipped the head of an ass, or that they refused to use perfumes, but that they made doctrinal statements concerning divine matters. This is the point at which Caecilius really draws the line. He calls the claim of the Christians to exclusive possession of the truth "arrogant and irresponsible" behavior. A contemporary of Fronto, and another famous critic of Christianity, Celsus raised the same criticism. In *True Word* he wrote: "They regularly discuss fundamental principles and make arrogant pronouncements about matters of which they know nothing."[5] Whether Fronto and Celsus knew each other or read each others' writing is not clear but they had very similar opinions on the Christians.

The Romans tolerated a remarkable degree of religious liberty, and they, therefore, found the Christians' exclusive claims to truth disconcerting. The statement by Caecilius, that no human being should claim to pass final judgment on divine matters, is quite consistent with the Roman mentality. The Romans believed that when Christians claimed exclusive possession of divine knowledge, they were capable of anything. This attitude encouraged the Romans to give credence to the most outrageous rumors about Christians. An irreconcilable difference existed between pagans and Christians on this issue. The pagan took the position that matters pertaining to the divine mystery were obscure and so should be left open to debate. The Christian, however, was convinced that he was in possession of the truth, because Jesus Christ embodied the ultimate revelation about God. The two great Christian thinkers of the second century, Irenaeus (died ca. 190) and Tertullian (ca. 150-220), eloquently pleaded for the superiority of Christianity precisely on this principle. *Veritas* meaning "Truth," is the word Tertullian used most frequently in his polemics with pagans and heretics, and he considered all his opponents victims of false belief.

The assurance with which the Christians proclaimed their faith did not diminish in subsequent centuries. St. Augustine, for example, wrote a book entitled *De Vera Religione (On True Religion)* in 390 arguing the falsity of all other religions (in particular the Manichaeans). The pagan attitude persisted as well. In 382 at the urging of Ambrose, the Christian bishop of Milan, Emperor Gratian had the altar and the statue of Victory removed from the Senate house in Rome. The noble and eloquent pagan Symmachus protested, but to no avail. After Gratian's death Symmachus took up the cause again, and addressed an ardent plea to the new emperor, Valentinian II.[6] In it he wrote: "We ask for peace and for our native indigenous gods. We cultivate the same soil, we are one in thought, we behold the same stars, the same heaven and the same world surrounding. Why should not each, according to his own purpose, seek the truth? The Great Mystery cannot be approached by one road. The divine mind distributed various thoughts and guardians in the cities; as various spirits in youth, so the fatal Genii are divided among nations."[7] By the time of Symmachus the situation had, of course, changed radically; now a pagan minority struggled for survival. Nevertheless, the noble plea made by Symmachus for religious tolerance is an admirable expression of the ancient Roman mentality.

In addition to attacking the Christians for their exclusive claim on truth Caecilius levels many other charges against them, including the wild generalization that they are ignorant, uncultured, rude, and boorish. Other charges are more specific: they recognize each other by secret marks, they meet at night, they make love to one another indiscriminately, they worship the head of an ass and the genitals of their high priests, and finally, they eat children. These charges, shocking as they are to us, were not without credence in antiquity. The Jews, for example, were often accused of worshipping the head of an ass.[8] It is possible that this accusation originated from the Egyptian sojourn of the Jews, as the Egyptians often represented their gods with animal heads. It was then probably transferred from the Jews to the Christians, as was the vague accusation regarding secret signs.[9] According to Justin Martyr (ca. 100-165) the Jews recognized each other by the secret sign of circumcision, and some pagans may still at this time have identified Christians with Jews.[10] But the secret sign referred to by Caecilius could have been anything: the sign of the cross, the sign of the fish, or even a mark on the body, or a movement of the hand. It is natural for covert and persecuted groups of people to adopt such signs. In more recent times secret societies such as the Freemasons have been suspected of using them.

We cannot so easily dispose of the description by Caecilius of the Christian communion service. Here he names Fronto, "our Cirtensian," as a witness, who had published a work containing charges against the Christians. It appears from Caecilius's speech that Fronto had two main impressions of the Christian services, namely that they had a libertine, sexually oriented character, and that they included ritual murder and cannibalism. This is no longer just rhetoric. Fronto either completely misunderstood the elements of Christian liturgy or he knew something we do not. The simplest way to explain this passage is to assume that Fronto misinterpreted the Christian use of certain words and practices in the liturgy. The Christians celebrated Holy Communion in memory of Christ's death, and they consumed the "body" and the "blood" of Jesus, which they symbolized with bread and wine.[11] But did Fronto know that? Furthermore, the following words by Jesus: "Truly, truly I say to you, unless you eat the flesh of the Son of man and drink his blood you have no life in you . . . ,"[12] may have made him gravely suspicious that the Christians practiced cannibalism during the Eucharist.

Ritual murder appeared in many forms in the ancient world, and it was thought to be an essential element of certain magical rites.[13] The best known example is in Horace's *Epode 5*, where the witch Canidia seeks to regain the love of Varus by magic. A boy is buried in the ground up to his neck, food is placed in front of his face but beyond his reach, so that he may die with desire for life and thus become a more potent force in the magical potion. After his death Canidia uses his marrow and dried liver for the preparation of a love-philtre. Tertullian also referred to such a gruesome rite when he rejected the pagan charges against Christians; "sorcerers call forth ghosts . . . they put boys to death in order to get a response from the oracle. . . ."[14] And Apollonius of Tyana was accused of killing a boy in order to use his entrails to predict the future.[15] The Senate prohibited human sacrifices in 97 B.C.,[16] and Emperor Hadrian later renewed this law for the whole empire,[17] yet references to such sacrifices are found still later. The *Historia Augusta* accused Emperors Commodus and Elagabalus of human sacrifices,[18] and Eusebius accused Emperor Valerian of such acts.[19] Also, according to Eusebius, Maxentius used magic, ripped up pregnant women, and at other times examined the insides of newborn babies.[20] In 172 the so-called "Bukoloi," an Egyptian band of robbers, revolted, killed the Roman centurian, took an oath over his entrails, and ate from them.[21]

Ritual murder was also a topic in ancient entertainment literature. In the second century A.D. Achilles Tatius, in the novel *The Adventures of Leucippe and Cleitophon*, described how Leucippe is killed by the "Bukoloi" who take out her insides, burn them on the altar, and then eat them.[22] A similar story is found in the *Phoinikika* by Lollianos, where Androtimos, the hero of the novel, witnesses the ritual murder of a boy who is sacrificed by a band of robbers. He is killed, his heart is taken out and roasted, then it is cut up and sprinkled with oil and flour. All the robbers eat of it and take an oath not to betray their leader.[23] No doubt Fronto knew of these stories, and he could also recall that the Catilinian conspirators (63 B.C.) supposedly pledged themselves to loyalty by drinking a mixture of blood and wine.[24] He may have heard the rumors that Antinous, the favorite of Hadrian, who died in 130, was a victim of a ritual sacrifice. The Druid custom of foretelling the future from the entrails of human sacrifices was well known to Romans, so was the ritual which they performed on certain holidays when they burnt prisoners of war in wooden boxes that looked like human figures. In the Celtic areas under Roman control (Gaul and Britain) legislative measures were taken to suppress such practices that Romans considered barbaric[25] but, as we have seen above, rumors of such monstrous crimes kept circulating in various parts of the empire.

It is understandable, therefore, that the news of a new outbreak of human sacrifice upset Fronto. But why did he mention children as the victims? Here again, he may have misinterpreted several things. First, the Romans knew of the sacrifices of first-born sons, mostly by the Carthaginians. Fronto's home town, Cirta, was about two hundred miles west of Carthage, and although this city was no longer the Carthage of the Phoenicians but was a Roman colony, Fronto, no doubt, knew about the religious practices of the ancient Carthaginians. Moreover, Tertullian claimed that in his own day human sacrifices were still performed in North Africa. He said: "Children were openly sacrificed in Africa to Saturn as lately as the proconsulship of Tiberius, who exposed to public gaze the priests suspended on the sacred trees overshadowing their temple—so many crosses on which the punishment which justice craved overtook their crimes, as the soldiers of our country still can testify who did that very work for the proconsul.[26] And even now that sacred crime still continues to be done in secret."[27] This could not have escaped the attention of Fronto, who may also have heard that Jesus was the son of God or, as many early Christian authors put it, the child of God. Here, then, was a "child" whose "flesh" and "blood" were consumed during the Christian service. Fronto could well have put two and two together and come up with a completely false interpretation of Holy Communion, and this would explain why Fronto charged the Christians with cannibalism and ritual murder.

Fronto's other main impression about Christianity was that it was sexually libertine. The Romans saw Christianity as a mystery religion from the Near East, and a comparison between it and other religious movements where sexual excess was coupled with ritual murder was inevitable. For example, Emperor Elagabalus (218-222), who was the hereditary priest of El-Gabal, the sun god of Emesa in Syria on the Orontes, alienated his Roman subjects by his sexually oriented religious rites and the rumors of human sacrifices.[28] Palestine and Syria-Phoenicia were too close to ignore a possible similarity in religious customs with the Christians. A Roman may have suspected a repetition of the Bacchanalian scandal that took place in 186 B.C. but remained well known through Livy's detailed description.[29] Here, too, we hear of nightly meetings, promiscuous rituals, and initiation ceremonies that included debauchery and murder. Livy judged the Bacchanalia to be *prava et externa religio*,[30] and similar expressions were used in characterizing Christianity by Tacitus (*exitiabilis superstitio*), Pliny (*superstitio prava, immodica*), and Suetonius (*superstitio nova ac malefica*). Were these associations with Eastern religions sufficient to turn Fronto against Christianity?

That is certainly possible, but still not quite probable. Fronto hated Christians, but he was a scholar, and a polished orator, who was not likely to make such a rash judgment. Something else must have affected his judgment of the Christians. What was it? The answer may be found in certain Gnostic-Christian groups that advocated some exceedingly bizarre—and to pagans like Fronto—repellent practices. Libertinism was a strain of early Christianity; soon, however, we find it limited to the above mentioned Gnostic sects.[31] In the second century the church father Irenaeus reported that some women, who had returned to the orthodox fold, admitted that they had engaged in promiscuous sexual activities as part of their earlier religious life. Irenaeus charged that the Gnostic Markos used to seduce women by talking to them in complimentary terms: "I am eager to make you a partaker of my Charis . . . the place of your angel is among us; it behooves us to become one . . . Adorn thyself as a bride who is expecting her bridegroom, that thou mayest be what I am and I what you are. . . ."[32] But we should resist the temptation to accept the judgment by Irenaeus that Gnostic leaders were lecherous men who used religious patter to gain sexual favors, until we have examined their religion more closely.

Irenaeus wrote about Simon, a Gnostic leader who "redeemed from slavery at Tyre, a city in Phoenicia, a certain woman named Helena. He was in the habit of taking her around with him, declaring that she was the first conception of his mind, the matter of all. . . ." Helena was a prostitute, and from this Irenaeus concluded about Simon's sect that: "the mystic priests belonging to this sect both lead profligate lives and practice magical arts. . . . They use exorcism and incantations, love potions, too, and charms. . . ."[33] Justin Martyr also mentioned Simon, who he said "was considered a god. . . . and almost all the Samaritans, and a few even of other nations, worship him, and acknowledge him as the first god; and a woman, Helena, who went about with him at that time, and had formerly been a prostitute, they say is the first idea generated by him."[34] Eusebius quoted this passage by Justin, and then with reference to Irenaeus he added that the secret rites performed by Simon's followers were so evil that they could not be put into writing and could not even be uttered by decent men.[35] On closer examination it appears that the prostitute Simon converted was a symbol of the fallen soul, temporarily imprisoned in the world of senses (the brothel) until liberated to return to its heavenly abode.[36] We can only imagine, however, how this theology found expression in the liturgy of Simon's Gnostic sect, and the nature of those unspeakably bad elements in it mentioned by Eusebius. The service must have had a strong Phoenician-Syrian element to it, that is, it was sexually oriented.

We know considerably more of another libertine Gnostic sect, the Carpocratians.[37] Irenaeus observed that "they lead a licentious life,"[38] but Clement of Alexandria gave a more detailed analysis of this aspect of their life in the third book of the *Stromateis*.[39] According to Clement the Carpocratians relied heavily on a book written by the son of Carpocrates, Epiphanes. H. Chadwick calls Epiphanes "an intelligent but nasty-minded adolescent of somewhat pornographic tendencies."[40] The Carpocratians believed that "wives should be common property," and they held services that were reminiscent of the one described in *Octavius*.[41] Clement wrote:

> These, so they say, and certain other enthusiasts for the same wickedness, gather together for feasts (I would not call their meeting an Agape), men and women together. After they have sated their appetites . . . then they overturn their lamps and so extinguish the light that the shame of their adulterous 'righteousness' is hidden, and they have intercourse where they will and with whom they will. After they have practiced community of use in their love-feast, they demand by daylight of whatever women they wish that they will be obedient to the law of Carpocrates—it would not be right to say the law of God.

Later Clement argued that the Carpocratians based this unrestricted promiscuity on the words of Jesus: "Give to everyone who begs from you;"[42] and he passed sharp judgment on the practitioners of such things: "These thrice wretched men treat carnal and sexual intercourse as a sacred religious mystery, and think that it will bring them to the kingdom of God," but it is "an insult to the name of communion to call Aphrodite Pandemos a mystical communion," more likely it leads to the brothels.[43]

Nowhere in the *Stromateis* do we hear of a connection between cannibalism and the Christians, thus it is unlikely that Fronto's criticism was aimed at the Carpocratians or the other libertines. We do have, however, in the *Panarion* by Epiphanius (ca. 315-403), a description of a Gnostic-Christian sect, called the Phibionites, whose practices were very close to what Fronto objected to.[44] Epiphanius believed that this sect was descended from the Nicolaitans, an early Christian splinter group, which, according to tradition, was founded by "Nicolaus, a proselyte of Antioch," one of the seven Hellenistic deacons of the first congregation.[45] Nicolaus supposedly believed that the flesh should be held in contempt, but his views led to libertinism and sexual excess. According to Epiphanius the Phibionites were very active, produced many books (Epiphanius reviewed several of them), and actively proselytized, striving to attract others, especially ortho-dox Christians, to their way of thinking.[46] They mostly wrote theo-logical treatises, in which they attempted to support their theories by applying allegorical interpretations to texts drawn from the Old and New Testaments. In one passage Epiphanius describes a Phibionite Communion service that is strangely reminiscent of the practices that Fronto ascribed to Christians:

> I will now come to the place of depth of their deadly story (for they have various false teachings about pleasure). First they have their women in common. And if a stranger appears who is of the same persuasion, they have a sign, men for women and women for men. When they extend the hand for greeting at the bottom of the palm they make a tickling touch and from this they ascertain whether the person who appeared is of their faith. After they have recognized each other, they go over at once to eating. They serve rich food, meat and wine even if they are poor. When they thus ate together and so to speak filled up their veins to an excess they turn to passion. The man leaving his wife says to his own wife: Stand up and make love with the brother [*Poiēson tēn agapēn meta tou adelphou*—"Perform the *agape* with the brother"]. Then the unfortunates unite with each other, and as I am truly ashamed to say the shameful things that are being done by them, because according to the holy apostle the things that are happening by them are shameful even to mention [*Eph.* 5.12] never-theless, I will not be ashamed to say those things which they are not ashamed to do, in order that I may cause in every way a horror in those who hear about their shameful practices. After they have had inter-course in the passion of fornication they raise their own blasphemy toward heaven. The woman and the man take the fluid of the emis-sion of the man into their hands, they stand, turn toward heaven, their hands besmeared with the uncleanness, and pray as people called "Stratiotikoi" and "Gnostikoi," bringing to the father who is the nature of all that which they have on their hands, and they say: "We offer to thee this gift, the body of Christ." And then they eat it, their

own ugliness, and say: "This is the body of Christ and this is the Passover for the sake of which our bodies suffer and are forced to confess the suffering of Christ." . . . [Here Epiphanius describes that the Phibionites do the same with the menstrual blood of the woman, and they call it "the blood of Christ."] They have intercourse with each other but they teach that one may not beget children. The infamy is committed by them not for the sake of begetting children, but for the sake of pleasure, because the devil plays with them and mocks the image formed by God. They bring the pleasure to its end, but they take to themselves the sperm of their uncleanness, not for the purpose of begetting children, but to eat their shame themselves. And if someone from among them is detected to have let the natural emission of semen go in deeper and the woman becomes pregnant, then hear, what even worse they do; they pull out the embryo in the time when they can reach it with the hand. They take out this unborn child and in a mortar pound it with a pestle and into this mix honey and pepper and certain other spices and myrrh, in order that it may not nauseate them, and then they come together, all this company of swine and dogs, and each communicates with a finger from the bruised child. And after they have finished this cannibalism finally they pray to God, saying, "We did not let the Archon of lust play with us but collected the mistake of the brother." And this they consider to be the perfect Passah. Many other horrible things are done by them. For when they again get into this rage among themselves, they smear their hands with their own emission. They stretch them out and pray with the besmeared hands naked in the whole body that through this practice they may find with God free conversation. But they take care of their bodies day and night, women and men, with creams, washings and foods, and devote themselves to the bed and to wine. They curse the man who fasts because they say that one should not fast, for fasting is the work of the Archon who made this *aion*. Rather one should nourish himself in order that the bodies may be strong, so that they may give the fruit in its time." [*Panarion* 26.4-5][47]

The obscenity described here is one of the most repulsive stories in ancient literature. But is it, as in the speech by Caecilius, just vicious talk reflecting the warped judgment of someone wracked by hatred for the people he described. After all, it does seem odd that Epiphanius knew such intimate details about the Phibionite meetings. According to him they were conducted in secret, and anyone unfamiliar with the sign (the tickling of the palm) was denied entry. Epiphanius knew that his credibility needed support, and, at the end of this chapter of the *Panarion*, he ruefully admitted that his knowledge of the Phibionites was based on personal experience.[48] As a young man he once made the acquaintance of some young women with stunningly attractive figures as well as faces—they were, he says, *eumorphoterai* and *euprosopotatai*. It later turned out that they were Phibionites who tried to save his soul by introducing him to their literature and their services. With a touch of nostalgia, Epiphanius confessed that they had sorely tempted him. He finally severed his connection with the Gnostics, but only, he claimed, through the power of God whom he praised for the victory by exclaiming: "Let us sing to the Lord, for He has triumphed gloriously; the horse and his rider he has thrown into the sea!"

For our purposes, the significance of the Phibionite service lies in the possibility that Fronto had heard of it, and had it in mind when he attacked the Christians, but failed to distinguish between Gnostics and Christians. This was a common mistake, as even within the Christian movement the boundaries between different sects were often blurred. Epiphanius reported that the church only expelled the Phibionites in Alexandria after he had exposed them; if this is so, then they existed under the name of Christianity for many years prior to his revelations.[49] They may have done so in Fronto's time; they were active then, and many bona fide Christians complained about the confusion in pagan minds between themselves and heretics. Justin Martyr, for example, proposed that the authorities arrest and convict criminals on the basis of their crimes, and not merely for bearing the name "Christian," because "all are called Christians." Later in the same book he named several Gnostic leaders and then said, "All who take their opinions from these men are called Christians. . . ."[50] Theological differences, both trivial and fundamental, among Christians had been common since apostolic times, when Hellenists murmured against the Hebrews, and Peter and Paul quarreled with each other.[51] We need to remember that all parties to such disputes were Christians. The libertine movements, such as the Phibionites or the group Fronto encountered, considered themselves Christians, probably better Christians than the others, because they believed that they were in possession of "knowledge" (*Gnosis*) superior to all other.

Even Gnostics of other persuasions condemned the sexual excesses of the Phibionite-type libertines, however. One of them judged the Phibionites with these ominous words: "This sin is more heinous than all sins and iniquities. Such men will straightaway be taken into the outer darkness and not be cast back anew into the sphere, but they shall perish, be destroyed in the outer darkness in a region where there is neither pity, nor light, and howling and grinding of teeth. . . ."[52] Another said: "Their God is evil . . . he is the enemy of the kingdom of heavens. . . ."[53] These two books were written during the third century, one toward the beginning of the century and the other toward the end. The existence of Phibionite-type heresies, therefore, can be traced back quite close to the time when Fronto lived and worked. We should now have little or no doubt that the excesses to which Fronto objected did exist, and that they existed under the name of Christianity.

In his righteous indignation Fronto called for the extermination of the depraved group that showed such a degree of moral decay. Epiphanius also passed harsh judgment on the "company of swine and dogs," and he based his criticism on personal experience. Both Fronto and Epiphanius seem to have assumed that the Phibionites were simply sex maniacs, but a closer examination of the records suggest a more complex explanation for Phibionite practices. First, the Phibionites were active in Alexandria, and in that city nobody needed to pose as a religious fanatic if he or she wished to engage in lustful activities. Furthermore, Epiphanius stated that sex was not the sole objective of their meetings; he also claimed that they ritually consumed unborn babies, although this fare so nauseated them that they had to use strong spices to be able to swallow just a little of it. It is difficult to believe that such a perversion could bring erotic or any other type of pleasure to anybody. Certainly the Phibionites did not like it, but they went through with it because their religion required it. Here then is the key point; the participants saw these rituals as part of a religious experience.

What kind of religion was Phibionitism? Epiphanius, who made no attempt at analysis, gave a few valuable hints in his report, from which we can reconstruct Phibionite theology. The Phibionites believed that the purpose of the work of Jesus Christ was the restoration of the primordial unity of the universe. The creation of the world and the creation of man had divided and reduced the creator's power, since everything in existence possessed a spark of his power. Salvation, therefore, consisted of collecting his power, and leading it back to its original condition. The Gnostics identified divine power with the creative, or generating, substances of the male and female bodies, and they concluded that their most sacred obligation was to physically collect these substances. The Nicolaitans supposedly stated: "We gather the power . . . from the bodies through the fluids of the begetting power...."[54] For this reason they did not want to have any children, because procreating would only further divide the divine power. This was the reasoning behind the gruesome custom of interrupting an accidental pregnancy and eating the unborn child. Rather than being a means of achieving sexual stimulation, it was a holy task for the Phibionites, by which the further scattering of the creator's power was prevented. When they did this they thought they were "co-workers with God" in the plan of salvation.[55]

In their books, according to the summaries provided by Epiphanius, the Phibionites invented stories to show that their peculiar beliefs and practices were true to the teachings of Jesus Christ. They also interpreted canonical words of Jesus, such as John 6:53: "if you do not eat the flesh of the Son of Man and drink his blood...," in ways that validated their rituals. Old Testament passages received similar allegorical treatment. The Phibionites went to great lengths to find in Old Testament texts some veiled allusion to male and female generative functions. So Psalm 1:3, for example, ("He is like a tree planted by streams of water which will give its fruit in its time"), became an important text in Phibionite theology. To these interpretations the Phibionites added revelations that they claimed came from Jesus, and visions that they attributed to outstanding Old and New Testament figures, such as Eve, Mary, and Philip. The main Phibionite articles of faith stated that intercourse was proper because it was an act of unification; the production of the male (and female) generative substances was also proper, so long as these substances were collected so as to assure salvation.[56]

Where did the Phibionites get these strange ideas from? Like other sectarian and heretical philosophies, their ideas may have come from an overemphasis on certain orthodox and legitimate aspects of Christianity. Originally this emphasis may have been quite harmless, but with the passage of time, and under the influence of pagan thought in a non-Christian milieu, such as that afforded by Alexandria in Egypt, it was carried to the point where the Christian element was almost lost, although some Christian ideas remained recognizable in Phibionitism. One such text that the Gnostics may have misinterpreted was Eph. 1:3ff., where Paul speaks about the unification of all things in Jesus Christ. The Phibionites' Eucharistic service, as described by Epiphanius, contained a number of recognizable elements of the orthodox Christian service.[57] Theirs, too, was a fellowship of eating together, which is perhaps the most ancient form of

Christian communion. The Phibionites understood this communion as an expression of unity among the faithful, and, indeed, performed sexual intercourse precisely because to them it was the most perfect union possible between two human beings, the path by which "two shall become one."[58] the Phibionites held a radical view of the unifying effect of the Eucharist, and they practiced sex as a liturgical act, believing that they were experiencing in a proleptic way something that would come in a perfect form only in the fullness of time. When, in their prayers of confession and dedication, they said "We offer to thee this gift, the body of Christ," they offered what they considered to be the very essence of man. This, however, was no longer in harmony with apostolic teaching, or mainstream Christianity. Fronto was quite right when he concluded, if this was Christianity, he did not want any part of it.

The charge that Christians practiced cannibalism was based on meager evidence, but it became a popular one, and Christians constantly had to defend themselves against it. When Pliny interrogated some Christians in 111, they took pains to emphasize that in the Eucharist they only ate "ordinary and harmless kind of food."[59] We can conjecture that these Christians knew of the rumors that were circulating about their meals, and they attempted to combat them. Later in the same century, Justin Martyr stated that those people who practiced "the upsetting of the lamp, promiscuous intercourse and the meals of human flesh" might go under the name of Christians but, in fact, were heretics.[60] In his *Dialogue with Trypho the Jew* Justin asked with some sarcasm, so as to mock the credulous nature of Trypho, "Have you also believed concerning us that we eat men; and that after the feast, having extinguished the lights, we engage in promiscuous concubinage?"[61] Tatian indignantly declared: "We are not man-eaters!"[62] Athenagoras, who sent a *Plea for the Christians* to the Emperor Marcus Aurelius and his son Commodus around 177, argued that because Christians were not murderers they could not be cannibals either, since one could not eat another person without first murdering him. Moreover, a cardinal Christian belief was the resurrection of the flesh, and it could not reasonably be supposed that people would eat flesh that they expect to be resurrected.[63]

Nevertheless, in 177, according to church historian Eusebius, during the anti-Christian violence in Lyons certain slaves, under the threat of torture, testified that their Christian masters were guilty of illicit intercourse and cannibalism.[64] Tertullian countered the charges with sarcasm. He described the alleged crimes as if they were parts of an initiation into a pagan mystery. When someone inquired into what the requirements for initiation into Christianity were, he would receive the following reply: "You must have a child still of tender age, that knows not what it is to die, and can smile under thy knife; bread, too, to collect the gushing blood; in addition to these, candlesticks, and lamps, and dogs—with tid-bits to draw them on to the extinguishing of the lights: above all things, you will be required to bring your mother and your sister with you." Then, in an attempt to further ridicule the charges, he raised the rhetorical question of what would happen to a candidate if he had no mother or sister, or if they refused to join him in the initiation.[65]

The Christians found it even more difficult to refute charges of sexual licentiousness, since, in fact, some so-called Christians did practice such licentiousness, as we have seen above. Orthodox Christians, therefore, tried to distinguish themselves from the heretics. Justin had already done this, and Irenaeus expressed the same opinion; the church is discredited, he argued, because the vices committed by Gnostics are simply transmitted to Christians.[66] Eusebius also believed that the Romans heard about the strange practices of the Gnostics and then applied them to the Christians. And so the suspicion spread that Christians practiced "unspeakable incest with mother and sister and took part in wicked food."[67] Clement felt the same way,[68] and Origen accused the Jews of starting these rumors: "The Jews .... when Christianity began to be first preached, scattered abroad false reports of the Gospel, such as that Christians offered up an infant in sacrifice, and partook of its flesh; and again that the professors of Christianity wishing to do the work of darkness, used to extinguish the lights in their meetings, and each one to have sexual intercourse with any woman he chanced to meet."[69] At one time, Origen said, these allegations had a great influence on the pagan population, but in his own day even most non-Christians dismissed them.[70] These rebuttals were supposed to be a vindication of Christianity, but at the same time they were also an open admission that such practices did indeed exist among religious groups that called themselves Christian.

Most early church fathers, therefore, attributed acts of licentiousness to Gnostic heretics, and it seems that cannibalism, too, was restricted to Gnostics, and even then, to a lunatic fringe only. Cannibalism and sexual licentiousness often appeared together, and not even Phibionites sacrificed or ate children unless they were under the influence of sexual excitement and frenzy. A psychiatric study could perhaps give us an idea of the extent to which the Phibionites' cannibalism was related to sadistic and unnatural sexual tendencies. In orthodox Christian congregations, however, sexual activity did not play a part in the service, nor did ritual murder. (How could each congregation kill at least 52 children a year—one every Sunday—and keep it secret?) But in Alexandria, Gnosticism was the only recognizable type of Christianity until the end of the second century.[71] The first orthodox Christian bishop of Alexandria, so far as we know, was Demetrius (189-231). Before him, when the church fathers referred to Alexandrian Christians they meant Gnostic heretics, whom they thoroughly condemned. Two gospels written in Alexandria, the so-called "Gospel of the Egyptians" and the "Gospel of the Hebrews," show every sign of being Gnostic creations, and it is no doubt for this reason that they have not been included on the list of legitimate (canonical) books of the New Testament. It was, therefore, natural for pagans in North Africa, such as Fronto, to confuse Gnostic aberrations with standard Christian behavior. Just as natural—perhaps even inevitable—was the subsequent spread of the confusion to other parts of the Roman empire.

Gnosticism is very difficult to pin down, and even today there is much debate concerning its origin.[72] All that can be said with certainty is that these people relied on inner knowledge (*gnosis* in Greek) as a guarantee of salvation, and they claimed that this knowledge came to them by way of a revelation other than the one contained in the Scriptures. They believed that the world was the creation of an evil god, and that material and physical limitations were the greatest hindrance of the soul in its upward thrust toward salvation. Therefore, the Gnostics regarded anything having to do with the physical side of existence with contempt. This contempt manifested itself in two diametrically opposed patterns of behavior. Some Gnostics were strict ascetics because they believed that sexual intercourse would only result in conception, and the consequent imprisonment of more souls in physical bodies. Others were the most extreme libertines, because they wanted to demonstrate their complete freedom from all physical inhibitions. The Phibionites were typical Gnostics; they not only practiced spiritual liberty but also prevented the entrapment of souls in human bodies.[73]

Traces of Gnostic heresies may be found in the New Testament, for example, in 1 and 2 Corinthians where Paul chastised his opponents who boasted of their "knowledge," or in 1 Tim. 6:20, which contains a definite warning against a "fasely named Gnosis." Jude, however, used such language and made such lightly veiled charges that it seems possible to believe that he had Phibionite-type heretics in mind: "ungodly persons" he wrote "secretly gained admission" to the church where they "pervert the grace of god into licentiousness." These heretics "defile the flesh, reject authority, and revile the glorious ones. . . . By those things that they know by instinct as irrational animals do, they are destroyed." Jude next described a Phibionite type service: "These are blemishes on your love feasts, as they boldly carouse together, looking after themselves; waterless clouds, carried along by winds; fruitless trees in late autumn, twice dead, uprooted; wild waves of the sea, casting up the foam of their own shame. . . ." With a final outburst against people who "follow their own passions," Jude closed his letter by reminding his readers to keep themselves holy. To be sure, he did not mention cannibalism, but he did mention Gnostics of a libertine sort who behaved in very much the same way as the Phibionites.[74]

Other books of the New Testament contain condemnations of licentiousness, too. Indeed, 2 Peter closely parallels Jude, and it is generally assumed that Peter used Jude as a source. Peter fiercely attacked persons guilty of licentious behavior, "and especially those who indulge in the lust of defiling passion and despise authority." He called these heretics "irrational animals, creatures of instinct" who "count it pleasure to revel in daytime. They are blots and blemishes, reveling in their dissipation, carousing with you. They have eyes full of adultery, insatiable for sin. They entice unsteady souls. They have hearts trained in greed. . . . uttering loud boasts of folly, they entice with licentious passions of the flesh men who have barely escaped from those who live in error. They promise them freedom, but they themselves are slaves of corruption. . . ." They came to the knowledge of Jesus Christ and then again became entangled in the defilements of the world. "It has happened to them according to the true proverb, the dog turns back to his own vomit, and the sow is washed only to wallow in the mire."[75]

Both Jude and 2 Peter were probably composed in the early part of the second century, which indicates that the libertine tradition in the

Christian Church was an early one. The charge of infanticide, however, was a broad generalization and it is safe to say that neither ritual killing nor anthropophagy were part of the Christian liturgy.

NOTES

1. The literature on Minucius Felix is extremely large. For an exhaustive bibliography see Johannes Quasten, *Patrology*, vol. 2 (Utrecht, Antwerp: Spectrum, 1953), pp. 159-63; and G. W. Clarke, *The Octavius of Minucius Felix* (New York: Newman Press, 1976), which is the best existing commentary on the book.

2. The most important literature on Fronto is listed in the *Oxford Classical Dictionary*, 2d ed. (Oxford: Clarendon Press, 1970), p. 449. See, in particular, E. Champlin, *Fronto and Antonine Rome* (Cambridge: Harvard University Press, 1980), pp. 64-66. On the debate over whether Minucius Felix based his dialogue on Fronto's work, see W. H. C. Frend, *Martyrdom and Persecution in the Early Church* (New York: Doubleday, 1967), p. 187-88; A. Henrichs, "Pagan Ritual and the Alleged Crimes of the Early Christians," in *Kyriakon. Festschrift Johannes Quasten*, ed. P. Granfield and Joseph A. Jungman, vol. 1 (Munich: Aschendorff, 1970), pp. 18-35; J. H. van Haeringen, "Circensis Noster, Minucius Felix 9.6.," *Mnemosyne* 3 (1935): 29-32; P. Frasinetti, "L'orazione di Frontone contro i cristiani," *Giornale italiano di filologia classica* 3 (1949): 238-54.

3. *Octavius* 1-13, E.T., *ANF* 4.177.

4. Ibid., 14.

5. Origen *Contra Celsum* 5.65, E.T., Henry Chadwick, *Origen, Contra Celsum* (Cambridge: Cambridge University Press, 1953). See also the discussion of Galen, below.

6. *Relatio de ara Victoriae*

7. E.T., W. W. Hyde, *Paganism to Christianity in the Roman Empire* (New York: Octagon Books, 1970), p. 216. See also John H. Smith, *The Death of Classical Paganism* (New York: Scribner's, 1976), pp. 151–52. Also, J. Wytzes, *Der Streit um den Altar der Viktoria* (Amsterdam: H. J. Paris, 1936); and A. Momigliano, ed., *The Conflict Between Paganism and Christianity in the Fourth Century* (Oxford: Clarendon Press, 1963).

8. See the remarks of G. W. Clarke, *Octavius*, to the relevant passages in the Octavius; and E. Bickerman, "Ritualmord und Eselskult," *Monatsschrift für Geschichte und Wissenschaft des Judentums* 71 (1927): 171-87; also A. Jacoby, "Der angeblische Eselskult der Juden und Christen," *Archiv für Religionswissenschaft* 25 (1927):265-82. Epiphanius *Panarion* 26.12.1-4 quotes a Gnostic document, called *Genna Marias*, which contained the statement that Zechariah saw in the temple the image of the Jewish god with the head of an ass. About Gnostic connotations see the references in E. Hennecke and W. Schneemelcher, *New Testament Apocrypha*, vol. 2 (Philadelphia: Westminster, 1963), p. 345; and Jean Doresse, *The Secret Books of the Egyptian Gnostics* (New York: Viking, 1960), pp. 41–42.

9. So, at least, claimed Tertullian *Ad nationes* 1.11 and *Apol.* 16. He

believed that Tacitus was the first to suggest this absurdity concerning the Jews in the *Histories* 5. 2-5. According to Josephus, however, Apion already believed that the Jews worshipped the head of an ass, see *Contra Apionem* 2.79-80 and 2.112-14. Plutarch *Symposium* 4.5 discussed the possibility that the Jews' refusal to eat pork was based on their worship of this animal. See references and comments in Menahem Stern, *Greek and Latin Authors on Jews and Judaism* (Jerusalem: The Israeli Academy of Sciences and Humanities, 1974).

10. *Dialogue* 16.

11. I Cor. 11. 24-25.

12. John 6.52.

13. See F. Schwenn, *Die Menschenopfer bei den Griechen und Römern* (Giessen: A. Töpelmann, 1915).

14. *Apol.* 23, E.T., *ANF* 3.37.

15. Philostratus *Vita* 7.11.20; 8.7.12; according to 8.5 Apollonius answered the accusation by Domitian with the words: "if I offered it, then I ate of it!" E.T., F. C. Conybeare, Loeb, 2:283; see also Juvenal *Sat.* 6.548ff. and Lucan *Pharsalia* 6.706ff.

16. Pliny *NH* 30.3, Pliny concluded from this that up until that time such rites were practiced, E.T., W. H. S. Jones, Loeb, 8.287.

17. Eusebius *Praeparatio Evangelica* 2.15.6.

18. *Heliog.* 8; also Dio Cassius 79.14.

19. *Hist. Eccl.* 7.10. For complete references see Theodor Hopfner, "Mageia," in Pauly, Wyssowa, and Kroll, *Realencyclopädie*, 28.330; and *Griechisch-Egypt. Offenbarungzauber*, vol. 1 (Leipzig: H. Haessel, 1921), pp. 162-64.

20. *Vita Const.* 1.36, *NPNF* 1.492.

21. Dio 71.4.1; on the question concerning whether this is a historical fact or hostile propaganda, see Albert Henrichs, *Die Phoinikika des Lollianos* (Bonn: Rudolf Habelt Verlag, 1972), pp. 48ff. Cf. Karl Kerényi, *Die griechisch-orientalische Romanliteratur in religionsgeschichtlicher Beleuchtung. Ein Versuch* (Tübingen: Mohr, 1927); and A. D. Nock's review of it in *Gnomon* 4 (1928):485-92.

22. Achilles Tatius 3.15.4.

23. See Henrichs, *Die Phoinikika des Lollianos*, p. 6. We may compare these stories with the Christian entertainment literature, such as the apocryphal "Acts of the Apostles." In one of these, "The Acts of Andrew and Matthias," the adventures of the two apostles are described in the land of the anthropophagi. See M. D. James, *The Apocryphal New Testament* (Oxford: Clarendon Press, 1955), pp. 453ff.

24. Sallust *Bellum Catilinae* 22; according to Plutarch *Cicero* 10.3.1 they killed a man and ate from the flesh; according to Dio 37.30.4 they killed a boy and ate from the flesh.

25. Dio 69.11. The subsequently established cult of Antinous in Antinoopolis had orgiastic character; on this refer to Origen *Contra Celsum* 3.36-38 and 5.53; Stuart Piggott, *The Druids* (New York: Praeger, 1975), pp. 108-21 and 193–201.

26. The Latin of this passage is not clear. "Militia patris nostri" may refer to the soldiers of Tertullian's father who was a centurion, according to Jerome *De Viris illustribus* 53; also see T. D. Barnes, *Tertullian* (Oxford: Clarendon Press, 1971), pp. 13-21.

27. *Apol.* 9, E.T., *ANF* 3.25; *Scorpiace* 7, E.T., *ANF* 640. See Lactantius

The Divine Institutes 1.21 for a description of human sacrifices in ancient Rome. Reference material concerning child-offerings in Tyre and Carthage was collected by Roland de Vaux, *Studies in Old Testament Sacrifice* (Cardiff: University of Wales Press, 1964), pp. 79ff.; and by Henrichs, *Die Phoinikika des Lollianos*, pp. 12ff. See also Lawrence E. Stager, "The Rite of Child Sacrifice at Carthage." in *New Light on Ancient Carthage*, ed. John G. Pedley (Ann Arbor: University of Michigan Press, 1980), pp. 1ff.; P. G. Mosca, *Child Sacrifice in Canaanite and Israelite Religion* (Ph.D. Thesis, Harvard University, 1975), may also be relevant although it was unavailable to me. Child sacrifice was thoroughly condemned by the Old Testament; see Lev. 18.21, 20.2-5; 2 Kings 23.10; Jer. 32.35,36; but compare with Gen. 22.1-14, when Abraham is commanded to sacrifice his only son, and Judges 11.34, when Jephtah sacrifices his only child. For further bibliography see Roland de Vaux, *Ancient Israel: Its Life and Institutions* (New York: McGraw-Hill, 1961), pp. 433ff., especially 441ff., on human sacrifice in Israel and its Canaanite origin; and his *Studies in Old Testament Sacrifice* (Cardiff: University of Wales Press, 1964), pp. 52-90.

28. *Heliog.* 8.

29. Livy 39.8-19.

30. Ibid., 39.14.3.

31. Morton Smith, *Clement of Alexandria and a Secret Gospel of Mark* (Cambridge: Harvard University Press, 1973), pp. 254-78, claims that it can be traced back to Jesus.

32. *Adv. Haer.* 1.6.3-4, 1.13.3, 1.23.2-3, E.T., *ANF* 1.348; also see Acts 8.9ff.

33. *Adv. Haer.* 1.23.4, E.T., *ANF* 1.348.

34. *Apol.* 1.26, E.T., *ANF* 1.171.

35. *Hist. Eccl.* 2.13.4.

36. R. M. Grant, *Gnosticism and Early Christianity* (New York: Columbia University Press, 1959), chap. 3, "Simon Magus and Helen, his Thought." More recently Henrichs, *Die Phoinikika des Lollianos*, pp. 21ff. See also Hermann Usener, "Legenden der Pelagia," in *Vortraege und Aufsaetze* (Leipzig und Berlin: Teubner, 1907), pp. 189-215.

37. All patristic references to Carpocrates have been collected by Smith, *Clement of Alexandria*, pp. 295-350, which includes a virtually complete bibliography up to 1960 and analyses of the important books.

38. *Adv. Haer.* 1.25.3, E.T., *ANF* 1.351.

39. Critical edition by O. Staehlin in *GCS*, 4 vols. (Leipzig: 1905-1936). In *ANF* the third chapter was not translated into English but into Latin in order to make it available to scholars only. There is, however, an English translation with notes by H. Chadwick in *Alexandrian Christianity*, ed. J. E. L. Oulton and H. Chadwick (Philadelphia: Westminster Press, 1954).

40. Oulton and Chadwick, *Alexandrian Christianity*, p. 25.

41. *Stromateis* 3.2.5. Oulton and Chadwick, *Alexandrian Christianity*, p. 42.

42. *Stromateis* 3.2.10, 3.4.27, 3.6.54; Oulton and Chadwick, *Alexandrian Christianity*, p. 45; see also Luke 6.30 and Matt. 5.42.

43. *Stromateis* 3.4.27-28; Oulton and Chadwick, *Alexandrian Christianity*, pp. 52-53. In addition to the Carpocratians, Clement also mentioned the followers of Prodicus and the *Antitactae* as practicing immorality, *Stromateis* 3.4.30-35, but he excused Nicolaus, 3.4.25f. See on this Chadwick's remarks in *Alexandrian Christianity*, pp. 29-30.

44. Epiphanius was for a while a monk in Egypt and later bishop of Salamis on the island of Cyprus. *Panarion* means medicine-chest. In the book Epiphanius describes eighty heresies and offers "medicine" against their "venom."

45. Rev. 2.6.15; Acts 6.5; Irenaeus *Adv. Haer.* 1.26.3; 3.11.1; Hippolytus *Refutation* 7.36; Tertullian *De praescriptione haer.* 33; *Adv. Marcionem* 1.29; *De Pudicitia* 19; Eusebius *Hist. Eccl.* 3.29.

46. For a survey see Stephen Benko, "The Libertine Gnostic Sect of the Phibionites According to Epiphanius," *Vigiliae Christianae* 21 (1967): 103-19.

47. Author's translation from K. Holl in *GCS*, vol. 25 (Leipzig: J. C. Hinrichs, 1915). A German translation is in Hans Leisegang, *Die Gnosis* (Stuttgart: A Kröner Verlag, 4. Auflage, 1955), p. 190f., and W. Forster, *Die Gnosis* (Stuttgart: Artemis Verlag, 1969), 1:405ff.

48. *Panarion* 26.17.1ff.

49. The *Panarion* was composed in 375, thus the expulsion must have taken place prior to this date.

50. *Apol.* 1.7, 26.

51. Acts 6.1f.; Gal. 2.1ff.

52. *Pistis Sophia* 147. C. Schmidt, *Koptisch-Gnostische Schriften I*, 2d. rev. ed., W. Till, *GCS* vol. 45 (Berlin: Akademie Verlag, 1954). See also G. R. S. Mead, *Pistis Sophia*, 2d. ed. (London: J. M. Watkins, 1921, repr. 1955).

53. *The Second Book of Jeu* 43, critical edition by C. Schmidt, *Koptisch-Gnostische Schriften*.

54. *Panarion* 25.2.2f., 25.3.2.

55. This philosophy was carried over to include other living matter, too. See *Panarion* 26.9.3-4, cf. *Panarion* 26.10.10.

56. According to Phibionite beliefs Jesus Christ himself revealed these things: "They say that he gave her a revelation taking her to the mountain and praying, and that he took from his side a woman and began to have intercourse with her, and thus taking his semen showed that 'we need to do the same thing in order to live,' and when Mary, dismayed, fell to the ground, he at once raised her up again and said, "Why did you doubt, O you of little faith?'" *Panarion* 26.8.1-2 and John 3.12 and 6.62 refer to the same thing. Also see Benko, "The Libertine Gnostic Sect of the Phibionites According to Epiphanius," p. 104f.

57. S. Fendt, *Gnostische Mysterien* (Munich: Kaiser Verlag, 1922), argues that the following liturgical characteristics were also part of the dinner fellowship of the Phibionites: the idea of eating together; the sentence, "Perform the *agape* . . . ," which sounds like a fixed liturgical formula; the prayer of dedication; and the closing confession.

58. Eph. 5.31.

59. William Melmath, *Pliny: Letters*, Loeb (London: William Heinemann, 1935), pp. 401-407.

60. Justin Martyr *Apol.* 1.26, E.T., *ANF* 1.172. Also *Apol.* 1.29: "promiscuous intercourse is not one of our mysteries. . . ."

61. Ibid., 1.199.

62. *Oratio* 25.

63. Athenagoras *A Plea for the Christians* 35, 36, see also 3.

64. *Hist. Eccl.* 5.1.14f. See also 5.1.26 and 5.1.52.

65. Tertullian *Apol.* 9.8, E.T., *ANF* 3.24; cf. *Ad Nat.* 1.7, which is an enlarged version of *Ap.* 9.8. The relationship between the accounts by Minucius Felix and Tertullian has been discussed many times; the literature on

this is available in J. Quasten, *Patrology* (Utrecht: Spectrum, 1953), 2:161-162.

66. *Apol.* 1.7, 1.26; *Adv. Haer* 1.25.3.

67. *Hist. Eccl.* 4.7.10ff., E.T., K. Lake, Loeb, 1:319.

68. *Strom.* 3.1.3; 3.18.107.

69. Origen *Contra Celsum* 6.27.

70. Ibid., 6.40.

71. See Walter Bauer, *Orthodoxy and Heresy in Earliest Christianity* (Philadelphia: Fortress Press, 1971), pp. 44ff.

72. It is impossible to define Gnosticism since it has never been a unified movement. The magnitude of the problem appears clearly in Barbara Aland et al., eds., *Gnosis: Festschrift für Hans Jonas* (Göttingen: Vandenhoeck & Ruprecht, 1978). In particular see the article in this volume by A. H. Armstrong, "Gnosis and Greek Philosophy," pp. 87-124; and Morton Smith, "The History of the term Gnostikos," in *The Rediscovery of Gnosticism*, ed. Bentley Layton (Leiden: E. J. Brill, 1981), 2:796-807. The following books may also be useful: Elaine Pagels, *The Gnostic Gospels* (New York: Random House, 1979); John Dart, *The Laughing Savior: The Discovery and Significance of the Nag Hammadi Gnostic Library* (New York: Harper & Row, 1976); Werner Foerster and R. M. Wilson, *Gnosis: A Selection of Gnostic Texts*, 2 vols. (New York: Oxford University Press, 1972); Hans Jonas, *The Gnostic Religion*, 2d. ed. (Boston: Beacon Press, 1970). The English translation of the Nag Hammadi texts is available in James M. Robinson, ed., *The Nag Hammadi Library* (New York: Harper & Row, 1977).

73. Clement *Stromateis* 3.5.40, divided the Gnostics into these two general groups. These are discussed by Chadwick in *Alexandrian Christianity*, pp. 22ff.

74. Jude 4, 7, 8, 10, 12-13, 16, 18. Clement of Alexandria thought that Jude spoke prophetically of the Carpocratians "and other similar sects," *Stromateis* 3.2.11; Oulton and Chadwick, *Alexandrian Christianity*, p. 45.

75. See, for example, Rev. 2:6, 14f., 20 ff., and 2 Peter 2:2, 7, 10, 12f., 21-22. All New Testament passages that show evidence of libertinism have been analyzed by Morton Smith, *Clement of Alexandria and a Secret Gospel of Mark* (Cambridge: Harvard University Press, 1973), pp. 258-62. According to Smith the libertine tradition in Christianity "derives from Jesus' baptismal practice." (p. 262) and continued in the movement of Carpocrates.

IV

The Kiss

I N THE SEARCH FOR THE formation of pagan attitudes toward Christianity, one aspect of early Christian life that has not been given adequate attention is the practice of the holy kiss. This gave rise to various rumors, and thus it is appropriate that we should examine this problem. We will, therefore, first trace the development of this practice in the early Christian congregations, and then ask whether the erotic element inherent in a kiss was indeed part of Christian theology, and, if so, what purpose it served. In this connection we will briefly review the attitude of the peoples of the eastern Mediterranean toward sex and religion in an effort to understand the early Christians in their own historical and cultural milieu. Finally, we will explore the idea of Christian love as a means to achieve mystical union with God.

"Greet all the brethren with a holy kiss." So Paul instructed the Thessalonians, and later the Corinthians and the Romans.[1] The same instruction in a slightly altered form also appears in 1 Peter: "Greet one another with the kiss of love."[2] A personal kiss, holy or not, involves the intimate touching of another person's body, and this touch may take various forms; in some societies rubbing noses together is a form of kiss, in western civilization it is the mouth that is brought into connection with a part of the body—hands, feet, cheeks, lips—but in either form the kiss creates a relationship between two bodies and carries with it a certain significance that both parties understand. It may signify respect and honor, such as kissing of the feet, or tender love, kissing the mouth, however, can easily become an erotic experience. Scholars who have investigated the origin of the kiss are divided in their conclusions. Some associate the kiss with breathing, others with eating.[3]

Those scholars who associate it with breathing point out that the two organs used for kissing, the nose and mouth, are both involved in the action of breathing. Breathing is an essential function of the human body and is so closely associated with the maintenance of life that the Hebrew word *Ruah* and the Greek word *Pneuma* can mean either breath, spirit, or life. Thus we read that "God formed man of dust from the ground, and breathed into his nostrils the breath of life; and man became a living being."[4] God "kissed" man, and so human life started on earth with a divine kiss; the transfusion of spirit or soul into the human body. The kiss, therefore, may have originated from an animistic notion that souls are transmitted by the organs through which the breath passes. For many societies kissing signifies an attempt to create or to maintain a life relationship through the fusion of souls and so it is often the symbol of initiation or reception of new members into an organization. But because the kiss is associated with the idea of the "breath of life" it can easily assume an erotic character. It is in sexual union that new life is created or transmitted on earth, and the mingling of breaths or souls in kissing is analogous to the union of bodies in intercourse. By the same token, during sexual intercourse, the parties kiss each other on the mouth, "and they become one flesh."[5] The kiss here plays the same role as the kiss of God in Gen. 2:7; conception takes place, and the breath of life is infused into a new human being. Equally cogent arguments have been advanced for the theory that the kiss had its origin in eating. Eating involves, of course, the consumption and absorption of food by the body. It can be said, then, that in food man recognizes something desirable, and seeks to unite with it; just as in kissing an attempt is made to unite with a desirable person.

Both of these theories contain a common element, they both emphasize the very close bond that is created or expressed by the kiss. Is the kiss, then, a subconscious expression of a desire to overcome separation, to recreate that primeval unity that existed before the creation of the world? Can we interpret the many works of art depicting lovers kissing each other on Hindu temples, Greek vases, and funerary monuments as calling attention not merely to the unity of mankind, but to the unity that existed and should exist between God and man? Possibly so, since temples were obviously places of worship, Greek art of this type was strongly connected with the cult of Dionysus, and funerary monuments were by their very nature religious objects. All of which may lead us to the hypothesis that kissing originated as a primitive religious experience, and only later did it take on other functions, such as the expression of respect, from which the religious aspect was missing. Gradually every form of kissing became secularized, so to speak, and its theological basis was pushed into the background or completely forgotten.

The Greek noun for "kiss" in the New Testament is *philema,* which comes from the verb *phileo.* The primary meaning of the verb *phileo* is "to love," but as a particular expression of love it can also mean "to kiss."[6] In the New Testament this is the verb used in the accounts of Judas kissing Jesus, and in the story about the sinful woman who annointed Jesus with expensive ointment "and kissed his feet."[7] To be sure, the writers of the New Testament used the verb *agapao* interchangeably with *phileo.* Still, what is significant for our present inquiry is that the noun "kiss" is derived from the verb "to love." A kiss is meant to signify personal affection—one kisses as an expression of love and intimate association. The monstrosity of the kiss of Judas lies in the fact that it was a kiss of betrayal, exactly the opposite of its supposed intention.

Completely missing from the New Testament, however, is the sort of kiss that is given in the service of Eros, and that fact has caused most Christian interpreters to exclude any erotic element from the meaning of the holy kiss in the letters of Paul and the kiss of love in I Peter. Such scholars understand these to be kisses that symbolize the unity of the church, that mysterious body in which the members relate to each other and to Jesus, as the vines relate to the vine stock. According to Paul, the Church was "destined in love" by God; in it there is forgiveness of sins through Jesus Christ, and a promise of the unification of all things in him. In the kiss, which the faithful exchange with each other, all these things become a reality: there is love, forgiveness of sins, and unity in the name of Jesus Christ.[8] Is such a chaste interpretation of the holy kiss or the kiss of love correct or not?

It is interesting that after the New Testament writings the liturgical kiss is not mentioned in the early church for almost a hundred years. Justin Martyr is the first Christian writer to refer to it again in the middle of the second century. He mentioned the kiss in connection with the eucharistic service, it occurred immediately after prayer and before the consecration and distribution of the elements.[9] From this period on many references to the kiss can be found in patristic literature, and it becomes a sign of peace and reconciliation so that it is often called the kiss of peace or simply peace.[10] In other kinds of ceremonies the kiss was also employed. After ordination a new bishop was kissed by the members of the congregation, and the newly baptized Christian was first kissed by the bishop and afterwards kissed the brethren in the congregation. Occasionally we read about the martyrs kissing each other before execution, or being kissed by other Christians when they were led away. The most frequently mentioned occasion for the holy kiss was the Eucharistic service.[11]

Thus the holy kiss was used on occasions when the Holy Spirit played some important role. In ordination the Holy Spirit is transmitted to the newly ordained person. In baptism the cooperation of the Holy Spirit is invoked since the benefits of baptism—membership in the church, forgiveness of sins, resurrection of the body, and life everlasting—are all believed to be works of the Holy Spirit. Similarly in the Eucharistic service, the vivifying power that restored the broken body of Christ is believed to be the Holy Spirit, and the benefits of Christ's death and Resurrection are imparted to the believer through the work of the Holy Spirit.

The early Christians probably derived the practice of the holy kiss from the life and ministry of Jesus. Indeed there is a passage in John 20:21-23 that may have been the origin of the holy kiss. In this passage the risen Christ appears to the disciples. He offers proof that he is really who he says he is, and then "Jesus said to them again, 'Peace be with you. As the father has sent me, even so send I you.' And when he had said this, he breathed on them, and said to them, 'Receive the Holy Spirit. If you forgive the sins of any, they are forgiven; if you retain the sins of any, they are retained.'" These verses describe the very first service of Christian ordination in history, in which Christ transmitted the Holy Spirit to the disciples by breathing on them. The question naturally arises, how did he breathe on them? Simply by blowing air in their direction, or holding out his palm and blowing on it? Although we have no information on this particular point, the answer that comes most readily to mind is that Jesus kissed the disciples. As we have already mentioned, an early animistic belief may have associated the kiss with the transmission of the spirit (breath of life); these verses from the gospel of John may reflect the same belief. At any rate the practice of the holy kiss in the early church involved communication with the Holy Spirit (pneuma-breath), and it may have been based on the kiss of Jesus mentioned in John.

Another passage in the New Testament, Luke 1, describes the

power of the Holy Spirit in a related context. In the account of the conception of Jesus, the angel Gabriel announces that the conception will take place when the Holy Spirit comes upon Mary (verse 35). To this Mary replies: "Behold, I am the handmaid of the Lord; let it be to me according to your word." The angel then leaves Mary. According to Christian belief at some point in this transaction Mary has become pregnant, although at exactly which point remains a question. Many interpreters believe that the words of Mary "let it be to me. . . ." express the active cooperation of the virgin with the divine will, and exactly at this instant the Holy Spirit is infused into Mary. How is he (the *pneuma*: spirit, breath, life) transmitted to her? Again, we lack information, but it would be logical to conjecture that it is in the form of a kiss by the angel, in the same way that Gen. 2:7 could be interpreted as referring to a divine kiss. It matters little if we attach a mere symbolic significance to the passage describing the conception of Jesus. The image of a kiss best expresses the idea of the love of God, the union of divine and human, and the infusion of spirit into man. In this connection it is worth noting that, just as life may arise by the kiss of God, so rabbinic literature raises the possibility that God can take life away by his kiss, and that the great saints of the Old Testament—Aaron, Abraham, Isaac, and Jacob—all died by a kiss of God.[12]

On what part of the body did the early Christians bestow their holy kiss? Today, when the kiss is employed in Christian service it is usually placed on the cheek of the other person, but this misses one of the important symbolisms of the kiss—that it is an exchange of breath or spirits—and logically that could only occur through the mouth. According to Augustine, Jesus breathed the Spirit into the mouth of the disciples,[13] and the early Christians kissed each other on the lips, even when the kiss was just a greeting, following this example. Cyprian wrote to the confessors Sergius, Rogatianus, and their colleagues, when they were in prison, that he longed to come and visit them and "kiss your lips, which with a glorious voice have confessed the Lord."[14] Cyril of Jerusalem explained that the kiss that friends usually exchanged was different from the one practiced by Christians in the liturgy, because the holy kiss "blends souls one with another."[15] Augustine, who is more explicit than Cyril, said that in the holy kiss "your lips approach the lips of your brother."[16] Chrysostom also admonished his congregation that the mouth is an honorable part of the body and is "the temple of Christ." "The mouth is the porch and entrance of the temple" through which we receive the Lord's Body and "it is for this reason chiefly that we here kiss."[17]

But kissing on the mouth poses problems. Ideally such a kiss should be chaste (parents and children may exchange a kiss on the lips), but it is not difficult to turn the emotion of a kiss on the mouth into an erotic experience of some kind. This must have been on the mind of Tertullian when he claimed that a pagan husband would not tolerate his wife "to meet any one of the brethren to exchange the kiss."[18] This matter did, in fact, cause problems very early in the Christian church. The apologist Athenagoras, a contemporary of Tertullian, reflected on it as follows: "We feel it a matter of great importance that those, whom we thus think of as brother and sister and so on, should keep their bodies undefiled and uncorrupted. For the Scripture says again, 'If one kisses a second time, because he found it enjoyable . . .' [The rest of the passage is missing] Thus the kiss, or rather the religious salutation should be very carefully guarded. If it is defiled by the slightest evil thought it excludes us from eternal life."[19] We do not know what Scripture Athenagoras quoted from, but obviously its author was familiar with some cases where the "brother and sister" liked the kiss so much that they wanted to try it a second time. Nor could these have been isolated occurrences; otherwise there would have been no need to lay down written rules against them. Athenagoras, too, recognized the danger of a holy kiss turning into a carnal one and warned that the liturgical kiss must be "carefully guarded."

No doubt, all sincere Christians took the warning by Athenagoras seriously. Yet we find that in subsequent years further warnings were necessary. A telling piece of evidence is in the book *Paedagogus*, in which Clement of Alexandria (died ca. 215), instructed people who had newly converted from paganism to Christianity how to conduct themselves in their daily lives. Clement admonished that a Christian girl's face must be clean, her eyebrows not let down, and her neck not stretched back, that Christian men should not spend time in barber shops and taverns, and that all Christians "must abandon a furious mode of walking, and choose a grave and leisurely, but not a lingering step." He set forth how Christians should dress when they go to church and how they should behave when they were in church. He wrote:

> And if we are called to the Kingdom of God, let us walk worthy of the
> kingdom, loving God and our neighbor. But love is not proved by a

kiss, but by kindly feelings. But there are those, that do nothing but
make the churches resound with a kiss not having love itself within.
For this very thing, the shameless use of a kiss, which ought to be
mystic, occasions foul suspicions and evil reports. The apostle calls
the kiss holy. When the kingdom is worthily tested, we dispense the
affection of the soul by a chaste and closed mouth, by which chiefly
gentle manners are expressed. But there is another, unholy kiss, full of
poison, counterfeiting sanctity. Do you know that spiders, merely by
touching the mouth, afflict men with pain? And often kisses inject
the poison of licentiousness. It is then very manifest to us, that a kiss
is not love.[20]

Clement then explained that to love means to love God, and to love
God in turn means to keep God's commandments, and not "that we
stroke each other on the mouth." He claimed that some people kissed
ostentatiously, without the least particle of grace. Yet, he believed
the kiss to be as great a mystery as prayer, and so Christians should
greet their neighbors with the same solemnity with which they said
their prayers. He advised men not to look at women at all, because of
the impossibility of looking without lust. Christians should not only
keep themselves chaste but also behave in such a way as to give no
ground for suspicion by outsiders. The words of Ecclus. 9:8 should be
remembered: "For by the beauty of women many have gone astray,
and at it affection blazes up like fire." This fire could lead to the
eternal fire that is the consequence of sin. Clement even advised
husbands not to kiss their wives in the presence of household
servants.[21]

Clement's remarks show not only that the kiss was a mouth-to-
mouth kiss, but also that it was indeed abused, that is, enjoyed by
some. Thus the practice that was meant as a symbol of the holiness of
the church became not infrequently an occasion for licentiousness,
and the situation hardly improved with the passage of time. *The
Apostolic Tradition* by Hippolytus, written in the second decade of
the third century, ordered that women sit apart from men in the
assembly and cover their heads. When the time came for the giving of
the kiss of peace, the baptized should embrace one another "men
with men and women with women. But let not men embrace
women."[22] Similarly, the *Ps. Clementine Epistle on Virginity*, written in the third or fourth century, advised that after prayer men kiss
men and women kiss the hands of men wrapped in men's garments.[23]
Tertullian, when he chided the frivolity of the conduct of the heretics, charged that "they exchange the kiss indiscriminately."[24] The
church order, composed around 380 in Constantinople or Syria and

called the *Apostolic Constitution*, ruled that during the liturgy men might only kiss men and women only kiss women.[25] The church historian Eusebius in his biography of Emperor Constantine reported that Constantine's coemperor, Licinius, forbade worship services by Christians in mixed congregations, possibly because the rumor of wild kissing and general promiscuity in the churches was already widespread.[26]

Eusebius also described an incident that he claimed took place in 311 in Damascus. A commander in the army used torture to force some women to confess that they had once been Christians and "that in their very churches, they committed licentious deeds, and innumerable other slanders, which he wished them to utter against our religion."[27] Did the holy kiss really degenerate into licentiousness in some congregations, or was this forced confession simply an attempt to discredit Christians during a wave of persecutions? Probably the latter, but the fact that such propaganda would have an effect among the population of Damascus shows that rumors did circulate in the cities concerning the Christian services.

Although the holy kiss gave rise to false rumors among non-Christians as well as temptations among the faithful, the church did not abandon it. The idea of the mystical union with God was so supremely important in this rite that it overrode all other considerations. The holy kiss maintained the unity of the church. The Holy Spirit guaranteed that unity, for one Spirit baptized Christians into one body, "and all were made to drink of one Spirit."[28] In the kiss, the Spirit was mingled, and the church became in a proleptic way a unity, the living body of Christ. This explains why the holy kiss occurred most frequently in the Eucharistic service. In the Eucharist the unity of the church was impressed on the senses of the believers as they drank from the same cup and ate of the same loaf of bread. The bread was a particularly important symbol because it represented "one body" that was consumed by all who thus became "one body" themselves. At the same time the Eucharist was a meal, and it reminded Christians of the time when the first believers ate together with Jesus after his Resurrection, which itself was a foretaste of the great messianic meal that believers will celebrate with Jesus in the kingdom of God.[29]

The Christian idea of universalism was not a new or even a biblical idea. The search for an ultimate "One" was present among the pre-Socratic Greek philosophers. Xenophanes (ca. 530 B.C.), for example, postulated that "There is one god, among gods and men the greatest, not at all like mortals in body or in mind."[30] He went on to define divine nature, and in so doing Xenophanes became the first philosopher to point the way toward a universalism that would fully flourish later in Christianity. Heraclitus of Ephesus (ca. 500 B.C.) also struggled with the problem of the unity of opposites, from which he proceeded to a discussion of the unity of all things and arrived at a statement that "looks suspiciously like monotheism."[31]

For our concern, however, Empedocles of Acragas (ca. 450 B.C.) is the most important of the early Greek philosophers. His famous "twofold tale" is worth quoting here:

> I shall tell thee a twofold tale. At one time it grew to be one only out of many; at another, it divided up to be many instead of one. There is a double becoming of perishable things and a double passing away. The coming together of all things brings one generation into being and destroys it; the other grows up and is scattered as things become divided. And these things never cease continually changing places, at one time all uniting in one through love, at another each borne in different directions by the repulsion of strife. Thus, as far as it is their nature to grow into one out of many, and to become many once more when the one is parted asunder, so far they come into being and their life abides not. . . . At one time it grew together to be one only out of many; at another it parted asunder so as to be many instead of one; Fire and Water and Earth and the mighty height of Air; dread Strife, too, apart from these, of equal weight to each, and Love in their midst, equal in length and breadth. Her thou contemplate with thy mind, nor sit with dazed eyes. It is she that is known as being implanted in the frame of mortals. It is she that makes them have thoughts of love and work the works of peace. They call her by the names of Joy and Aphrodite. . . .[32]

Empedocles talked about the unification and separation of the four elements (fire, air, water, earth), which result in the creation and the destruction of mortal things. He believed that Love unites and Strife separates, which brings us close to our own problem.

The following passage by Empedocles discusses the contest between Love and Strife which "is manifest in the mass of mortal limbs. At one time all the limbs that are the body's portion are brought together by Love in blooming life's high season; at another, severed by cruel Strife, they wander each alone by the breakers of life's sea. It is the same with plants and the fish that make their homes in the water, with the beasts that have their lairs on the hills

and the seabirds that sail on wings."[33] A leading scholar of Empedocles has written that "Since Love has among her titles Aphrodite . . . it
would appear that we have here a reference to sexual love . . . Possibly
heterosexuality was the source of Empedocles' idea of Love operating
between different things."[34] If so, Empedocles laid the groundwork
for the later Christian interpretation of sexual union as a religious
experience; but other scholars have seriously questioned this
interpretation.[35] Plato (ca. 429-347) saw love (Eros) as the mediator
between God and man that alone is able to bridge the chasm that
exists between divine and mortal. It is only through love that man
can approach God. But when people love, they desire first to unite
with the object of their love, Plato argued, and to procreate. Procreation is the union of man and woman "and is a divine thing, for
conception and generation are an immortal principle in the mortal
creature." It, therefore, provides a sort of eternity and immortality,
and it is this that mortals seek through love. When men desire to have
children "that universal love and interest is for the sake of
immortality."[36]

In Jewish thought, Moses formulated the idea of one God who
transcends all. The great Shema, "Hear, O Israel: The Lord our God is
one!"[37] is not so much a protest against polytheism, as it is an
affirmation of the uniqueness of God as Creator.[38] In Jewish belief
God represented unity, and to believe in God meant to strive for unity
since eternity was really just "another word for unity."[39] The desire
for eternity is thus a natural desire on the part of the creation for a
union with God, the Creator.

Early Christian theology developed these ideas and made them into
a central theme of Christian theology. The church fathers maintained that the life, death, and Resurrection of Jesus Christ must be
understood in terms of God's ultimate aim of restoring unity to the
universe, which was thought somehow to have been broken and
scattered as a result of the destructive workings of sin. Paul made this
clear in Eph. 1:3ff., when he said: "Blessed be the God and Father of
our Lord Jesus Christ, who has blessed us in Christ with every
Spiritual blessing in the heavenly places. . . . He destined us in love to
be his sons through Jesus Christ, according to the purpose of his will.
. . . In him we have redemption through his blood. . . . For he has made
known to us in all wisdom and insight the mystery of his will,
according to his purpose which he set forth in Christ as a plan for the
fullness of time, to unite all things in him, things in heaven and

things on earth. . . ." Similarly, in Rom. 5, Paul drew a comparison between the "one man" Adam, through whom sin spread over mankind, and the "one man" Jesus Christ, through whom grace and life will be given to all men. The same thought is again developed in the passage about the Resurrection of the dead in 1 Cor. 15:22 where we read that "as in Adam all die, so also in Christ shall all be made alive." Paul heightened the mystery of the unification to cosmic levels when he wrote in 1 Cor. 15:28 that after everything had been subjected to Jesus, then Jesus "himself will also be subjected to him who put all things under him, that God may be everything to everyone." Paul argued that history had changed its course since the appearance of Jesus Christ. Before his arrival there was a scattering and separation from God, but now the movement had been reversed, and all things were being brought back together in God.

Pursuing Paul's line of speculation, that great Christian of the second century, Irenaeus, wrote that universal salvation is a recapitulation, a work of summing up, a bringing together.[40] St. Augustine drew on the ideas of his predecessors when he argued that salvation meant the restoration of the image of the first Adam as the final act of redemptive history: "Adam has been scattered over the whole world. He was in one place and fell, and as in a manner broken small, he filled the whole world: but the mercy of God gathered together the fragments from every side, and forged them by the fire of love, and made one that was broken. . . . He will gather together His elect with Him. . . ."[41]

Origen, the Christian theologian from Alexandria (ca. 185-ca. 254), presented his views on the eschatological union of the universe with God in a systematic way in his treatise *De principiis.* He began with the statement that God is the center of the transcendental world. From God emerges the Logos, and through the Logos the spiritual world is created. Some spiritual beings leave God, and thus the world arises. Further away from God, physical existence takes form, and so the process continues down to the state of hell and the condition of the devils. Origen, therefore, saw a gradual movement away from the center and God. God, however, seeks to recover those who have fallen; he sustains them, and, in an attempt at unification, he sends the Logos (Jesus Christ) to lead fallen creation back to him. The fall is not final. The redemptive will of God touches all the cosmos and every entity within it, even God's enemies will ultimately be restored.[42] The final consummation, when all things will be subject to

Christ, means a returning to the one. "For the end is always like the beginning: and, therefore, as there is one end to all things, so ought we understand that there was one beginning; and as there is one end to many things, so there spring from one beginning many differences and varieties, which again, through the goodness of God, and by subjection to Christ, and through the unity of the Holy Spirit, are recalled to one end, which is like unto the beginning. . . ."[43]

Origen believed that his cosmology was biblical, and he applied it to the individual Christian's mystical ascent to union with the Logos.[44] First, man must understand himself and his place in the cosmos, which makes him conscious of the presence of sin and also desirous of overcoming sin. When he begins to mortify his flesh and to fight against evil, then his mystical ascent begins. Slowly by conscious efforts and divine grace he rises to a spiritual union with Christ, which Origen compared to a spiritual marriage.[45]

Plotinus, a pagan philosopher, developed a very similar system of belief. The similarity could be due in part to the fact that both men may have had the same teacher, an Alexandrian scholar named Ammonius Saccas. Plotinus (205-270), a native Egyptian, conceived of all existing reality as a tightly structured hierarchical order. The ground of all existence from which everything else flows is the "One," or the "Good," which supersedes human understanding. He is absolute, without origin, above space or time, and infinite. He is Light, and all other modes of existence are the result of his expansion, or creative overflow. The first and highest reality emanating from the One is the divine "Mind" that is the intermediary, the divine intelligence, the link between the One and lower grades of reality. Next in this descending order is the "Soul," which is now so far from unity with the One that it must create space and time to apprehend its objects. Thus, the Soul stands between Mind and Nature; in its relation to Mind, Soul is divine but its activity (in a downward direction) is spatial-temporal. The lowest creative power is "Nature," which projects "Matter," that is, the physical world. The quality of every reality in this structure is, therefore, dependent on its proximity to the One, but nothing exists outside the sphere of the One, and ultimately even Matter is the result of the expansion, or overflow of the One. Plotinus does not see Matter as "evil," as it is in many Gnostic systems and sometimes in Christian thinking; it is just the end of the creative process.

What, then, is man? Man is a microcosm that unites all these

principles in himself: the individual soul is created after the image of
the Mind, although it inhabits a corporeal body. Looking upward, so
to speak, man is able to rise to the level of the divine Mind and may
even achieve momentary unity with the One. For the occupation of a
body is a humiliation for the soul, and its most important task is to
escape from the body, rise to a higher existence and to its original
condition.

The activity of the life flowing from the center, from the One,
toward lower and further levels of existence means a gradual loosen-
ing of the unity that is within the One. This centrifugal movement
away from the One, however, is accompanied by another centripetal
movement toward the One, an upward thrust that ultimately leads
back to a perfect union with the One. Man can achieve this goal
through contemplation and introspection until the soul sees light
and feels the presence of God in a state of mystical union. The
essence of this mystic union is Love (Eros), for the soul desires union
with its origin not because of curiosity, but because the same power
motivates it that motivates lovers to unite.[46]

Though this sketch is all too brief, it does show that Plotinus's
philosophy bordered on Christian thinking at a number of points. It is
no wonder, therefore, that Neo-Platonism exercised such an im-
mense influence on later Christian thinkers. For example, Paul's
words in Eph. 1:3-10 and the theories of Irenaeus and Augustine
express many of the ideas developed by Plotinus. The basic issue of
religion, according to both Christian thinkers and Plotinus and his
Neo-Platonist followers, is the mystical union of the individual soul
with God. This is achieved by "love" (agape) according to Paul and
"love" (Eros) according to Plotinus. The holy kiss in Christianity
symbolized this union and, moreover, the stark physical character of
a mouth-to-mouth kiss was an actualization and realization of the
Christians' hope to overcome separation and to find union in and
with God.

The Christian idea of mystical union expressed by the holy kiss,
therefore, made full use of the physical side of existence, but the
Platonic and Neo-Platonic ideas did not. Although both Christianity
and the Platonic and Neo-Platonic systems saw "love" as the uniting
force, in the Platonic and Neo-Platonic systems, Eros was thought of
as driving the soul upward away from the sensual and sensible. So
arose the mistaken notion that physical love and religion have nothing to do with each other. Anders Nygren, who made a sharp distinc-

tion between *agape* and *eros*, declared that "Sensual love has no place in a discussion of love in the religious sense, whether in the context of Eros or of the Agape motif."[47] In the English translation his reference to physical love is "vulgar Eros" as opposed to "heavenly Eros" similar to the Greek distinction between "Pandemos" and "Uranios" Eros. Greek literature, however, provides us with several examples of love in a religious context where the sexual aspect is obvious. Hesiod (ca. 700 B.C.), a Greek poet, named Eros among the first three powers born in the universe, from which all other gods descended.[48] Aristophanes (ca. 457-ca. 385) developed the same thought in his comedy *The Birds*. He wrote:

> There was Chaos at first, and Darkness, and Night, and
>   Tartarus vast and dismal;
> But the Earth was not there, nor the Sky, nor the Air, till
>   at length in the bosom abysmal
> Of Darkness an egg, from the whirlwind conceived, was
>   laid by the sable-plumed Night.
> And out of that egg, as the Seasons revolved, sprang Love,
>   the entrancing, the bright,
> Love brilliant, and bold with his pinions of gold, like a
>   whirlwind, refulgent and sparkling!
> Love hatched us, commingling in Tartarus wide, with
>   Chaos, the murky, the darkling,
> And brought us above, as the firstling of love, and first to
>   the light we ascended
> There was never a race of Immortals at all till Love had
>   the universe blended;
> Then all things commingling together in love, there arose
>   the fair Earth, and the Sky,
> And the limitless Sea; and the race of the Gods, the
>   Blessed, who never shall die.
> So we then the Blessed are older by far; and abundance of
>   proof is existing
> That we are the children of Love. . . .[49]

In these early cosmogonies Eros is instrumental in bringing harmony out of chaos and in organizing the universe. Love accomplishes this by bringing elements together into a creative union that results in the coming into being of earth, sky, sea, and, eventually, all creatures. Eros, so our ancestors believed, was a fundamental principle of all existence. Thus, it is no wonder that they even thought about agricultural productivity, their primary requirement for survival, in terms of creative love. Only when the sky and earth united would there be a fruitful harvest. The most primitive agrarian religious rites reflect this faith. Archaeologists have discovered many votive clay figurines that show couples performing intercourse, which were clearly meant to encourage the fruitfulness of the soil. The origins of this belief go back to the dawn of our civilization, to Mesopotamia, where "the power manifest in fertility in all its forms was personified in the Goddess who was the incarnation of the reproductive forces."[50] The same belief existed throughout the ancient Mediterranean, and it formed the basis for the sacred marriage (*hieros gamos*).

In Mesopotamia the people celebrated the sacred marriage during the New Year's Festival. The king and the queen engaged in sexual intercourse in a chamber of the ziggurat, a temple tower. They imitated the creative union of the goddess Inanna (Ishtar) and the shepherd god Dumuzi (Tammuz), who were responsible for the renewal of life at the turn of the year. Winter, the time of sterility, was over, and the vital forces in nature would be aroused again. Similar rites were celebrated in Syria, Anatolia, and Egypt.[51] In Greece the sacred marriage was part of the festival of Anthesteria (in February). This solemn ceremony was preceded by strict requirements; the Archon Basileus had to marry a virgin who had been carefully selected for him. Every year on the twelfth day of the month Anthesterion, the basilinna (the wife of the Archon Basileus) was taken to the Acropolis in a procession, and there, in the former royal residence, called the Bukolion (meaning, ox stall) she engaged in sacred intercourse with Dionysus, who was represented, it is assumed, by her husband. This ensured "the process of fertility over which Dionysus had control."[52] In addition, these rites served as a reminder of the primeval cosmogony related by Hesiod and Aristophanes, and, in a symbolic way, the Archon Basileus and his wife re-enacted the divine union that would end chaos. This great mystery made the faithful observer feel that he was part of the whole divine order.

The idea of sacred marriage had an important place in Jewish thinking, too, as has been shown by Raphael Patai's book *The Hebrew Goddess*.[53] References to this phenomenon are mostly found in the Qabbalah, which is the Hebrew term for traditional lore. Its roots may go back to the first century A.D. and beyond that to ancient Near Eastern mythology. According to Hebrew mythology the sacred marriage was performed by the divine King and his twin the "Matronit" who regularly performed divine intercourse on the eve of the Sabbath.

Their union resulted in the creation of human souls and angels. In imitation of the generative forces of the cosmos, pious Jews customarily had their marriage relations on Friday nights, too. "Human marriages were intended to be like the divine ideal and failure to imitate the divine example diminished the image of God. 'When is a man called complete in his resemblance to the Supernal?' The Zohar (a book of the Qabbalah) asked and gave answer: When he couples with his spouse in oneness, joy and pleasure, and a son and daughter issue from him and his female. This is the complete man resembling the Above. . . ." It is also a part of Jewish tradition that the cherubim in the holy of holies of the temple represented the male and female aspects of the deity and that they were shown there in a sexual embrace. There are many references to this in the Talmud and in later Jewish mysticism, which used the example of the Cherubim to emphasize the "sanctity of sex and the cosmic necessity of sexual intercourse between man and wife."[54]

Eros as a force that unites man and woman even in the face of death is also the theme of *Antigone* by Sophocles. He praised the power of love in the following hymn:

> Where is the equal of love?
> Where is the battle he cannot win,
> The power he cannot outmatch?
> In the farthest corners of earth, in the
>   midst of the sea.
> He is there; he is here
> In the bloom of a fair face
> Lying in wait;
> And the grip of his madness
> Spares not god or man,
> Marring the righteous man,
> Driving his soul into mares of sin
> And strife, dividing a house.
> For the light that burns in the eyes of
>   a bride of desire
> Is a fire that consumes.[55]

Bultman has shown how deeply *Antigone* is rooted in the Greek religious experience.[56] He called attention to the two basic motifs of the play, Hades and Eros, death and love. These are the two overriding forces in human affairs, irresistible, transcendental powers that supersede all laws made by man. Hades and Eros are both divine, and they determine our fate and limit our freedom. To try to challenge them is hubris.

The Dialogue on Love (Erotikos) written by Plutarch around 116-117 is closer to the era of the early Christians.[57] This spirited treatise written in praise of Eros contains many passages that place sexual relations directly in the sphere of the divine. Although Aphrodite is the goddess of the physical act of intercourse, "intercourse without Eros is like hunger and thirst, which can be sated, but never achieve a noble end. It is by means of Eros that the goddess removes the cloying effect of pleasure and creates affection and fusion."[58] To the objection that it is impious to identify the gods with our passions, Plutarch replied that if Ares is a god, so is Eros. "So the warlike, inimical, and antagonistic element has a divinity, while the affectionate, sociable, coupling impulse is to be left without a god? When men slay and are slain, is there a god . . . but when they desire marriage and an affection that will lead to concord and co-operation, [the Greek words are ὁμοφροσίνη and κοινωνία] is there no god to witness and direct, to lead and help us?"[59] Like Sophocles, Plutarch connected Eros with Hades. Plutarch concluded from the legends of Alcestis, Protesilaos, and Orpheus and Eurydice, that Eros is "the only one of the gods whose commands are obeyed by Hades." Then he compared the festivals in honor of Eros with the mysteries at Eleusis and said: "So though it is true, my friend, that it is a good thing to be initiated into the mysteries of Eleusis, I observe that celebrants of love's mysteries have a higher place in Hades."[60] Plutarch believed that those who love have a greater prospect of immortality, and that love is stronger than death.[61] He praised married life in which the lovers "though separated in body, forcibly join their souls and fuse them together, no longer wishing to be separate entities, or believing that they are so."

What kind of love, then, did the early Christians have in mind when they talked about the Church, Jesus Christ, and God?[62] Paul wrote in Eph. 2:24 that "a man shall leave his father and mother and be joined to his wife, and the two shall become one." The text itself, in fact, says that man and woman "become one flesh," which can mean nothing else but sexual union. Paul continued: "This is a great mystery and I take it to mean Christ and the church."[63] The church is a body that brings into the context of the present the future experience of union with God, and the relationship of church to Christ can be expressed only by the image of intercourse, the intermingling in body and spirit of man and woman engaged in the act of love. It is the unifying aspect of love that concerns us here, because this is the underlying meaning of the term in the most important passages in the New Testament. Love, in this sense, is the key concept of Christian theology and the cornerstone of the church. "God so loved the world that he gave his only Son"[64] is the concise message of the gospel, and because of this Christians are reminded: "Beloved, let us love one another; for love is of God, and he who loves is born of God and knows God. He who does not love does not know God; for God is love."[65] If there is no knowledge of God apart from love, are we to conclude that a religious experience of God is by nature an erotic experience of some sort?

As in ancient Greek literature, the Christians used words and phrases to refer to marriage relations and procreation that they also used to express religious ideas. Redemptive history begins with the love of God, whose wish to bring his world back to a perfect union, results in a "new creation."[66] Born again Christians are the "children of God," they call God "Father" because he sent the "Spirit" into their hearts, and that same "Spirit" is in Jesus Christ, the Son of God, the first born of the new creation, who was conceived by a kiss of God.[67] The religio-erotic terminology is unmistakable in these ideas but it appears in an even more open form in 1 John 3:9. "No one born of God commits sins because God's nature abides in him. . . ." In the original, the Greek word for "nature" is "sperma," i.e. sperm. The "sperm of God," the life substance of God, is in the man who is born of God—in short, that man has been fathered by God. No wonder that Christian theologians of the patristic period defined love along Greek philosophical lines.[68]

The most important aspect of love—Christian love—is that it unites, as does erotic love too, and it is at this point that the two notions of love meet. The church is explained by means of sexual imagery, and sex is viewed as a matter pertaining to the sphere of the divine. It is logical, therefore, that early Christians usually explained the Song of Songs, that most erotic of all canonical writings of the Bible, as referring to the passionate desire of the human soul, or of the church, for God. The sentence: "O that he would kiss me with the kisses of his mouth," (Song of Songs 1:2), has been interpreted in a spiritual sense, but in the light of the above discussion the allegorization is not really such a radical departure from the literal meaning. The kiss, as the meeting and touching of lips and the mingling of breaths (spirits), carries in itself an element of creative fusion, and sexual union, as we have seen, was thought of in strongly religious terms.[69] From this point it is an easy transition to the kiss of God that creates and redeems the world by the infusion of his Spirit.

Nowhere does this mystery appear deeper and more real than in the celebration of the Eucharist. This is *agape*, a love feast, in which the communicants "eat the body" and "drink the blood" of Jesus Christ. Thus they become one with him—Christ is in them, and they are in Christ, according to the imagery used by Paul—and they are assured of eternal life. At the same time the bond of union is established among the communicants, and they become the body of Christ. It was in the Eucharistic service that the holy kiss was practiced, and it is interesting, to say the least, that this kiss, a very physical sign of love and union, may have been thought of as a holy marriage between Christ and his "spotless bride," the church.[70] In this connection J. J. Perella quoted the seventeenth-century, Roman Catholic Bishop J. B. Bossuet:

> In the ecstasy of human love, who is unaware that we eat and devour each other, that we long to become part of each other in every way, and, as the poet said, to carry off even with our teeth the thing we love in order to possess it, feed upon it, become one with it, live on it? That which is frenzy, that which is impotence in corporeal love is truth, is wisdom in the love of Jesus: 'Take, eat, this is my body': devour, swallow up not a part, not a piece but the whole.[71]

Is it possible that in the subconscious mind of the early Christians some vague memory of holy marriage was still alive? That sacramental intercourse that from time immemorial had demonstrated to believers the creative power of the gods, that power that did away with the primeval chaos and established law and order in the universe, made man, and assured the continued fertility of the land. In the Christian Eucharist the sacramental intercourse is reduced to the holy kiss and to the eating and drinking of the "body" and "blood" of Jesus, and the "union of love" is consummated in this way. This must be the reason why the early Christians, and modern day Christians too, have liked to quote in their communion services the words of Psalm 34:8: "O taste and see that the Lord is good." The sense of taste is called upon here for the knowledge of God and, of course, the organs of taste are the mouth, the lips, and the tongue. Thus an equally sacramental interpretation could be given to Song of Songs 1:2, 4:11, and 5:13 when the bridegroom extols the delight of uniting with his bride in a kiss. Since bride and groom, or even husband and wife, imagery is common in the Bible for the description of God's relation to his people, or the relation of Jesus to the church, it would be quite natural to interpret these words, too, with reference to the Eucharist: "Your lips distil nectar my bride; honey and milk are under your tongue."[72]

The practice of the holy kiss, therefore, could and occasionally did lead to unholy acts. This, in turn, spread rumors among the non-Christians about licentious behavior in Christian services. But the holy kiss for the early Christians was more than just a form of greeting, as it was in secular usage. There it could be simply an expression of friendship and good will, but among Christians it assumed a deeper meaning; it symbolized the unity, the belonging together of Christians, in the Church of Jesus Christ. Through the kiss the Holy Spirit was transmitted and received, and the kiss represented the life giving breath of God. Hence the importance of the kiss in the services of ordination, baptism, and the Eucharist.

The Christians believed that the holy kiss through the Holy Spirit established unity. This faith raised Christian theology to eschatological levels. They saw the work of God in the world as the unification of the universe, and through the holy kiss the Christian, in a proleptic way, tasted that unity. An important element of the holy kiss was the concept of love, for which Christians preferred to use the word *agape*. The idea of sexual love, however, cannot remain immaterial when it is accompanied by such a stark physical act as a kiss. Naturally, therefore, Christian authors used the imagery of marriage relationships and sexual symbolism to explain theological concepts. A comparison between the Christian holy kiss and the pagan holy marriage shows that the principles behind both were similar; they both tried to effect a relationship with the divine for the purpose of attaining life. In Gnostic groups these principles sometimes degenerated into promiscuity; in the mainstream church, however, they continued in the Eucharist.

NOTES

1. 1 Thess. 5:26; 1 Cor. 16:20; 2 Cor. 13:12; Rom. 16:16.
2. 1 Pet. 5:14.
3. See N. J. Perella, *The Kiss Sacred and Profane* (Berkeley and Los Angeles: University of California Press, 1969); Ch. Nyrop, *The Kiss and Its History* (London: Sands, 1901), pp. 175ff.

4. Gen. 2:7.
5. Gen. 2:24.
6. To the following see Gustave Stählin, φιλέω, κτλ, *Theologisches Wörterbuch zum Neuen Testament* (Stuttgart: Kohlhammer Verlag, 1975), 9.112-69; K.-M. Hofmann, "Philema Hagion" (Ph.D. Dissertation, University of Erlanger, 1938); Klaus Thraede, "Ursupünge und Formen des Heiligen Kussus," *Jahrbuch für Antike und Christentum* 11/12 (1965-1969):124-80.
7. Mark 74:44; Matt. 26:48; Luke 22:47, 7:38, 45.
8. Eph. 1:3ff.
9. *Apol.* 1.65.2, E.T., *ANF* 1.185.
10. See, for example, Tertullian *De oratione* 18; Augustine *Sermo* 227.
11. Hippolytus mentioned the use of the holy kiss for the consecration of a bishop, after prayer, and for confirmation. See *The Apostolic Tradition of St. Hippolytus of Rome*, ed. Gregory Dix (London: SPCK, 1937).
12. See Stählin, φιλέω, κτλ, p. 125f.
13. *Sermo* 42. *De Elisaeo* II, *MPL* 39. 1830; Augustine talks about Elisha raising a dead child in the following way: "He went up and lay upon the child, putting his mouth upon his mouth, his eyes upon his eyes, and his hands upon his hands; and as he stretched himself upon him, the flesh of the dead child became warm." This, Augustine says, prefigures the work of Christ who resuscitated the human race by his Spirit. "The Lord gave the same Spirit to the disciples when he breathed upon them and said, 'Receive Holy Spirit' Because he somehow placed mouth over mouth when he gave the Spirit by breathing." In *Ioannis Ev. Tractatus* 32.6. Augustine says that Jesus breathed upon the faces of the disciples. The Gnostic *Gospel of Bartholomew* 4.71 also refers to the kiss of Jesus: "Jesus put off his mantle and took a kerchief from the neck of Bartholomew," pronounced a benediction, "And when he had ceased the apostles kissed him, and he gave them the peace of love."
14. *Epistula* 6:1.
15. *Catechetical Lectures* 23.3, E.T.: *NPNF* Series 2, 7:153.
16. Quoted in Perella, *The Kiss Sacred and Profane*, p. 24.
17. *Homily* 30.2; 2 Cor. 13:12, "Greet one another with a holy kiss." "What is 'holy'? not hollow, not treacherous, like the kiss which Judas gave to Christ. For therefore is the kiss given, that it may be fuel unto love, that it may kindle the disposition, that we may so love each other, as brothers brothers, as children parents, as parents children; yea rather even far more. For those things are a disposition implanted by nature, but these by spiritual grace. Thus our souls bound unto each other. And therefore when we return after an absence we kiss each other, our souls hastening unto mutual intercourse. For this is that member which most of all declares to us the workings of the soul. But about this holy kiss somewhat else may yet be said. To what effect? We are the temple of Christ; we kiss then the porch and entrance of the temple when we kiss each other. See ye not how many kiss even the porch of this temple, some stooping down, others grasping it with their hand, and putting their hand to their mouth. And through these gates and doors Christ both had entered into us, and doth enter, whensoever we communicate. Ye who partake of the mysteries understand what I say. For it is in no common manner that our lips are honored, when we receive the Lord's Body. It is for this reason chiefly that we here kiss." E.T., *NPNF* First Series, 12:418.
18. *Ad uxorem* 2.4, E.T., *ANF* 4.34. Tertullian came close to equating the kiss with marital union. See *De virginibus velandis* 11.7. "it is a betrothal

that [virgins] are veiled because then both in body and in spirit they have mingled with a male, through the kiss and the right hand. . . ."

19. *Legatio* 32, E.T.; in Cyril C. Richardson, *Early Christian Fathers*, Library of Christian Classics (Philadelphia: Westminster Press, 1953), 1:337.

20. *Paedagogus* 3.11, *ANF* 2.291.

21. Ibid., 3.12.

22. Dix, *Apostolic Tradition*, p. 29.

23. *Ps. Clementine Epistle on Virginity* 2.2.5.

24. *De praescr. haer.* 41.3.

25. *Apostolic Constitution* 2.57, E.T., *ANF* 7.421-22, 486, 8.11. In the assemblies of the church women had to sit apart from men and when the time came for the Eucharist they had to "let the deacon who is at the high priest's hand say to the people, 'Let no one have any quarrel against another; let no one come in hypocricy.' Then let the men give the men, and the women give to the women, the Lord's kiss. But let no one do it with deceit, as Judas betrayed the Lord with a kiss." For the dependency of the *Ap. Const.* on Hippolytus, *Ap. Trad.*, see Dix, *Apostolic Tradition*, p. lxxi.

26. *De vita Constantini* 1.53.

27. *Hist. Eccl.* 9.5.2, E.T., J. E. L. Qulton, Loeb (Cambridge: Harvard University Press, 1953), 2.338-39.

28. 1 Cor. 12:13.

29. Luke 24:30; John 21:4ff.; Rev. 3:20.

30. *Frg.* 23, in *The Worlds of the Early Greek Philosophers*, ed. J. B. Wilbur and H. J. Allen (Buffalo, N.Y.: Prometheus Books, 1979), p. 52.

31. Michael C. Stokes, *One and Many in Presocratic Philosophy* (Cambridge, Mass.: Harvard University Press, 1971), p. 106.

32. John Burnet, *Early Greek Philosophy* (New York: Macmillan, 1892).

33. Ibid. Also see Wilbur and Allen, *Early Greek Philosophers*, p. 145.

34. Stokes, *Presocratic Philosophy*, p. 165. See also M. R. Wright, *Empedocles: The Extant Fragments* (New Haven: Yale University Press, 1981).

35. Stokes, *Presocratic Philosophy*, p. 165.

36. *Symposium* 201-207, E.T. by B. Jowett, *The Dialogues of Plato* (New York: Random House, 1937), 1:327ff. See also Paul Friedländer, *Plato* (Princeton: Princeton University Press, 1969), 3:26–27.

37. Deut. 6:4.

38. "The term 'one' is just as inapplicable to God as the term 'many'; for both unity and plurality are categories of quantity, and are, therefore, as inapplicable to God as crooked and straight in reference to sweetness, or salted and insipid in reference to a voice," Maimonides, *The Guide of the Perplexed* I. 57, in A. J. Heschel, *Man Is Not Alone: A Philosophy of Religion* (New York: The Jewish Publication Society, 1951), p. 115.

39. Heschel, *Man Is Not Alone*, p. 112.

40. *Adv. Haer.* 5.1ff.

41. *In Ps.* 96.15.

42. *De principiis* 1.6.1, E.T., *ANF* 4.260.

43. *De principiis* 1.6.2, E.T., *ANF* 4.260.

44. The most important passages were collected by J. Quasten, *Patrology* (Utrecht: Spectrum, 1953), 2:94ff.

45. In his meditation on the mystical union of the soul with the Logos, Origen, too, used the words of the Song of Songs 1.2 "Let him kiss me with the kisses of his mouth." These are the kisses of the Word of God. In *Canticum Canticorum* 1.1, *MPG* 13.85. An analysis of Origen's commentary, with special emphasis on his interpretation of the love present in the

Song of Songs is in Anders Nygren, *Agape and Eros* (Philadelphia: Westminster, 1953), pp. 387-92.

46. See Michael Grant, *The Climax of Rome* (New York: New American Library, 1968), pp. 139-50, and Anders Nygren, *Agape and Eros*, pp. 186-99. From among the many numerous publications dealing with Plotinus, the following were especially helpful: John N. Deck, *Nature, Contemplation and the One* (Toronto: University of Toronto Press, 1967); J. M. Rist, *Plotinus: The Road to Reality* (Cambridge: Cambridge University Press, 1967); Joseph Katz, *Plotinus' Search for the Good* (New York: Columbia University Press, King's Crown Press, 1950); Edgar Früchtel, *Weltentwurf und Logos* (Frankfurt: Klostermann, 1970).

47. Nygren, *Agape and Eros*, pp. 660, 208. Nygren has argued that *agape* is God's love and involves a downward movement, but *eros* is self-love and involves an upward movement; *agape* is sacrificial; *eros* is acquisitive. Nygren's thesis has been severely criticized but this is not our concern here.

48. *Theogony* 120.

49. Benjamin Bickley Rogers, *Five Comedies of Aristophanes* (New York: Doubleday, 1955), p. 34.

50. E. O. James, *The Ancient Gods* (New York: Putnam's 1960), p. 78.

51. Ibid., 94, 110ff; also see H. Frankfort, *Kingship and the Gods* (Chicago: University of Chicago Press, 1948), pp. 295ff.

52. James, *The Ancient Gods*, p. 133; J. G. Frazer, *The Golden Bough* (New York: Macmillan, 1935), 2: 120-70; C. Kerényi, *Dionysos*, Bollingen Series (Princeton: Princeton University Press, 1976), pp. 290-315. It is also possible that the Eleusinian mysteries included a sacred marriage between Zeus and Demeter, Pluton and Persephone, who were represented by the hierophant and the chief priestess. See James, *The Ancient Gods*, 165.

53. Patai, *The Hebrew Goddess* (New York: Ktav Publishing House, 1967).

54. Marvin H. Pope, *Song of Songs*, The Anchor Bible (Garden City, N.Y.: Doubleday, 1977), pp. 165, 157.

55. E. F. Watling, ed., *Sophocles: The Theban Plays* (Baltimore: Penguin, 1947), pp. 126-62.

56. Rudolf Bultmann, "Polis und Hades in der Antigone des Sophokles," in Hans Diller, ed., *Sophokles* (Darmstadt: Wissenschaftliche Buchgesellschaft, 1967), pp. 311-24.

57. Plutarch *Moralia*, E.T., W. C. Helmbold, Loeb (London: Heinemann, 1961), 9:438.

58. Ibid., 756 E.

59. Ibid., 757 C.D.

60. Ibid., 761 F. Alcestis offered to die in place of her husband, Admetus, and was rescued from the underworld by Heracles; Protesilaus offered himself as a patriotic sacrifice at Troy and was brought back by Hermes; Orpheus descended to Hades to retrieve his wife, Eurydice.

61. See R. Flacelière, *Love in Ancient Greece* (London: F. Muller, 1962), pp. 47–48.

62. From among the many words in the Greek language to express the idea of love (*philia, agape, eros, charis, pathos*), *eros* is completely missing from the vocabulary of the New Testament. It occurs in Ignatius *Romans* 7.2: "My love (Eros) has been crucified, and there is no material passion in me."

63. Eph. 5:31-32. The debate concerning whether Paul wrote Ephesians ought not to detain us here.

64. 1 John 3:16.

65. 1 John 4:7-8.

66. 1 John 3.16; Gal. 5.15; 2 Cor. 5.17.

67. 1 John 3.1; Rom 8.15f; Gal. 4.6.

68. Augustine *De ordine* 2.18.48: "What about love? Does not it want to become one with that what it loves?" *De Trinitate* 8.10.14 "What, then, is love except a certain life which couples or seeks to couple together some two things, namely, him that loves, and that which is loved? And this is so even in outward and carnal loves," E.T., *NPNF*, first series, 3.124. Also see Perella, *The Kiss Sacred and Profane*, p. 46ff.; Oliver O'Donovan, *The Problem of Self-Love in St. Augustine* (New Haven: Yale University Press, 1980), pp. 131ff.; G. Quispel, "God is Eros," in *Early Christian Literature and the Classical Intellectual Tradition, In Honorem Robert M. Grant*, ed. William R. Schoedel and Robert L. Wilken, Théologie Historique 53 (Paris: Beauchesne, 1979), pp. 189-205; Cornelia J. DeVogel, "Greek Cosmic Love and the Christian Love of God: Boethius, Dionysus the Areopagite and the Author of the Fourth Gospel," *Vigiliae Christianae* 35 (1981):57-81 (DeVogel's work is in reply to Quispel's "God is Eros".)

69. This idea is commonplace in Greek and Roman literature as has been shown by Stephen Gaselee, "The Soul in the Kiss," *The Criterion* (1923-1924):349-359. From this collection of texts let us only mention one: Aristaenetus *Ep.* 11.19, 20-24: "This is the power and meaning of the kiss; the lovers' souls hurry to one another through their mouths and meet upon their lips and very sweet is the intermingling of souls." Gaselee, "The Soul in the Kiss," p. 352.

70. 2 Cor. 11.2, and Eph. 5.23ff.

71. Perella, *The Kiss Sacred and Profane*, p. 3.

72. See, for example Hosea; Ps. 45; Matt. 9.15; 25.1ff; John 3.29; Rev. 19.7ff; and Eph. 5.23-33. As an example of the sacramental interpretation of the Song of Songs see Ambrose, *De sacramentis* 5. 2. 5-8: "Thou has come to the altar; the Lord Jesus calls thee or thy soul or the Church and says, 'Let her kiss me with the kisses of her mouth.' Wouldst thou apply it to Christ? Nothing sweeter. Wouldst thou apply it to thy soul? Nothing pleasanter. 'Let her kiss me.' He sees that thou art clean from all sin because thy sins are purged away. Therefore he judges thee worthy of the heavenly sacrament and therefore he invites thee to a heavenly banquet. 'Let her kiss me with the kisses of her mouth.' Yet on account of what follows it is thy soul or human nature of the Church which, seeing itself cleansed from all sins, and worthy to be able to approach the altar of Christ (for what is the altar but the type of the body of Christ?), has seen the wondrous sacraments and says, 'let him kiss me with the kisses of his mouth,' that is, let Christ imprint a kiss on me. Why? 'Because thy breasts are better than wine.' That is, the sensation which thou suppliest are better, thy sacraments are better, than wine. . . . Even in those days Solomon represents the marriage of Christ and the Church, or of the spirit and flesh and soul." *CSEL* 73.61, E.T., T. Thompson and J. H. Shrawley, *St. Ambrose On the Sacraments and On The Mysteries* (London: SPCK, 1950), pp. 96-97. Perella, *The Kiss Sacred and Profane*, pp. 37ff has further references to the interpretation of the Song of Songs.

-V-

Magic and Early
Christianity

MANY PAGANS BELIEVED that Christians were involved in harmful magical practices, but to what extent, if at all, was this suspicion founded on facts? Two second-century Roman works, which include veiled references to this suspicion, cast some light on this problem: a passage in Apuleius's *Metamorphoses*, and Lucian's satire *Alexander the False Prophet*. We shall explore the explicit pagan charges that linked magic with Christianity, and then we shall examine those Christian practices that were most likely to remind pagans of magic. Throughout our investigation we shall apply the basic principles of Greco-Roman magic to Christian practices, because this is the way pagans must have seen these practices. Moreover, the Christians themselves also applied the categories of contemporary magic to their own practices. Thus, to fully understand the early Christians it is necessary to approach them from the viewpoint of Greco-Roman magic.

A possibly common misunderstanding about Christian life may be seen in the second-century Roman novel (the only surviving complete Roman novel) that is generally known as *The Golden Ass* or *Metamorphoses*. A delightful and entertaining story, the work has as its hero a man called Lucius who becomes interested in magic and accidentally turns himself into an ass. Unable to reverse the transformation, he is obliged to serve many masters and to undergo many trials. Since, however, he retains his human mind, he observes, understands, and remembers much that occurs to him. Finally, he is restored to human form by the gracious intervention of the goddess Isis and dedicates his life to her service. While still an ass Lucius is at one point sold to a baker whose wife he characterizes in the following passage:

> The baker who purchased me was otherwise a good and very modest
> man but his wife was the wickedest of all women and he suffered
> extreme miseries to his bed and his house so that I myself, by Her-
> cules, often in secret felt pity for him. There was not one single vice
> which that woman lacked, but all crimes flowed together into her
> heart as into a filthy latrine; cruel, perverse, man-crazy, drunken,
> stubborn, obstinate, avaricious in petty theft, wasteful in sumptuous
> expenses, an enemy to faith and chastity, she also despised the gods
> and instead of a certain religion she claimed to worship a god whom
> she called 'only'. In his honor she practiced empty rites and cere-
> monies and she deceived all men and her miserable husband, drinking
> unmixed wine early in the morning and giving up her body to con-
> tinual whoring.[1]

The description of this woman could be a hostile view of a Christian. She rejected polytheism and worshipped an only god, she drank
wine in the morning (which may be a misunderstanding of the daily
celebration of the Eucharist), and she was promiscuous (which could
be the charge of libertinism that we have seen in the discussion of
Octavius). It is also possible, however, that Lucius is describing a
Jewish proselyte, that is θεοσεβής (meaning, god-fearer), somebody
who adopted many Jewish practices without formally becoming a
Jew. But what did Apuleis mean by his reference to "empty rites and
ceremonies"? Before discussing this question further, we need to
know more about Apuleius.

Apuleius (his first name may have been Lucius, unless this was
attached to him because he was identified with the hero of *Metamorphoses*) was born in Medaurus, North Africa (Numidia) sometime around 123; the date of his death is unknown. He came from a
financially solid background and received a good education, first at
Carthage, then in Athens and Rome. His father, who attained the
highest municipal office of duumvir, left him an inheritance of two
million sesterces. Apuleius could now afford to travel extensively,
and this he did for a time, after which he returned to North Africa. In
the city of Oea (Tripoli) he married a rich widow, Pudentilla, who was
several years older than he, being just over the age of forty. Her
disgruntled relatives brought legal action against Apuleius, however,
on the grounds that he had won Pudentilla by sorcery for her money.
The trial took place before the proconsul sometime between 155 and
161. Apuleius defended himself in a lengthy speech, the text of which
survives and is called *Apologia*.

In his defense Apuleius characterized one of his accusers, Aemilianus, with the following words:

> "I know that some persons, among them that fellow Aemilianus,
> think it a good jest to mock at things divine. For I learn from certain
> men of Oea who know him, that to this day he has never prayed to any
> god or frequented any temple, while if he chances to pass any shrine,
> he regards it as a crime to raise his hand to his lips in token of
> reverence. He has never given first fruits of crops or vines or flocks to
> any of the gods of the farmer, who feed him and clothe him; his farm
> holds no shrine, no holy place, nor grove. But why do I speak of grove
> or shrines? Those who have been on his property say they never saw
> there one stone where offering of oil has been made, one bough where
> wreaths have been hung. As a result, two nicknames have been given
> him: he is called Charon, as I have said, on account of his truculence
> of spirit and of countenance, but he is also—and this is the name he
> prefers—called Mezentius,[2] because he despises the gods. I therefore
> find it the easier to understand that he should regard my list of
> initiation in the light of a jest. It is even possible that, thanks to his
> rejection of things divine, he may be unable to induce himself to
> believe that it is true that I guard so reverently so many emblems and
> relics of mysterious rites. . . ."[3]

Aemilianus "regards it as a crime to raise his hand to his lips in token
of reverence" when he passes a shrine. Likewise, Octavius rebuked
Caecilius when he "raised his hand to his mouth, as is the custom of
the superstitious common people, and pressed a kiss on it with his
lips."[4] This similarity suggests that the accuser of Apuleius may have
been a Christian. Aemilianus's refusal to offer sacrifices or to maintain altars on his property also fits the behavior of a Christian,
although his preference for the name of the arch-atheist Mezentius
does not, which suggests that Aemilianus was a person who did not
care for religion in general.

Apuleius had to defend himself against the charge of magic. His
accusers made a number of specific charges against him. In particular,
they produced one of his letters in which he wrote about tooth-
powder; he explained that this was a harmless substance that served
no other purpose but cleanliness. His accusers also pointed out that
he owned and used a mirror, but, he replied, so did Socrates and
Demosthenes, among others, and philosophers should use a mirror.
Moreover, his accusers continued, he had sought out a particular kind
of fish for the purpose of making magical charms. No, Apuleius
answered, he had merely tried to satisfy his interest in science and

medicine, following Aristotle.[5] Then came the charge that he, together with a few accomplices, had taken a boy to a secret place with a small altar and lantern and there pronounced magical incantations over the boy, who fell in a faint to the ground and awoke out of his wits. Apuleius proved that the boy was an epileptic.[6] His accusers next charged him with hiding certain secret objects in a magical cloth. These turned out to be emblems and mementos of his initiation into various mystery cults, and he refused to reveal what they were. Bird feathers and smoke had been discovered in his house; his accusers claimed these indicated that he had performed secret nocturnal rites. Apuleius called this a poor lie. Then he was accused of having fashioned a seal for himself out of a rare wood, allegedly endowed with magical powers and adorned with the figure of a gruesome corpse; Apuleius produced the seal, and the figure on it turned out to be that of a cheerful god. Finally, Apuleius proved false the charges that he had bewitched his wife and married her for her money.[7]

Apuleius won his case, but his reputation as a magician survived. St. Augustine, in a letter written in 412, some two hundred and fifty years after the trial, referred to Apuleius as such, but even St. Augustine had some laudatory things to say about him.[8] Augustine declared, however, that those who compared pagan magicians with the holy prophets and even with Christ were in great error, for Christ and the prophets were "incomparably superior to magicians of every name." Earlier in his letter Augustine ridiculed those who subjected Christ to any sort of comparison with such persons as Apollonius of Tyana or Apuleius.[9] Lactantius (ca. 240-ca. 320) voiced similar sentiments in his response to Hierocles when he claimed that Jesus "gained belief in His divinity, which could have happened neither to Apollonius, nor to Apuleius, nor to any of the magicians. . . ."[10]

Apuleius, therefore, had the reputation of being both a philosopher and a magician. Ramsey MacMullen has shown that Apuleius and other philosophers, spiritual descendants of Pythagoras, claimed powers "to do more than other mortals."[11] Apuleius was a "theurgos", a name attached to the highest, most respected class of magicians who, instead of dragging down divine power into the physical sphere by incantations, potions, and other material means, tried to lift up the soul into the divine sphere by a clear knowledge of the divine. Such divine men or "theurgoi," as distinct from regular magicians and tricksters, were thought to be capable of accomplishing superhuman things. One such person who gained renown in the second century was Apollonius of Tyana, a contemporary of Jesus, who supposedly survived until the time of Domitian. His biographer, Philostratus (ca. 170-ca. 244?), credited him with the ability to fore-tell the future, to exorcise demons, and even to restore life. Apollo-nius was a Neo-Pythagorean, and many of the miracles attributed to Pythagoras were also attributed to him. According to MacMullen, Peregrinus Proteus belongs in this group of divine men, as no doubt does Apuleius, who, although he fiercely defended himself against the particular charges of practicing magic, still found some good words for magicians and the performance of magic.[12] According to Apuleius the true definition of a magician is to be found in the original Persian meaning of the word; magician is the Persian word for priest, and therefore magic is nothing else than the worship of the gods.

> "Do you hear, you who so rashly accuse the act of magic? It is an act acceptable to the immortal gods, full of all knowledge of worship and of prayer, full of piety and wisdom in things divine, full of honor and glory.... If that is so, why should I be forbidden to learn the fair words of Zalmoxis or the priestly love of Zoroaster? But if these accusers of mine, after the fashion of the common herd, define a magician as one who by communion of speech with the immortal gods has power to do all the marvels that he will, through a strange power of incantation, I really wonder that they are not afraid to attack one whom they acknowledge to be so powerful."[13]

Apuleius may, indeed, have dabbled in magical arts. He had an inquisitive soul and studied everything that came within his reach including philosophy, zoology, medicine, geometry, music, and po-etry. Now, philosophy, as we have seen above, was used as a means to bridge the chasm that divides the divine and the human. Animals were long considered to be sacred to various divinities with whom they stood in a sympathetic relationship, and the medical use of plants and herbs in ancient magic is well attested. It would not be at all surprising, therefore, if Apuleius had experimented with these things. He was by nature superstitious, as is abundantly evident in *Metamorphoses*. This book may contain his own conversion to, and initiation in, the mysteries of Isis, where the priests seem to have taken advantage of his sincerity and credulity. These traits of his character, his reverence for the holy talismans of his initiations, and his later reputation, make it seem entirely possible that the depiction

of him as a magician was close to the truth. He was certainly sensitive toward matters pertaining to magic, and it is at least an open
question whether in the description of the baker's wife his reference
to "empty rites and ceremonies" referred to certain Christian practices that he did not understand and thus classified simply as some
sort of elementary, lower-class magic by uneducated people. One,
unfortunately damaged, passage in the *Apologia* even suggests the
possibility that he knew of Jesus and classified him as a magician. "If
you can prove that I have made the very slightest profit out of my
marriage, I am ready to be any magician you please—the great Car-
mendas himself or Damigeron or *his* . . . Moses . . . or any sorcerer of
note from the time of Zoroaster and Ostanes till now."[14] If the letters
"his" refer to Jesus (such as "ihs", the first three letters of the name of
Jesus in Greek: IHΣ) then we have here an important reference.
Moreover, the fact that Greek and Roman authors often mentioned
Moses and Jesus together strengthens this hypothesis, although it is
by no means certain.[15]

Alexander of Abonuteichos also developed a very negative attitude
toward Christianity, albeit for different reasons. Lucian of Samosata
(ca. 115-ca. 200), described Alexander's activities in detail, and in
perhaps an even more sarcastic and angry tone than he had used in
recounting the life and death of Peregrinus Proteus.[16] Apart from
some minor references on inscriptions and coins, Lucian is our only
source about Alexander. His account is naturally hostile, but we
must keep in mind that Lucian knew Alexander personally, and thus
the essential facts in his account are probably true. His essay, *Alexander the False Prophet*, is addressed to Celsus, who may be the same
Celsus who wrote *True Word*, an anti-Christian tract, but this has
not been proven.[17]

Alexander, Lucian tells us, while still a young man became associated with a physician who used his profession to practice magic,
incantations, enchantments, charms for love affairs, and for success
in business ventures. This physician-magician learned his trade from
the famous Apollonius of Tyana, which fact, Lucian assured his
readers, showed immediately what sort of man Alexander was. After
the death of his teacher, Alexander formed a partnership with a
Byzantine writer of choral songs, and the two together cheated a rich
lady from Pella in Macedonia out of much money. In Pella Alexander
saw many tame serpents that were kept as pets by children and
women, and they gave him the idea for deception. He and his associ-

ate decided that the best way to make money was to establish a prophetic shrine. They took painstaking care to make their oracle appear genuine. In the temple of Apollo in Chalcedon they buried, and then conveniently discovered, bronze tablets that predicted that Asklepios and his father Apollo would soon move to Abonuteichos in Pontus. This prophecy so excited the people of Abonuteichos that they immediately began to build a temple for Asklepios. In the meantime, Alexander's associate died, leaving Alexander alone to carry out the scheme. He let his hair grow long, dressed in a white and purple tunic, wore ringlets, and claimed descendance from the mythical hero Perseus. He produced a Sibylline oracle that purported to foretell the birth of a prophet, with whom he identified himself. To give the illusion of prophetic madness he chewed the root of the soapwort plant, which produced foam around his mouth. He also constructed an artificial head that looked quite human and whose mouth could be opened and closed by pulling horsehairs.

Alexander was now ready to bring the hoax to its lurid climax. He went to the place where the temple was to be erected and hid a goose egg containing a newly born snake in a pool of water. Snakes supposedly had healing powers and were associated with Asklepios. In the morning he made his way to the market place, clad only in a loin cloth. Tossing his long hair as though in a religious frenzy, he announced that the god was about to arrive. He followed this announcement with a volley of unintelligible words, screamed at the top of his lungs. Then he raced to the building site, chanting and praying on the way and "found" the previously hidden goose egg. When he broke it, and the people saw the tiny snake wriggling in his palm, they were convinced that Asklepios had indeed been born anew in their city! Alexander retired to his home and stayed there for a few days until the news had spread and the city was full of people who had flocked in from the surrounding district.

Alexander next presented himself and his "god" to the people. He sat on a couch in a little, semidark room, with a huge, tame snake (which he had picked up in Pella) coiled around his neck. The snake's tail reached to the floor and its head was under Alexander's arm, while an artificial head was tucked to one side of his beard so as to look as though it belonged to the snake. Alexander bade the people enter. They were ushered in through one door and immediately crowded toward the other, but what they saw during the brief interval when they were in the room filled them with amazement—the tiny snake grown to a huge size in a few short days and bearing a human head! Soon paintings and statues of the god appeared and Alexander named him: Glycon. Alexander may have used this name to identify Asklepios as a benevolent god.[18]

The stage was thus set for Alexander to achieve his real purpose, namely, to make a fortune for himself. He announced that the god would dispense prophecies at the price of one drachma and two obols each. His business grew so great that he took in as many as seventy or eighty thousand drachmas a year. Out of his revenues he paid his many accomplices: writers of oracles, informers, clerks and others. Alexander's scheme was exceedingly intricate. Requests were handed to him in sealed scrolls, he removed the seals, read the contents of the scrolls, attached answers to them, resealed them in such a way as to make it appear that the original seals had been unbroken, and then returned them to his clients. Lucian described in detail how the seals were removed and subsequently restored. Alexander's hoax was probably not an isolated case, but was rather a common practice among professionals in the business. This is shown by the Christian presbyter and bishop of Rome, Hippolytus (c. 170-c. 236), whose life slightly overlapped with Lucian's and Alexander's. In his book, *Refutation on All Heresies* Hippolytus dealt with, among others, astrologers, magicians, and assorted charlatans, and he described deceptions similar to those perpetrated by Alexander.[19] He does so, he said, with hesitation, "perceiving the danger lest, perchance, any knavish person, taking the opportunity [afforded by my account], should attempt [to imitate these tricks]. . . ."[20]

Alexander's fame spread and eventually reached the highest circles in Rome. P. Mummius Sisenna Rutilianus, a man of consular rank, went to Abonuteichos to consult the oracle and came under Alexander's influence to such an extent that, although by this time in his sixties, he married Alexander's daughter. Around 167, when Marcus Aurelius fought the Marcomanni and Quadi, Alexander advised the emperor to throw two lions in the Danube to assure victory. The lions swam to the other shore, however, and a great disaster befell the empire, the invading tribes occupied several provinces and came near to the gates of Aquileia in Italy. Alexander talked himself out of this embarrassing situation by resorting to the well-known explanation given by the Delphic oracle to Croesus: the oracle was right, but its interpreters had failed to understand which side would gain the victory that it foretold. Alexander later petitioned the emperor to change the name of Abonuteichos to Ionopolis—perhaps because the son of Apollo, and thus the brother of Asklepios, was Ion, or because the Greek word "to heal" is ἰᾶσθαι and Asklepios was the god of healing. The petition was granted. (The modern name of the community, Ineboli, comes from Ionopolis.) Coins were even minted "bearing on one side the likeness of Glycon and on the other that of Alexander."[21]

Lucian reported that Alexander's oracles consisted mostly of advice on the ordinary vicissitudes of life, and only in a small number of cases did they deal with medical problems, in spite of the fact that the shrines of Asklepios were places of healing. Some of his oracles were simply unintelligible gibberish such as: "MORPHEN EUBAR-OULIS EIS SKIAN CHNECKHIKRAGE LEIPSEI PHAOS" or "SABARDALACHOU MALACHAATTEALOS EN."[22] This is a common characteristic of many magical papyri and Gnostic documents. Lucian would have done a service to scholarship and posterity had he asked for an interpretation of Alexander's unintelligible sayings. Instead he tried to expose Alexander as a fraud, an endeavor that nearly cost him his life. When he accused Alexander before the governor of Bithynia-and-Pontus he was politely ignored. Alexander had good connections with Rutilianus, a man of consular rank, who probably protected him. And so Alexander died a natural death before his seventieth year, sometime around 170. The cult he established survived for another century.

But two groups of people in particular did question the credibility of Alexander's story, the Epicureans and the Christians. And so Alexander castigated them both. He called Epicurus "impervious," and publicly burned one of his books, scattering the ashes in the sea.[23] This is an understandable reaction since the Epicureans, who believed that natural causes could explain all physical phenomena, steadfastly refused to lend credence to Alexander's hoax. Alexander put the Christians in the same category with atheists, and he excluded them from his services. In his writings on Alexander, Lucian twice referred to Alexander's treatment of the Christians and Epicureans:

> When at last many sensible men, recovering as it were from profound intoxication, combined against him [Alexander] especially all the followers of Epicurus, and when in the cities they began gradually to detect all the trickery and buncombe of the show, he issued a promulgation designed to scare them, saying that Pontus was full of

atheists and Christians who had the hardihood to utter the vilest abuse on him; these he bade them drive away with stones if they wanted to have the god gracious. . . .[24]

He established a celebration of mysteries, with torchlight cere- monies and priestly offices, which was to be held annually for three days in succession in perpetuity. On the first day, as at Athens, there was a proclamation, worded as follows: "If any atheist or Christian or Epicurean has come to spy upon the rites, let him be off, and let those who believe in the god perform the mysteries, under the blessing of Heaven." Then, at the very outset, there was an "expulsion" in which he took the lead, saying: "Out with the Christians," and the whole multitude chanted in response, "Out with the Epicureans."[25]

Lucian observed that Alexander based his ceremonies on the Eleusin- ian mysteries of Athens, and the ritual of expulsion was a part of this ancient religious rite. Celsus, in fact, chided the Christians for invit- ing sinners to their services while the mysteries excluded them.[26] Alexander also based the sacred marriage of his liturgy on Eleusinian examples, and a torchlight procession was part of the closing services.[27] The practice of excluding certain groups from religious ceremonies was widespread. The earliest Christian liturgy, the *Didache*, called on certain people to leave the service; first, in an ordinance that only those previously baptized could take part in the Eucharist and then, in the call after the service: "If anyone is holy, let him come; if anyone is not, let him repent."[28] The Christians obviously viewed the Eucharist as a mystery from which the uniniti- ated should be excluded. Such restrictions were taken seriously. Suetonius, for example, wrote that Nero "in his journey through Greece did not venture to take part in the Eleusinian mysteries, since at the beginning the godless and wicked are warned by the herald's proclamation to go hence."[29] The hierophant forbade Apollonius of Tyana to enter the mysteries because of the suspicion that he was a magician.[30]

But Alexander did not exclude the Christians from his ceremonies because he thought that they were morally deficient, but because he was afraid that they might expose his fraud. Many Christians lived in Pontus, and undoubtedly Alexander, like many others, called them atheists. The Christians did not believe in Glycon and, along with the Epicureans, would have treated him with scorn. It is also possible that Alexander's fear of the Christians was based on his knowledge that Christians were well-known exorcists, and so their presence at his meetings might have "broken the spell." Lucian, in another satire, referred to an exorcism, possibly performed by a Christian:

> Everyone knows about the Syrian from Palestine, the adept in it, how many he takes in hand who fall down in the light of the moon and roll their eyes and fill their mouths with foam; nevertheless, he restores them to a health and sends them away normal in mind, delivering them from their straits for a large fee. When he stands beside them as they lie there and asks: 'Whence came you into his body?' the patient himself is silent, but the spirit answers in Greek or in the language of whatever foreign country he comes from, telling how and whence he entered into the man; whereupon, by adjuring the spirit and, if he does not obey, threatening him, he drives him out. Indeed, I actually saw one coming out, black and smokey in colour.[31]

A very similar incident is related in Mark 5:1-19, when Jesus exorcises the Gadarene demoniac and sends the unclean spirit into the swines. Morton Smith suggested that either Mark inspired Lucian's story, or both Mark and Lucian drew on common knowledge of exorcists' practices.[32] Lucian's exorcist could have been a Palestinian Jew, or, just as he says, a "Syrian from Palestine" who had nothing to do with Christianity. In either case, the picture is characteristic, and if Lucian had heard such stories, Alexander may have heard them too. If he did, his strict rule not to permit Christians to attend his services makes good sense: he was afraid that the superior power of the Christians to identify and drive out demons might spell disaster for his fraud.

Eusebius (260-340) made it clear that the Christians had a reputation for disrupting pagan ceremonies by their mere presence. In his *Ecclesiastical History*, Eusebius quoted Dionysius, bishop of Alexandria (ca. 264–265), concerning the causes of the persecution of the Christians under Valerian. According to Dionysius, Valerian favored Christians "until the master and chief of the Egyptian magicians [Macrianus], persuaded him to abandon this course, exhorting him to persecute and slay these pure and holy men, as enemies and obstacles to their wicked and detestable incantations. For there were, and still are, men who, by their very presence, or when seen, and only breathing and speaking, are able to dissipate the artifices of wicked daemons."[33] Lactantius (c. 240-c. 320) also blamed the Christian disruption of pagan ceremonies as the initial cause of the persecution under Diocletian, which began in 303. While Diocletian was in the

East, he sacrificed animals and had their livers examined. In the
midst of these sacrifices, some of his attendants put the sign of the
cross on their foreheads.

> At this the demons were cleared away, and the holy rites interrupted.
> The soothsayers trembled, unable to investigate the wanted marks on
> the entrails of the victims. They frequently repeated the sacrifices,
> as if the former had been unpropitious; but the victims, slain from time
> to time, afforded no tokens for divination. At length Tages, the chief
> of the soothsayers, either from guess or from his own observation,
> said, 'There are profane persons here, who obstruct the rites. . . .' At
> this Diocletian became angry and ordered all those in the palace to
> sacrifice. [34]

The Romans interpreted such powers, described by Lactantius and
Eusebius, as the signs of magicians, and Celsus openly accused
Christians of being magicians. He argued "that it is by the names of
certain demons, and by the use of incantations, that the Christians
appear to be possessed of miraculous power; hinting, I suppose, at the
practices of those who expel evil spirits by incantation. . . ."[35] He even
asserted that "he has seen in the hands of certain presbyters belonging to our faith barbarous books, containing the names and marvel-
lous doings of demons. . . ." Then, to make the charge even worse, he
claimed that these presbyters "professed to do no good, but all that
was calculated to injure human beings"; they were involved in evil
magic.[36] Similarly, the investigating magistrate in the case against
the Christian Achatius said: "You are magicians, because you are
introducing some kind of new religion."[37] In the *Passion of Perpetua
and Felicitas* 16 the tribune treated these two Christians harshly
because he had received information from certain people that made
him fear that "they would be secretly removed from the prison by
magic incantations."[38] Hadrian's much debated letter to Servianus
counts the Christian presbyters, along with Samaritans and the chief
of the Jewish synagogue, as "astrologers, soothsayers, anointers."[39]
These observers of Christianity, then, believed that Christians were
in the possession of secrets that enabled them to manipulate supernatural powers as they wished.

Christians always rejected this charge and steadfastly objected to
being called magicians, and they maintained that, as Achatius supposedly answered to Marianus, Christians "abhor magical arts."[40]
Christian authors also argued that although Apollonius of Tyana and
Apuleius were indeed magicians, Christ was not, because—and here

the argument becomes somewhat shaky—Christ was incomparably greater than those men. The church fathers, however, liberally accused Christian heretics, especially Gnostics, of being magicians. When he discussed the followers of Carpocrates, Irenaeus said that they "practice also magical arts and incantations; philters, also, and love potions; and have recourse to familiar spirits, dream-sending demons and other abominations, declaring that they possess power to rule over, even now, the princes and formers of this world; and not only them, but also all things that are in it." These men, Irenaeus stated, were sent by Satan to bring dishonor to the Church, but he claimed that, in fact, the name of Christ and Christians have no fellowship with them.[41] Hippolytus made a similar judgment concerning the Carpocratians; they "practice their magical arts and incantations, and spells and voluptuous feasts." He argued that they were sent by Satan to discredit the Church.[42]

But in spite of their criticisms against heretic Christians for practicing magic, orthodox Christians, themselves, also exorcised demons. The references to exorcisms are so numerous that only a selection can and need be given. Justin Martyr, for example, pointed out that Christians prayed to be preserved from demons by Jesus Christ "the power of whose name even the demons do fear; and at this day, when they are exorcised in the name of Jesus Christ . . . they are overcome"; "The concealed power of God was in Christ the crucified, before whom demons, and all the principalities and powers of the earth, tremble"; "When we exorcise all demons and evil spirits, have them subjected to us"; "every demon, when exorcised in the name of this very Son of God . . . is overcome and subdued."[43] Justin Martyr also claimed knowledge of Jewish exorcists who used incantations and fumigations exactly like those of the pagans; whenever they invoked the names of their kings and prophets they were unsuccessful, whereas if they exorcised in the name of the God of Abraham, Isaac, and Jacob the outcome was uncertain.[44] "Numberless demoniacs throughout the whole world, and in your city [Rome], many of our Christian men exorcising them in the name of Jesus Christ, who was crucified under Pontius Pilate, have healed and do heal, rendering helpless and driving the possessing devils out of the men, though they could not be cured by all the other exorcists and those who used incantations and drugs."[45]

According to Irenaeus, Christians performed miracles to promote the welfare of other men. "Some do certainly and truly drive out devils," others heal the sick, know the future, raise the dead. Yet the

Church does nothing "by means of angelic invocations or by incantations, or by any other wicked curious art; but directing her prayers to the Lord . . . and calling upon the name of our Lord Jesus Christ" the Church works miracles for the advantage of mankind. The name of Christ, therefore, conferred benefits, but the names of Simon, Alexander or Carpocrates did not.[46] Tertullian stated that the authority Christians had over demons stemmed "from our naming the name of Christ. . . . So at our touch and breathing, overwhelmed by the thought and realization of those judgment fires, they leave at our command the bodies they have entered, unwilling and distressed, and before your very eyes put to an open shame. . . ."[47] "We not only reject those wicked spirits: we overcome them; we daily hold them up to contempt; we exorcise them from their victims, as multitudes can testify."[48]

Given the important role that exorcism appears to have played in early Christian life, we should not be surprised that it attracted the attention of outsiders. Nor should we be surprised that these outsiders assumed exorcism was some sort of magical art. There were so many exorcists that the church occasionally had to warn against impostors and those who would take advantage of sincere Christians by using exorcism as a pretense to get into homes to do things that they were not supposed to do. The pseudo-Clementine *De Virginitate*, probably written in the first half of the third century, warns that these impostors "gad about among the houses of Virgin brethren and sisters, on pretense of visiting them, or reading the Scriptures to them, or exorcising them. For as much as they are idle and do no work, they pry into those things which ought not to be inquired into and by means of plausible words make merchandise of the name of Christ."[49] The exorcist, the treatise continues, should adhere to certain rules: the prayers and adjurations should be framed intelligibly, not filled with great quantities of elegant words that may be impressive but bring no help to the afflicted. Terrible words that frighten people are to be avoided also, as is talkativeness and noise. The exorcist should approach the sick person "without guile and without covetousness . . . but with the meek and lowly spirit of Christ [and] make the adjuration with fasting and with prayer. . . ."[50] It is not difficult to visualize the abuses that may have occasioned these warnings. The impostors pronounced a stream of mysterious words that, like others that we find in Gnostic texts and magical papyri, make no sense today and probably never did. They were designed merely "to excite the celebrant," as Morton Smith has said, and to overawe the inflicted person by suggesting to him that the exorcist had a superior knowledge.[51] False prophets who stayed too long and upon departure asked for money were a well-known phenomenon, and the case of these professional exorcists was probably no different.[52]

Yet the Christian church accepted speaking in tongues (glossolalia) as a spiritual gift, and it was widely practiced, especially in the Pauline churches. Similar to the garbled speeches of the magicians, glossolalia manifested itself by many unintelligible exclamations. Paul recognized the dangers of the practice and insisted that it be closely regulated, stipulating, among other things, the necessity of interpretation.[53] But the practice continued. The *Didache*, for example, advises people to treat prophets who make "ecstatic utterances" with respect. This work quickly adds, however, that not everybody who makes "ecstatic utterances is a prophet," and it sets forth ways to recognize genuine prophets.[54] Celsus claimed that he had seen preachers who assumed the "motions and gestures of inspired persons" and at the end of their preaching "added strange, fanatical and quite unintelligible words, of which no rational person can find the meaning for so dark are they, as to have no meaning at all; but they give occasion to every fool or impostor to apply them to suit his own purposes." Origen accused Celsus of lying, because there were no prophets in his time. Origen also argued that the words of Isaiah, Ezekiel, and the other prophets did make sense.

It is, however, clear that Celsus did not speak about prophets in the Old Testament sense but about preachers of his own day; he even claimed that when he questioned some of these preachers, they admitted to him that their ambiguous words "really meant nothing." Origen himself acknowledged that some sort of glossolalia was still present in his own day, when he wrote: "the Holy Spirit gave signs of his presence at the beginning of Christ's ministry, and after His ascension He gave still more; but since that time these signs have diminished, although there are still traces of His presence in a few who have had their souls purified by the Gospel, and their actions regulated by its influence."[55] The reference to the Pentecostal speaking in tongues is unmistakable, and so is the fact that Origen was aware of the continuing practice. The magical papyri and the literature of the Gnostics give us a good idea of what such speeches may have been like; Alexander of Abonuteichos provides but one good example.[56] Few pagans though could clearly see a difference between genuine Christian glossolalia and the fraudulent gibberish of lower-class magicians and exorcists.

Another component of magic is the use of powerful names and the Christians accomplished their miracles of exorcism through the name of Jesus.[57] Origen pointed out that certain names are endowed with great powers, and some names in other languages are efficacious against specific demons and are endowed with a variety of properties.[58] Then, Origen addressed the charge made by Celsus that Christians exorcised by incantations; Origen stated that Christians used only the name of Jesus. "Such power, indeed, does the name of Jesus possess over evil spirits, that there have been instances where it was effectual, when it was pronounced even by bad men. . . ."[59] He reaffirmed this point a few lines later by adding: "it is clear, that Christians employ no spells or incantations, but the simple name of Jesus, and certain other words in which they repose faith, according to the holy Scriptures." This enabled the Christians not only to cast out evil spirits but also to perform cures and foresee certain events.[60] Moreover, "the name of Jesus can still remove distractions from the minds of men and expel demons, and also take away diseases; and produce a marvelous meekness of spirit and complete change of character. . . ."[61] Then in a curious passage, which indicates that such exorcisms were mostly popular among the uneducated classes, Origen stated that Christians do all these things "without the use of any curious arts of magic, or incantations, but merely by prayer and simple adjurations which the plainest person can use. Because for the most part it is unlettered persons who perform this work; thus making manifest the grace which is in the word of Christ, and the despicable weakness of demons. . . ."[62]

In addition to the name of Jesus, Christians also used the sign of the cross in their exorcisms. Justin Martyr wrote about the power of the cross, and he found symbols of it in the sail of a ship, the shape of the plough, mechanical tools, the human form, and even the Roman *vexilla*, (the banner).[63] Tertullian mentioned the crossing of oneself as an established custom among Christians: "At every forward step and movement, at every going in and out, when we put on our clothes and shoes, when we bathe, when we sit at table, when we light the lamps, on couch, on seat, in all the ordinary actions of daily life, we trace upon the forehead the sign."[64] Tertullian's contemporary, Hippolytus of Rome wrote: "And when tempted always reverently seal thy forehead (with the sign of the cross). For this sign of the Passion is displayed and made manifest against the devil if thou makest it in faith, not in order that thou mayest be seen of man, but by thy knowledge putting it forward as a shield."[65]

Lactantius wrote in a similar vein. Those who have marked on the highest part of their body the sign of the cross ("the sign of the true and divine blood") will be safe, he asserted.[66] Lactantius also confirmed that the sign of the cross was widely thought to be a great terror to demons. "When adjured by Christ, they flee from the bodies, which they have besieged." Just as Christ, when he was living among men, cast out demons by his word, so now his followers "in the name of their Master, and by the sign of His passion, banish the same polluted spirits from men." Then Lactantius repeated what he had said in *De Morte persecutorum*: In pagan sacrifices, if someone stands by with the mark of the cross on his forehead, the sacrifices are not favorable and the diviner can give no answer.[67] "But of what great weight this sign is, and what power it has, is evident, since all the host of demons is expelled and put to flight by this sign." Cyril of Jerusalem (died 386) sang the praises of the cross with the following words: "Be the Cross our seal made with boldness by our fingers on our brow, and on everything; over the bread we eat, and the cups we drink; in our comings in and goings out; before our sleep, when we lie down and when we rise up; when we are in the way, and when we are still. Great is that preservative; it is without price . . . it is the sign of the faithful, and the dread of the devils . . . for when they see the cross, they are reminded of the Crucified; they are afraid of Him. . . ."[68] Many non-Christians interpreted the making of the sign of the cross as an act of magic, as is clearly shown by Tertullian. He advised against the marriage of a Christian woman to a pagan man because (among many other reasons) when she put the sign of the cross on her bed and on herself he would interpret this as some work of magic.[69] Exactly like pagan magicians, the Christians used the sign and symbol of the cross as a device (φυλακτήριν) to assure divine protection for themselves, and they claimed that the cross was more powerful than pagan magic symbols, and it was thus able to confound the demons and bring pagan magic to naught.[70]

The Christians, therefore, exorcised demons by invoking the name of Jesus and by making the sign of the cross. This presupposes, of course, a firm belief in demons, and indeed we find that in this respect Christians were no different from their pagan neighbors. "We affirm indeed the existence of certain spiritual essences," wrote Tertullian, "nor is their name unfamiliar." Philosophers like Socrates and Plato acknowledged that demons existed. The Bible teaches that fallen angels become wicked demons bent on the ruin of mankind, and they are the instigators of diseases, violent passions, lusts, errors, and so forth.[71] The simple fact that Christians expelled demons proved their existence.[72] Indeed, early Christians felt constantly surrounded by demons: they sensed them lurking under the statues and images, and behind pagan oracles and divinations.[73] They possessed people, but when they were adjured by Christians they yielded immediately, and could even be seen leaving: "You may see them at our voice, and by operation of the hidden majesty, smitten with stripes, burnt with fire, stretched out with the increase of a growing punishment, howling, groaning, entreating, confessing whence they came and when they depart...."[74] Christians believed that one of the main occupations of demons was to stir up hostility against them.[75] In reply to Demetrius, the procounsul of Africa who had denounced the Christians on the grounds that war, famine, and pestilence came upon the world because they did not worship the gods, Cyprian countered by arguing that these gods were demons who left the bodies that they possessed with howling and groaning when they were adjured by Christians.[76]

Tatian, in his Address to the Greeks, was the first Christian author to leave us his thoughts about the origin and works of demons.[77] He believed that demons have a body like fire or air, they foster superstitions and deceive men, and will at the end be severely punished for their wickedness. Later, Tertullian (ca. 160-ca. 220) dealt with this problem in his *Apology*.[78] He believed demons to be spiritual beings who have wings and can be everywhere in a moment. They dwell in the air, close to the stars and the clouds, and possess great deceptive power. They pretend to be gods but when they are confronted with a Christian they will readily admit that they are demons. Christians have power over them. The third-century *Pseudo-Clementine Homilies* presents a view of demons that was shared by Christians, Jews, and pagans alike. Demons lust after physical pleasures such as meat, drink, and sex, but because they are spirits they cannot have them. The best way to get rid of them, therefore, is abstinence.[79] They employ various devices to deceive those in whose souls they have taken up residence, but the baptized can drive them out, not only from their own souls but from others, too, sometimes simply by looking at them, because demons fear Christians.[80]

Later, when paganism presented a fully developed demonology through the works of Neo-Pythagorean and Neo-Platonic philosophers (especially Porphyry's *Letter to Anebo*, Iamblichus's *De Mysteriis* and the works by Proclus), Christians quickly followed suit. Lactantius had already distinguished between two kinds of demons, one of heaven, the other of the earth, the latter of which were wicked. These contaminated spirits wander the world, deceiving and possessing men, and afflicting them with disorders. From these earthly demons the magicians derived their power.[81] Augustine in the *De civitate dei* described the prevailing demonology based largely upon Porphyry's work, and he criticized the pagan notion that simply because the demons inhabit the air they are mediators between God and men. Demons are "false and deceitful mediators, who through their uncleanliness of spirit frequently reveal their misery and malignity, yet by virtue of the levity of their aerial bodies and the nature of the bodies they inhabit, do continue to turn us aside and hinder our spiritual progress; they do not help us towards God, but rather prevent us from reaching Him."[82] Power has been delegated to the demons "at certain appointed and well-adjusted seasons" to stir up hostility against the city of God.[83] Augustine sharply rejected magic because it depended on the assistance of evil spirits, and he claimed that Christians did not propitiate but rather exorcised "the hostile power of the air."[84] Their method was true piety, prayer to God in the name of Jesus Christ, whom Augustine acknowledged as the only mediator between God and men. In another treatise, *De Divinatione Daemonum*, Augustine analyzed the demons' power to predict the future, their knowledge of nature and life, and their aerial bodies that permit them to enter human bodies and affect people's minds, without their presence being detected.[85]

This was perfectly sound doctrine, but it is clear that when Christians accepted the existence of demons who inhabited the air and discussed their influence on human life, they were really talking in the context of contemporary pagan magic, which was based on the assumption that demons can be made to obey the will of the person who knows how to approach them properly. The use of the name of Jesus in exorcism meshed perfectly with the pagan assumption that there is an existential relationship between the name and its bearer. Knowing the true name of a divinity gave the magician extraordinary power over this divinity, as Apuleius said.[86] The Christians, therefore, used the name of Jesus in their exorcistic formulas in the same way that non-Christian magic relied on the power of the name and the force that a proper formula exerts on spiritual beings. The same can be said concerning the sign of the cross as a physical means to achieve spiritual ends. These practices presupposed a belief in an affinity between the spiritual and material worlds, which can affect each other. Moreover, this cosmic sympathy and antipathy meant that the divine existed in the material (animals, plants, minerals, the human body, and the voice). The secret was to find out which material contained which divine element in the purest and most abundant form.[87] The preparation of magic potions, the use of amulets, the myriads of magical prescriptions and closely defined formulas were based on this presupposition. Pagan magic also maintained that the souls of persons who were victims of violent death lingered around the place of their death, and some power of their οὐσία was attached to the material that caused their death, to the clothing that they wore, and the earth in which they were buried. Were Christians influenced by such ideas when they used the cross in word and in sign? Certainly it cannot surprise us if pagans thought so, and if they also associated the same powerful οὐσία with the food that Christians ate, that is, the Body and Blood of the crucified Jesus.

Some Christian authors used surprisingly candid language when they discussed magic. Origen, for instance, argued that magic is "not an altogether uncertain thing, but is, as those skilled in it prove, a consistent system."[88] Similarly, Augustine believed that it was possible to produce miracles by magic, because

> devils are attracted . . . not by food like animals, but like spirits, by such symbols as suit their taste, various kinds of stones, woods, plants, animals, song, rites. And that men may provide these attractions, the devils first of all cunningly seduce them . . . and thus make a few of them their disciples, who become the instructors of the multitude. For unless they first instructed men, it was impossible to know what each of them desires, what they shrink from, by what name they should be invoked or constrained to be present. Hence the origin of magic and magicians.[89]

A reader of *De civ. dei* will have no argument with the statement that Augustine "fully accepted all the superstitions of his age, both as to theurgic and goetic magic and explained everything by the power of demons."[90] He mentioned a list of materials charged with divine potency, the proper use of which could bring beneficial results. One such material was a bag of earth from Jerusalem, where Jesus died and rose again. This bag was hung up in the bedroom of Hesperius "to preserve him from harm." After his house was exorcised, since he no longer needed special protection, he buried the bag of earth. Thereafter, Christians frequently gathered at the burial place, and a paralytic was healed when he visited there. Other materials mentioned by Augustine as having magical import were oil mixed with the tears of a presbyter who prayed for a young woman (when a woman was anointed with this mixture she was freed from the devil); flowers used in a procession that bore the relics of a saint (they restored the sight of a blind person) and a dress that had been taken to a shrine (when it was put on the body of a dead woman she was restored to life). As far as human faculties were concerned, the voice could work the most powerful magic. Augustine believed that hymns sung at evening prayer drove the demon from a young man. The list goes on and on: objects, words, rites, and formulas endowed with magical properties forced demons to yield and enticed the divine power to condescend to lend assistance in time of need in the form of a desired service.[91]

Christians believed the sacraments to be especially important, because it is in them that the divine is connected with the material. Ignatius referred to the Eucharist as the "medicine of immortality (φάρμακον ἀθανασίας) and the antidote which wards off death."[92] It is well known that the word φάρμακον was widely used in the sense of magic potion, charm, or poison, as well as for medicine, and Ignatius was by no means an exception when he employed the word to describe the effect of a sacrament.[93] Thus the magic element could not have been very far from the minds of the fathers when they talked about the sacraments in this sense. According to Irenaeus, the Logos present in the bread and wine effected immortality, but other authors emphasized the importance of the Eucharistic prayer.[94] For Augustine, the Eucharist was the "daily medicine of the Lord's body," although he also stressed the importance of the attending word.[95] No wonder that we hear about countless miracles involving the Eucharist. Typically these fall into one or the other of two categories, sympathetic or antipathetic, depending on whether their results were beneficial or harmful. One such sympathetic miracle involved Hesperius, an acquaintance of Augustine's, who had a farm that was haunted by evil spirits until the Eucharist was offered.[96] Hippolytus also believed in the magical powers of the Eucharist; he advised people to take it before they ate anything else, "for if he partakes with faith, even though some deadly thing were given to him, after this it cannot hurt him."[97]

Tertullian's treatise *De Baptismo* is a good example of the Christians' belief in the efficacy of their sacraments. It also clearly shows how much early Christian ideas were constrained by the times. In baptism the act is simple, but the effect is great: a man is dipped in water, a few words are spoken, and when he rises he has attained eternity. Tertullian explained the importance of water: it is an age-old substance that is dignified by the fact that even before creation it was the seat of the Holy Spirit.[98] There existed, therefore, an eternal sympathy between God and water, so that water became the regulating power in creation; through the "dividing of the waters" the dry land was made. It was from water again that living creatures were made, "that it might be no wonder in Baptism if waters know how to give life."[99] The material substance "which governs terrestrial life acts as agent likewise in the celestial."[100] These statements on the benefits of baptism by Tertullian are in line with pagan principles of magic, but Tertullian had much more to say. The Spirit of God, which hovered over the waters, continues to linger over the water of baptism, and it thus has a spiritual quality and the power to sanctify. "All waters, therefore, in virtue of the pristine privilege of their origin, do, after invocation of God, attain the sacramental power of sanctification."[101]

Tertullian recognized that the pagans also knew the rites of sprinkling houses, temples, and cities; that in the Eleusinian mysteries people were even baptized; and that the pagans attributed other miracles to water. But he argued that in all these instances evil angels are active in the element, while a holy angel of God is active in Christian baptism. The holy angel prepares the way for the coming of the Holy Spirit to the baptized; the names of Father, Son and Holy Spirit are mentioned, which give the assurance of salvation; to these names, that of the Church is added, because it is the body of the three. Two more acts follow, first the anointing with a blessed unction, and then the laying on of hands in invitation to the Holy Spirit. Just as it is possible by means of human ingenuity to summon a spirit into water, so in the rite of baptism the Holy Spirit willingly descends through cleansed and blessed bodies. Tertullian then discussed a variety of matters concerning baptism, such as the type of baptism in the Red Sea, the water from the Rock, the baptism of John, and the fact that Jesus did not baptize. He next gave directions concerning who can baptize, who can be baptized, and what times are most suitable for the administration of the sacrament. The place, the day of the month, and even the hour of the day could be more or less propitious in magical rituals. Tertullian recommended Passover (Jesus had pointed out the place of Passover with a reference to water: "You will meet a man carrying water," Mark 14:13) and Pentecost; still, since every day is the Lord's, every time is all right. Tertullian finished his treatise by giving advice on how a person should behave before and after baptism.[102] Properly administered, baptism never failed to produce miraculous results. Augustine listed two such miracles. A gouty doctor in Carthage, the night before his baptism, had a dream in which he saw black, woolly-haired boys who tried to prevent him from accepting the sacrament. He understood that these were devils and resisted them, although they caused him much pain. The next day, during his baptism, not only did his pain disappear but also his gout. Similarly, an old comedian, who lived near Carthage, was cured of paralysis and a hernia when he was baptized.[103]

So the Christians used objects, rites, words, and formulas charged with divine potency to force demons to yield, all in accordance with well-known, contemporary rules of magic. Although most cases could be classified as sympathetic magic, there are also examples of antipathetic magic. Cyprian related one such example; a child who had been given food offered to the idols subsequently refused to take the cup of the Eucharist, and when it was forced into her mouth she began to cry and vomit: the elements of the Eucharist and the pagan sacrificial food had rejected each other. "So great is the Lord's power, so great is his majesty" cried Cyprian, who professed to be an eyewitness to this event. Another example of antipathetic magic involved a pagan woman who secretly went to the Christian Eucharistic service and had terrible pains afterwards as if she had taken poison.[104]

Ancient magical rites were usually performed at night, in seclusion, and in silence. The night air, according to Plutarch, is full of lights and powers that come like seeds from the stars.[105] Because a profane sound could break the spell and make the whole ritual invalid, according to Pliny, strict formulas were adopted during these meetings. An attendant maintained silence, and a piper played so that nothing but the prayer could be heard.[106] Ancient literature is full of references to nightly rituals in which magic was performed.[107] Philostratus put the following words in the mouth of Apollonius of Tyana: "wizards do not affect temples of the gods as their places of reunion;

for such places are inimical to those who deal in magic, and they cloak their art under the cover of night and of every sort of darkness, so as to preclude their dupes from the use of their eyes and ears."[108] Apollonius believed that magicians used darkness to fool people, as Alexander was accused of doing.[109] According to Apuleius, magic is "as mysterious an art as it is loathly and horrible; it needs as a rule night watches and concealing darkness, solitude absolute and mur-mured incantations, to bear which few free mean are admitted. . . ."[110]

The Greeks and Romans, therefore, closely associated magical practices and nightly meetings. Tertullian realized the potential dan-gers that this posed for Christians. In a treatise addressed to his wife, Tertullian described the difficulties a Christian woman could face who had to live with a pagan husband. He could hinder her in the performance of her religious duties, especially attendance at nightly meetings. What pagan husband, Tertullian asked, "will willingly bear her being taken from his side by nocturnal convocations, if need so be? Who, finally, will without anxiety endure her absence all the night long at the paschal solemnities? Who will, without some suspi-cion of his own, dismiss her to attend that Lord's Supper which they defame?[111] Then he wrote: "Shall you escape notice when you sign your bed, or your body? when you blow away some impurity; when even by night you rise to pray? Will you not be thought to be engaged in some sort of magic? Will not your husband know what it is which you secretly taste before taking any food? and if he knows it to be bread, does he not believe it to be that bread which it is said to be? And will every husband, ignorant of the reason of these things, simply endure them, without murmuring, without suspicion whether it be bread or poison?"[112] Tertullian's warnings neatly summarize the suspicions pagans had about Christians: they meet at night, perform secret rites, and partake of food that may or may not be harmful. Given these suspicions, for many the conclusion was inevi-table that Christians were involved in some sort of magic.

Tertullian, in this treatise, made a veiled reference to the Christian wife's secrets, which the pagan husband may keep for her sake. Indeed, secrecy was another hallmark of pagan magic, this being one of the reasons why it was performed under cover of darkness. Formu-las, true names, ingredients in potions, and other parts of the rites were well-kept secrets. The initiates of mystery religions were also under a strict rule of secrecy, and Tertullian, in fact, likened Chris-tianity to the mystery religions in this respect.[113] When we turn to early Christianity, however, we find that the sources are not always consistent concerning secrecy. We know that the Eucharist was only available to the initiated.[114] So, too, was baptism, which was the ceremony of initiation. It is probably because of this that Celsus called Christianity a "secret system of belief."[115] Origen admitted that there were certain secret doctrines of Christianity that were not divulged to the multitude. But he pointed out that such discretion was not unique to Christianity, but rather was common to many philosophical systems and mysteries. More to the point, Origen contended that the basic teachings of the Christians were well known to all, and, therefore, he argued that it was absurd to call Christianity a secret doctrine.[116]

In an indirect way Tertullian also acknowledged a certain secrecy in Christianity when he chided the heretics that "they cast to the dogs that which is holy, and their pearls they will fling to the swine," he meant that they provide access to their services to everybody without distinction, and he accused them of being frivolous, merely human, without seriousness, without authority.[117] This secretive element in early Christianity has been called *disciplina arcani*, or the rule of secrecy;[118] eventually it included, in addition to baptism and the Eucharist, the Lord's Prayer and the baptismal creed. But the *disciplina arcani* was never uniformly followed; in the second century, Justin Martyr did not know it, and Hippolytus placed little emphasis on it.[119] In later centuries many Christian authors treated the principle in a very liberal way. From the fifth century on it quickly disappeared—everybody was Christian and there was nothing to be kept secret. For second-century pagans the most suspicious Christian secret was their celebration of the Eucharist and, as we have seen above it was in this connection that the worst rumors arose.

Tacitus and Pliny also associated Christian rituals with magical practices. Morton Smith has presented a strong case for the hypothesis that both Pliny's letter and the remarks made by Tacitus make good sense only if one presupposes that the Romans had already formed the opinion of Christianity that "it was an organization for the practice of magic."[120] It is, of course, not necessary to assume that this was the only way Romans or Greeks viewed Christianity; as a matter of fact, one conclusion from our investigations so far is that Christianity must have been many things to many people inside and outside of the Christian community. But, as far as the charge of

magical practices is concerned, it is clear that Christians were no
better and no worse than their contemporaries. They believed in
demons and exorcisms; they attributed supernatural power to material elements when used in connection with precise formulas and
under specific circumstances; they identified certain names as having unusual potency; they preferred nights and daybreaks for their
meetings; they warded off evil by signs and symbols; they ate food
charged with divine energy; and they spoke in tongues. These are all
characteristics of the working of magic, and with these, Christians
opened themselves to the pagan charge, "They are magicians."

One final question needs to be examined. What was legal and
illegal magic in the eyes of Roman law?[121] Certain elements in the
official Roman religion were based on magical principles, such as
haruspicium (the examination of the insides of animals) and auspi-
cium (flights of birds, natural phenomena). In addition to these,
Greek and Roman literature contains such a large number of references to magical arts from the lowest to the highest level of society
that it appears that magic was an accepted form of religious piety that
ran parallel to other religious institutions. Apart from occasional
temporary measures, such as expulsion of astrologers from the city,[122]
there were three major monuments in the history of Roman law that
cast light on the Roman attitude toward magic. These are the Twelve
Tables (ca. 451 B.C.), the laws of Sulla (81 B.C.), and the legislation
enacted by later Christian emperors.

The text of the Twelve Tables survives only in later references to it
by Roman authors. From these authors we learn of the following
stipulation. "If any person had sung or composed against another
person a song (carmen) such as was causing slander or insult to
another . . . he should be clubbed to death."[123] Whether the carmen in
this sentence and the verb associated with it, occentare, signify a
magical idea or a simple defamatory verse is open to question. Very
clear, however, is Table VIII.8, which made it a crime to move
someone's crops from one field to another by means of magic.[124] The
Twelve Tables, in short, enunciated basic arguments against magic
for the purpose of preventing people from doing harm to others.[125]

The law enacted under Sulla, known as Lex Cornelia de sicariis
et veneficis ("The Cornelian Law Concerning Assassins and
Poisoners"), is described in the Sentences of Paulus (ca. 210) and the
Digest by Justinian. The following statements describe which magi-

cal activities were prohibited by the Romans and the punishment prescribed for them:

> Persons who celebrate, or cause to be celebrated impious or nocturnal rites, so as to enchant, bewitch, or bind anyone, shall be crucified, or thrown to wild beasts. . . . Anyone who sacrifices a man, or attempts to obtain auspices by means of his blood, or pollutes a shrine or a temple, shall be thrown to wild beasts, or, if he is of superior rank, shall be punished with death. . . . It has been decided that persons who are addicted to the art of magic, shall suffer extreme punishment; that is to say they shall be thrown to wild beasts, or crucified. Magicians themselves shall be burned alive. . . . No one shall be permitted to have books on the art of magic in his possession, and when they are found with anyone, they shall be publicly burnt, and those who have them, after being deprived of their property, if they are of superior rank shall be deported to an island, and if they are of inferior station shall be put to death; for not only is the practice of this art prohibited, but also the knowledge of the same (*Sentences of Paulus* 5.23.15-18).[126]

Digest 48.8 deals with the Cornelian law and quotes the opinions of Marcianus, Ulpian, and others. Of particular interest here is the opinion of Marcianus, who made a careful distinction between harmful poisons (*mala venena*) and those that are not harmful, such as love philters and drugs that are used for medicinal purposes. Persons who made poisons designed to kill people were punished with either decapitation or crucifixion.[127]

The legislation enacted by the Christian emperors from Constantine on are in the Code of Justinian 9:18 and in the *Codex Theodosianus* 9.16. In 312 Constantine forbade a haruspex to visit the house of another one; in 321 the same emperor forbade magical arts that endangered the health of other people but permitted those used for medicinal purposes or for the general welfare of mankind.[128] Constantius in 357 forbade magic altogether: "Chaldeans, magicians, and others who are commonly called malefactors on account of the enormity of their crimes shall no longer practice their infamous arts." A law published in 358 called magicians the "enemies of the human race" and classified the following as magicians, those who used magic verses, sorcerers, haruspices, soothsayers, augurs, diviners, interpreters of dreams.[129]

These are the three milestones in Roman legal history as far as magic is concerned. Clearly, the most important was the Cornelian law, in which the evil intent and the harmful consequences of magic were emphasized. The extermely severe provisions of the *Sentences of Paulus* 5.23.17, which ordained that magicians be thrown to wild beasts, crucified, or burned alive and which made no distinction among different kinds of magic or different kinds of magicians, were not strictly enforced. Magic as a discipline, as a form of religion, or as a doctrine was not suppressed; nor were magicians brought to court just because they were magicians. Although in principle magic was outlawed by the Cornelian law, in practice it was tolerated. Even when the law was applied, special circumstances were present. For example, when Apuleius was accused of performing magic he was also accused of causing a boy to fall sick and of using witchcraft to induce his wife to marry him because he craved her money. Magic became a crime, and thus subject to prosecution, when some sort of harm was associated with it, and only in Christian times were all sorts of magic universally forbidden. This means that, as far as the Christians were concerned, the provisions of the *Lex Cornelia de sicariis*, as described in the *Sentences of Paulus* 5.23.17, may have been invoked in only one instance, namely the persecution under Nero as described by Tacitus, in which the punishments meted out were the same as those listed by Paulus. But this passage in Tacitus is not clear and does not permit a definitive interpretation.

The question now arises as to why the Christians rejected the charge of practicing magic so vehemently. One reason may be that they were so totally immersed in the culture of their age that what they believed in and practiced appeared to them as a universally accepted form of religious experience, in no way outside of or contrary to accepted standards. In point of fact, what we now recognize as magical practices in early Christianity could not be considered as deviant behavior when compared to the average Greco-Roman piety of the age. Another reason for the Christians' protest may be that they associated magic with harmful practices and evil purposes. There are extremely few instances of these in early Christianity. The cursing of the fig tree by Jesus could be classified as such, and the New Testament also describes the invocation of death in the story of Ananias and Sapphira, which was probably the worst of all magical practices.[130] Furthermore, Paul punished a magician by the name of Bar Jesus, or Elymas, with blindness, and he said: "You son of the devil, you enemy of all righteousness, full of deceit and villainy, will you not stop making crooked the straight path of the Lord? And now the hand of the Lord is upon you, and you shall be blind and unable to see the sun for a time."[131] Twice in Paul's letters we read that he "delivered to Satan" certain people.[132] This sort of activity definitely falls into the category of harmful "black" magic, and indeed we find many references to it in non-Christian magical papyri. These incidents should be contrasted, however, with the words Paul wrote in Ephesus: "a number of those who practiced magic arts brought their books together and burned them in the sight of all; and they counted the value of them and found it came to fifty thousand pieces of silver."[133] The main thrust of Paul's activity, therefore, and that of the early Christian church generally, opposed magic that used illegal means and that was directed to destructive ends. Indeed, early Christian literature does not provide us with examples of magical arts that could be even remotely compared to the many disgusting and repulsive stories that we run across in Greco-Roman literature.[134]

According to the Cornelian law, magic was illegal and, although it was not always enforced, there was still the threat of legal action. But these considerations must have been secondary to the Christian belief that in Jesus Christ God entered the human situation in an absolute and perfect way; this made the mediating role of demons, and in consequence magic, unnecessary. Demons had served a purpose at one time because without their existence any communication between the physical and spiritual world would have been impossible. But with Jesus Christ this condition had been superseded; in Jesus and through Jesus the Christian had direct access to God. What the Christians did was not, therefore, in their eyes magic (they did not use the services of demons), but rather a legitimate exercise of a privilege granted to them by God.

Nevertheless, there was a firm and genuine conviction by pagans that Christians were involved in magic, despite the latter's indignant and persistent denial of the charge. The Christians acknowledged that there was such a thing as magic, but they attributed it to the workings of evil demons. The Christians did, however, engage in activities that must have looked suspicious to all outsiders. Of course, we must distinguish between the appearance of magic and that which was truly magic. Not every *carmen* was an incantation, and not everything done at night necessarily involved the conjuring of spirits; Pliny had already learnt that. But the important point is that too often Christian authors talked like magicians; they boasted of their ability to summon powers from another world, and they claimed that by manipulating the correct elements under the correct circumstances they could force the divine to do their will. They may have claimed that this was not magic, but it certainly looked like magic to others. After the patristic period we find that the church increasingly absorbed and sanctified pagan magical practices; the veneration of relics and the use of incense, charms, and bells were integrated into the life of the church. This peculiar Christian brand of magic was not merely tolerated but promoted as long as it was within the ecclesiastical framework.

NOTES

1. *Metamorphoses* 9.14. Author's translation. See the comments of M. Stern, vol. 2, pp. 201-202, particularly fn. 7, p. 202.

2. Mezentius figures in Virgil's *Aeneid* 7-10 as an atheistic tyrant who is killed by Aeneas.

3. *Apol.* 56, E.T., H. E. Butler, *The Apologia and Florida of Apuleius of Meadaura* (1909; reprint ed., Westport, Conn.: Greenwood Press, 1970), pp. 97-98.

4. Octavius 2, 3, *ANF* 4.173-74.

5. Apuleius *Apol.* 6ff., 13ff., 27ff.

6. Ibid., 42ff. Apollonius of Tyana was also accused of being a magician. One of the charges against him was that he sacrificed a boy at night and examined his entrails to ascertain Nerva's chances of becoming emperor. Philostratus *Life* 7.20.

7. *Apol.* 53-66. But, as Lynn Thorndike, *History of Magic and Experimental Science* (New York: Macmillan, 1929), 1:233, points out, three times before he made this statement in the *Apologia*, Apuleius mentioned Mercury in connection with magical practices. Also see H. Remus, "Pagan-Christian Conflict over Miracle in the Second Century" (Ph.D. Dissertation, University of Pennsylvania, 1979), pp. 117-188, who examines the "social and cultural factors" that figured in the bringing of charges against Apuleius.

8. *Ep.* 138.19.

9. *Ep.* 138.18, 20. Apuleius is also mentioned in *Ep.* 120, 136. Augustine also citicized Apuleius and his teaching on demons in *De civ. dei* 8.14; 9.3, 6, 8; 10.27; see also 18.18: Augustine could not decide, whether Apuleius was really transformed into an ass as he described in *The Golden Ass* or not.

10. Hierocles wrote two books to the Christians around the time of the Diocletian persecutions, ca. 303, urging them to leave their "foolishness." Lactantius *The Divine Institutes* 5.3.

11. MacMullen, *Enemies of the Roman Order* (Cambridge: Harvard University Press, 1966), p. 95ff.

12. Ibid., pp. 99ff. Galen was also accused of practicing magic, and,

although he sharply rejected philters and love charms, his works do contain magical devices. See Thorndike, *History of Magic and Experimental Science*, 1:165-181.

13. *Apol.* 25-26; Butler, *Apologia and Florida*, p. 56.

14. Butler, *Apologia and Florida*, p. 141; T. R. Glover, *The Conflict of Religions in the Early Roman Empire* (Boston: Beacon Press, 1960), p. 230.

15. See, for example, Epictetus and Galen.

16. Remus, *Pagan-Roman Conflict*, pp. 313-51 and 383-85, gives a good review of recent scholarly works on Lucian.

17. *True Word* was written about 180, as was *Alexander the False Prophet*. See A. M. Harmon, *Lucian*, Loeb (London: Heinemann, 1961), 4:174, fn. 1.

18. MacMullen, *Enemies of the Roman Order*, p. 118.

19. Ibid., 4.34.

20. *ANF* 5.38. See also *Refutation* 4.28 concerning other secret magical rites that call to mind the fact that Alexander, according to Lucian, claimed the power of speech for his snake (Harmon, *Lucian*, p. 58). Cf. Irenaeus *Adv. Haer.* 1.13.2.

21. Lucian *Alexander* 58. A. H. Harmon, *Lucian*, p. 250, notes that coins with the new name of the city and also with the name of Glykon and the image of a snake with a human head continued to circulate until the middle of the third century.

22. Lucian *Alexander* 51.

23. Ibid., see chaps. 25, 47.

24. Harmon, *Lucian*, chap. 25, see especially p. 209.

25. Ibid., chap. 38, p. 225.

26. Origen *Contra Celsum* 3.59. See S. Angus, *The Mystery Religions and Christianity* (London: J. Murray, 1925), p. 80 for further references from ancient literature. Also Harold R. Willoughby, *Pagan Regeneration* (Chicago: University of Chicago Press, 1929), p. 44.

27. Harmon, *Lucian*, 38, 39; Lactantius *Epitome of the Divine Institutes* 23, E.T., *ANF* 7.229.

28. *Didache* 9.5; 10.6.

29. *Nero* 34. On the other hand, Augustus was initiated in the mysteries in 21 B.C., see Suetonius *Augustus* 93, and Hadrian was "admitted to the highest grade" in 128 A.D., Dio 69.11.9.

30. Philostratus *Vita* 4.18.

31. *Philopseudes—The Lover of Lies* 16, E.T., Harmon, *Lucian*, 3:345.

32. Smith, *Jesus the Magician* (San Francisco: Harper and Row, 1978), p. 57.

33. Eusebius, *Hist. Eccl.* 7.10.1-4.

34. *De morte persecutorum* 10, E.T., *ANF* 7.304.

35. Origen *Contra Celsum* 1.6, E.T. *ANF* 4.398.

36. Ibid., 6.40. E.T., *ANF* 4.591.

37. *Acta Disputationis Sancti Achatii V.:* "Martianus ait: Ubi sunt magni socii artis tuae, vel doctores hujus artificiosae fallaciae? Respondit Achatius: Nos omnia meruimus a Deo et meremur; sectam vero magicae artis horremus. Martianus ait: Ideo magi estis, quia novum nescio quod genus religionis inducitis." P. Theodor Ruinhart, *Acta Martyrum* (Ratisbonae, 1759), p. 201. The text has been printed by O. Gebhardt in his edition of the *Acta Martyrum* (Berlin: A. Duncker, 1902), p. 119, but omitted by H.

Musurillo as being spurious in his *The Acts of the Christian Martyrs* (Oxford: Clarendon Press, 1972), p. xii. The martyrdom of Achatius is traditionally dated around 250 A.D..

38. *"Incantationibus aliquibus magicis"* see Musurillo, *The Acts of the Christian Martyrs*, p. 124.

39. *Historia Augusta, Saturninus* 8, E.T., D. Magie, *SHA*, Loeb, 3.397-401. The *Historia Augusta* is a much debated work. The time of its authorship (under Constantine?) is questionable and even the name Flavius Vopiscus is spurious. See on this topic A. Chastagnol, "Recherches Sur l'Histoire Auguste: Avec un Rapport Sur Les Progrès de la Historia Augusta—Forschung Depuis 1963," *Antiquitas* 4 (1970):6. Also spurious is the story of Cyprian of Antioch (not to be confused with Cyprian of Carthage) who supposedly lived in the third century and, before his conversion to Christianity, was a professional magician. Eventually he became bishop of Antioch and a martyr. His *Confession* is a mine of information concerning pagan divination and magic. See Thorndike, *History of Magic and Experimental Science*, 1:428ff, who mentions several other legendary stories about Christians accused by pagans of being magicians and then martyred. Similarly legendary are the many references to magic and magicians in the N.T. Apocrypha. Finally, Priscillian, the bishop of Avila and six of his followers were beheaded on the charge of magic in 385 but the circumstances of their condemnation are so tainted by ecclesiastical and imperial politics that it is difficult to make a clear judgment. Literature in Altaner, *Patrologie*⁷ (1966), p. 374 and the *Oxford Classical Dictionary*² (1970), p. 878.

40. See also Hippolytus *The Apostolic Tradition* 16.21-22: "A magician shall not even be brought for consideration (i.e. to be admitted as a catechumen). A charmer or an astrologer or an interpreter of dreams or a maker of amulets, let them desist or let them be desisted." Dix, *The Apostolic Tradition*, p. 27. Magicians are put here in the same category as soldiers, military governors, harlots, sodomists, gladiators, charioteers, makers of idols and schoolmasters (!)

41. *Adv. Haer.* 1.25, *ANF* 1.350. Similarly *Adv. Haer.* 2.31.2, *ANF* 1.407.

42. *Refutation* 7.32, *ANF* 5.113.

43. *Dialogue* 30, 49, 76, 85, *ANF* 1.209, 220, 236, 241.

44. *Dialogue* 85, *ANF* 1.241. This statement is remarkable, in that the God of Abraham, Isaac and Jacob is the same as the God of Jesus Christ whose power Justin had just affirmed. Theophilus also mentioned that exorcism in the name of God, and not strictly in the name of Jesus Christ, was practiced among Christians: "even to this day the possessed are sometimes exorcised in the name of the living and true God; and these spirits of error themselves confess that they are demons. . . ." *Ad Autolycum* 8, *ANF* 2.97.

45. *Apol.* 2.6, *ANF* 1.190.

46. *Adv. Haer.* 2.32.4-5, *ANF* 1.409.

47. *Apol.* 23, *ANF* 3.33.

48. *Ad Scapulam* 2, *ANF* 3.106, cf. *De anima* 1: Christianity does not introduce new gods but expels the old demons.

49. *De Virginitate* 1.10, *ANF* 8.58.

50. *De Virginitate* 1.12; *ANF* 8.59.

51. Smith, *Jesus the Magician*, p. 193.

52. *Didache* 11.5-6.

53. 1 Cor. 12-14.

54. *Didache* 11.7-8.

55. Origen *Contra Celsum* 7.9; see also 7.8, 10, 11, 12, *ANF* 4.614–15.

56. Lucian *Alexander* 51.

57. This is obviously based on new Testament texts, such as Phil 2.9-10; Acts 3:6; 16:18; also Mark 16.17; 1 Cor. 5.4. See also Rev. 19.12 about the secret name of Jesus "which no one knows but himself." Also Rev. 2.17; 3.12; 14.1. The numerical value of the letters that make up the name of ΙΗΣΟΥΣ (10 + 8 + 200 + 70 + 400 + 200) is 888 (compare *Oracula Sibyllina* 1.325), which may be a contrast to 666, the name of the Antichrist in 13.18. Thus the name of Jesus as a "true name" would have a powerful magic force. About "true names" and their numerical value a brief but clear summary is in Hopfner, pp. 339ff.

58. Origen *Contra Celsum* 1.24, *ANF* 4.406.

59. Origen *Contra Celsum* 1.6, *ANF* 4.398. The power of the name of Jesus is also underscored by the treatise on *Rebaptism,* falsely attributed to Cyprian. This treatise claims that even people outside the church use the name of Jesus successfully, but when these people come to the last judgment and say: "Lord, have we not . . . in Thy name cast out demons . . . ," the Lord will tell them, "I never knew you; depart from me, ye who work iniquity." Matt. 7:22 ff. and Mark 14:27. In this connection we may also remember that according to Acts 19:13 ff., the itinerant Jewish exorcists who tried to use the name of Jesus were less successful: the evil spirit refused to leave and attacked them.

60. Origen *Contra Celsum* 1.46, *ANF* 4.415.

61. Origen *Contra Celsum* 1.67, *ANF* 4.426.

62. Origen *Contra Celsum* 7.4, 7.67, *ANF* 4.612.

63. *Apol.* 1.55, *ANF* 1.181.

64. *De Corona* 3, *ANF* 3.94.

65. *The Apostolic Tradition* 37.1; Dix, 68–69.

66. *The Divine Institutes* 4.26, *ANF* 7.129.

67. *The Divine Institutes* 4.27, *ANF* 7.129-130.

68. *The Epitome of the Divine Institutes* 5, *ANF* 7.243. The spurious *Passio Quatuor Coronatorum* relates the curious story of the four Christians in Diocletian's stone quarry in Pannonia whose tools broke less frequently than the others' because they were Christians and made the sign of the cross on all their works. Cyril of Jerusalem *Catechetical Lectures* 13.36; *PG* 33.816.

69. *Ad uxorem* 2.5. We find similar statements in the works of the later fathers. For example, Ambrose *De Fide ad Gratianum* 1.3; Augustine *De civ. dei* 22.8; John Damascene *De fide orthodoxa* 4.11.

70. Franz Joseph Dölger, "Beiträge zur Geschichte des Kreuzzeichens, IV," *Jahrbuch für Antike und Christentum* 6 (1963):7-34. Also see E. Dinkler, "Zur Geschichte Des Kreuzes-Symbols," *Zeitschrift für Theologie und Kirche* 48 (1951):148-172; W. Michaelis, "Zeichen, Siegel, Kreuz," *Theologische Zeitschrift* 12 (1956):505-525; Johannes Schneider, σταυρός "*Theologisches Wörterbuch Zum Nt.* 7 (1964) 572-584.

71. *Apol.* 22, *ANF* 3.36.

72. *De testimonio animae* 3.

73. Minucius Felix *Octavius* 27; Cyprian *Quod Idola* 7, ANF 5.467.

74. Cyprian, *Quod Idola, ANF* 5.467; see also *Ep.* 75:15: "the devil is scourged and burned and tortured by exorcists, by the human voice, and by divine power," *ANF* 5.402. Similarly in *Ep. 1 to Donatus* 5, *ANF* 5.276.

75. *Octavius* 28; Cyprian *Quod Idola* 7; Augustine *De civ. dei* 10.21.

76. *Ad Demetrium* 15, *ANF* 5.462; also see Lactantius *The Divine Institutes* 2.15.

77. Tatian *Oratio ad Graecos* chaps. 7-18. Also see Athenagoras *Apology* 24-27, and Minucius Felix *Octavius* 27.

78. Tertullian *Apol.* chaps. 22, 23, and 24. Tertullian shows similarities here with a lesser known work of Apuleius, *On the God of Socrates* in which Apuleius describes the prevailing pagan doctrine on demons. He relies on Plutarch, especially his *de defectu oracularum* and *de Iside et Osiride*, and Plato's *Timaeus*; no doubt Tertullian knew these works, too.

79. *Pseudo-Clementine Homilies* 8, 9.10.

80. For a full discussion see Hans Joachim Schoeps, "Die Dämonologie der Pseudoklementinen," in *Aus Frühchristlicher Zeit* (Tübingen: Mohr, 1950).

81. *The Divine Institutes* 2.15-17.

82. *De civ. dei* 9.18. *NPNF* 2.176.

83. *De civ. dei* 10.21. John J. O'Meara, *Prophyry's Philosophy from Oracles in Augustine* (Paris: Études Augustiniennes, 1959), p. 145 claims that in chap. 10 of *De civ. dei*, Augustine was confronting especially the "philosophy from Oracles" by Prophyry.

84. *De civ. dei* 8.19. References to magic and magicians appear scattered in many works by Augustine.

85. *De civ. dei* 10.22; *De Div. Daem.* in *CSEL* 41. Later John of Damascus (ca. 650) made an attempt to reconcile the existence of demons with that of angels and both with the idea of monotheism in *De Fide Orthodoxa* 2.4.

86. Apuleius *Apol.* 26; 7; see also Hippolytus *Refutation* 7.32; Lactantius *The Divine Institutes* 2.17. Cf. Pliny *NH* 28.3.10ff. on the question of whether words have power. See, on this problem: W. Heitmüller, *Im Namen Jesu* (Göttingen: Vandenhoeck and Ruprecht, 1903); B. Jacob, *Im Namen Gottes* (Berlin: S. Calvary, 1903). T. Hopfner, "Mageia," in Pauly, Wissowa, and Kroll, *Realencyclopädie der classischen Altertumswissenschaft*, vol. 28 (Stuttgart: Druckenmiller Verlag, 1928), pp. 301-94. Also, David E. Aune, "Magic in Early Christianity," in *Aufstieg und Neidergang der römischen Welt*, vol. 23/2 (Berlin: De Gruyter, 1980), pp. 1507-57, which has an excellent up-to-date bibliography on the subject.

87. Hopfner, "Mageia," p. 310ff.; Aune, "Magic and Early Christianity," p. 1513, fn. 17 for bibliography. Remus, *Pagan-Christian Conflicts*, pp. 106-107, cites examples from non-Christian literature where crucifixion gives the opportunity to obtain potent magical objects.

88. Origen *Contra Celsum* 1.24; cf. Apuleius *Apol.* 25.

89. *De civ. dei* 21.6. See also Hopfner, "Mageia," p. 312.

90. Henry Charles Lea, *Material Toward a History of Witchcraft*, ed. Arthur C. Howland, (New York: T. Yoseloff, 1957), 1:121. Cf. Charles Alva Hoyt, *Witchcraft* (Carbondale: Southern Illinois University Press, 1981).

91. *De civ. dei* 22.8-10.

92. *Eph.* 20.2.

93. Hopfner, "Mageia," 320; Liddel-Scott, *A Greek-English Lexicon* (New York: Harper, 1883), p. 861. For further sacramental use of φάρμακον Lampe, *A Patristic Greek Lexicon*, p. 1472 has numerous references from patristic literature.

94. Irenaeus *Adv. Haer.* 5.2.2; Barnabas 2.10; *Didache* 9.1-4, 10.2-6; Hermas *Mand.* 10.3.2; *1 Clem.* 52.2ff.; Justin *Apol.* 1.66; *Dial.* 41.117.

95. Augustine *Ep.* 54.3; *Sermo* 234.2; and concerning Baptism in *Jo. Ev.*

Tr. 80.3: "Take away the word and what is the water but water only? The word is added to the element and it becomes a sacrament."

96. Augustine *De civ. dei* 22.8, 9, 10.

97. Hippolytus *The Apostolic Tradition* 32.2-4. See also Ps. Aug. *Sermo* 279.5, *MPL* 39.2237, which recommends that sick people should partake of the body and blood of Christ. But is this still religion? The Jewish scholar, Abraham Heschel, although he did not mention Christianity, argued that "the essence of religion does not lie in the satisfaction of a human need. It is true that man, seeking to exploit the forces of nature for his own profit, does not recoil from forcing supernatural beings to do his pleasure. But such intentions and practices are characteristic, not of religion, but of magic, which is ... the deadly enemy of religion, its very opposite. ... As long as man sees in religion the satisfaction of his own needs, a guarantee of immortality ... it is not God whom he serves but himself." Heschel, *Man is Not Alone. A Philosophy of Religion* (New York: The Jewish Publication Society of America, 1951), pp. 232f.

98. Gen. 1.1-2.

99. Ibid., 1.20.

100. Tertullian *De Baptismo* 3, *ANF* 3.670.

101. Ibid., 4.

102. A comparison of this treatise by Tertullian with the baptismal liturgy by Hippolytus in *The Apostolic Tradition* (chaps. 19 to 22) shows how many of the principles and ideas discussed by Tertullian were integral parts of congregational life.

103. Augustine *De civ. dei* 22.8-10.

104. *De lapsis* 25, 26, *ANF* 5.444.

105. Plutarch *De Iside et Osiride* 80b: "for the light of day is single and simple, and Pindar says that the sun is seen 'through the lovely ether,' whereas the night air is a coalescence and fusion of many illuminations and powers which flow down like seeds to one centre from all the stars. ..." See also 79b. E.T., J. Gwyn Griffiths (Cardiff: University of Wales Press, 1970), pp. 249, 245. Magical elements in Plutarch's essays and his demonology were analyzed by Thorndike, *History of Magic and Experimental Science*, 1:200ff.

106. *NH* 28.3.11. Cf. Morton Smith, "The Origin and History of the Transfiguration Story," *Union Seminary Quarterly Review* 36.1 (1980): 39-44. See also Hopfner, "Mageia," pp. 305, 321, 373.

107. K. J. Dover, *Theocritus* (London: Macmillan, 1971), pp. 9ff.; also Pindar *Olympic Odes* 1.73ff: "He drew near unto the foaming sea, and alone in the darkness called aloud [for Poseidon]"; Tibullus 1.8.17: "Has some old woman bewitched you with her spells, or with blanching herbs in the silent night hours?" E.T., F. W. Cornish, Loeb, 217–218.; Ovid *Metamorphoses* 7.180ff.: O Night, faithful preserver of mysteries. ... Hecate, who knowest our undertakings and comest to the aid of the spells and arts of magicians: and thou, O Earth, who dost provide the magicians with thy potent herbs ... be with me now," E.T., F. J. Miller, Loeb, vol. 1.

108. Philostratus *Vita* 2.295 E.T., F. C. Conybeare, Loeb.

109. See Philostratus *Life* 8.7; Horace *Epode* 5.5. In *Philopseudes* 14 (*Lover of Lies*) Lucian writes about a "Hyperborean" magician who through a rite performed about midnight brings up Hecate and pulls down the moon.

110. *Apol.* 47. Butler, *Apologia and Florida*, p. 84.

111. Tertullian *Ad uxorem* 2.4, *ANF* 4.46.

112. Tertullian *Ad uxorem* 2.5, *ANF* 4.47.

113. Tertullian *Apol.* 7 and 8.

114. *Didache* 9.5, Hippolytus, *The Apostolic Tradition* 23.13.

115. Origen *Contra Celsum* 1.7, *ANF* 4.399.

116. Ibid.

117. Tertullian *De Praescriptione haereticorum* 41.

118. Jean Daillé in J. N. D. Kelly, *Early Christian Creeds* (London: Longmans, 1960), p. 168. See also F. X. Funk, "Das Alter der Arkandisziplin," in *Kirchengeschictliche Abhandlungen und Untersuchugen*, 3 (1907):42-52; H. Clasen, "Die Arkandisziplin in der alten Kirche" (Ph.D. dissertation, University of Heidelberg, 1956); J. Leipoldt, "Arkandisziplin," *RGG³*, 1 (1957):606-7; Douglas Powell, "Arkandisziplin," *Theologische Realencyclopaedie*, ed. T. Klauser (Stuttgart: Hiersemann, 1957), 1:667-76.

119. See, however, Hippolytus *The Apostolic Tradition* 23.13-14. "And we have delivered to you briefly these things concerning Baptism and the Oblation because you have already been instructed concerning the resurrection of the flesh and the rest according to the Scriptures. But if there is any other matter which ought to be told, let the bishop impart it secretly to those who are communicated. He shall not tell this to any but the faithful and only after they have just been communicated. This is the white stone of which John said that there is a new name written under it which no man knows except him who receives (the stone)"; Dix, *The Apostolic Tradition*, pp. 42-43.

120. Smith, *Jesus the Magician*, p. 53. See E. von Dobschütz, "Charms and Amulets," in *Encyclopedia of Religion and Ethics*, ed. James Hastings (New York: Scribners, 1926), 3.414.

121. Cf. Smith, *Jesus the Magician*, pp. 75ff; Ramsey MacMullen, *Enemies of the Roman Order* (Cambridge: Harvard University Press, 1966), pp. 95-127; Hopfner, "Mageia," pp. 348ff.

122. See Suetonius *Lives of the Twelve Caesars Augustus* 31, *Tiberius* 36, *Vitellius* 14; for further references see Kleinfeller, "Magia" in Pauly, Wissowa, and Kroll, *Realencyclopädie*, 396-98.

123. E. H. Warmington, *Remains of Old Latin*, Loeb (Cambridge: Harvard University Press, 1961), 3:474-5.

124. Apuleius *Apol.* 47; Virgil *Ecl.* 8.99; Pliny *NH* 28.18; Tibullus, 1.8 17-22.

125. MacMullen, *Enemies of the Roman Order*, p. 324; p. 124 states: "It was a capital crime to commit magic if that is the right way to put it," and he then quotes Apuleius, *Apol.* 47—but Apuleius here clearly refers to harmful magic and does not have in mind a law forbidding magic per se. It may be significant that Apuleius often refers to magic as *magica maleficia* (*Apol.* 9, 42, 61, 63). He seems to believe that what really makes a magical art illicit and harmful is the *maleficium*, the evil deed, the injury done to others. And, if Thorndike is right the magistrate hearing his case may have taken a similar view. The accusers of Apuleius charged that a woman had an epileptic seizure because he bewitched her, and the magistrate asked whether the woman died or what good did her seizure do to Apuleius. "This is significant as hinting that Roman law did not condemn a man for magic unless he were proved to have committed some crime or made some unjust gain thereby." Thorndike, *History of Magic and Experimental Science*, 1:235. Also see Hopfner, "*Mageia*," p. 385.

126. See *Corpus Iuris Civilis*, E.T., S. P. Scott (Cincinnati: Central Trust Co. 1973), 1:326-327.

127. Marcianus 48.8.3; A milder punishment is provided for the administration of love philters by the *Sentences of Paulus* 5.23.14.

128. *Cod. Just.* 9.18.3-4.

129. Ibid., 9.18.5–7.

130. Mark 11:13ff., Acts 5.

131. Acts 13:6-12.

132. 1. Cor. 5:3-5, and 1 Tim. 1:19-20.

133. Acts 19:19.

134. See, however, Morton Smith, "Pauline Worship as Seen by Pagans,"
Harvard Theological Review 73 (1980):241-49.

Pagan Criticism of Christian Theology and Ethics

M OST PAGAN CRIITCS of Christianity, despite their deep-seated
antipathy toward Christians, had had little direct contact
with either them or their religion. It is not surprising, therefore, that
their views on Christianity were either inaccurate or false. No pagan
made a serious effort to study Christian teachings or to observe
Christians in action until the end of the second century. Then, two
pagan scholars almost simultaneously turned a critical yet objective
eye toward Christianity. They have left us valuable clues as to how
educated and unbiased pagans may have regarded the new religion.
One was the medical doctor Galen, whose references to Christians,
although few, are important to us mainly because of their objectivity.
The other was Celsus, who wrote the first important scholarly criticism of Christianity.

Galen

Galen was born around 129 in Pergamum, Asia Minor. Pergamum
was a great cosmopolitan city that had been at one time the capital of
one of the successor states of Alexander's empire. The library of
Pergamum was nearly as famous as that of Alexandria, and it was
here that the new writing material, parchment, was developed. Pergamum was bequeathed by its last king to Rome and was annexed
between 133-129 B.C. as the province of Asia. Thus, by the time of
Galen's birth the city had already been part of the Roman empire for
two and a half centuries. Pergamum was the seat of one of the seven
churches mentioned in Rev. 1:11, and some citizens still held to the
doctrine of the Nicolaitans. Furthermore, the "throne of Satan" was
supposedly located there, perhaps a reference to the magnificent altar

of Zeus, the outstanding architectural sight of the city.[1] Clearly Christians lived in Galen's native city. He may even have known some as a child, although if so they left no profound impression on him.

At his father's urging, the seventeen-year-old Galen enrolled as a student in the Asklepieion, the medical school of Pergamum. The school was primarily a shrine to the healing god Asklepios, from whom it took its name. According to Greek mythology, the father of Asklepios was Apollo, and it was Apollo himself who taught Asklepios the art of healing. So skilled did Asklepios become in healing and in the administration of drugs—he could supposedly even raise the dead—that he was elevated to godhood by Zeus. He became the patron god of Greek physicians, and whenever they failed in the treatment of the sick, they held out the hope of a miraculous healing at his nearby temple. It was believed that Asklepios imparted his healing powers to those who sought his help through the medium of their dreams as they slept in his temple. The patients were required to lie down overnight in a sacred hall and wait for the appearance of the god, who sometimes appeared in human guise and at other times in that of a serpent.[2] The healing was done in several ways, either through direct intervention, by the god appearing in the form of a young man, or through the placement of a drug on the wound, or through the use of a serpent, which touched the sick part of the body with its tongue so making it sound again. The records contain many stories of miraculous healings. Given the essentially religious orientation of Greek medicine, it is quite understandable that Galen acquired a deep sensitivity toward religious matters.[3]

Galen's religious inclinations were no hindrance to his medical research, which today appears brutal and repulsive. Although Galen never used human specimens, he practiced vivisection on a host of animals. By chopping the spinal cords of live animals piece by piece he was able to observe how the hapless creatures progressively lost their powers of feeling and movement. When he severed their optic nerves he noted that the animals could no longer see. He opened their skulls to examine their brains, but he advised others not to use an ape for this experiment so as to "avoid the unpleasant expression" on its face, which perhaps appeared too human even for Galen.[4] He made some important medical discoveries through these experiments. Around 158 he was appointed physician to the gladiators of Pergamum, and he was now able to extend his learning even further. Many of the men whom he was called on to treat were badly wounded. Far from flinching at the sight of mangled bodies, Galen welcomed the opportunity to study the functions of the human heart and intestines and the working of the human anatomy in general.

For Galen this was more than technical research. In the complex order of the body and the specialized functions of its organs Galen sought and found God. He believed that the body was filled with spirits that controlled its activity; hence to him the study of anatomy was a demonstration of divine truth and a proof of the existence of God. In his own mind, Galen established a close connection between experimentation and religion. He had no respect for religions that were based on faith alone, because in his opinion faith was a poor substitute for experienced truth. It was on this point that Galen criticized both Judaism and Christianity. There are four references to Christians in Galen's writings.

> One might more easily teach novelties to the followers of Moses and Christ than to the physicians and philosophers who cling fast to their schools.
>
> .   .   .
>
> In order that one should not at the very beginning, as if one had come into the school of Moses and Christ, hear talk of undemonstrated laws, and that where it is least appropriate.
>
> .   .   .
>
> If I had in mind people who taught their pupils in the same way as the followers of Moses and Christ teach theirs—for they order them to accept everything on faith—I should not have given you a definition.
>
> .   .   .
>
> Most people are unable to follow any demonstrative argument con-secutively; hence they need parables, and benefit from them [Galen understood by parables tales of rewards and punishments in a future life] just as now we see the people called Christians drawing their faith from parable (and miracles), and yet some acting in the same way (as those who philosophize). For their contempt of death (and of its sequel) is patent to us every day, and likewise their restraint in cohabitation. For they include not only men but also women who refrain from cohabiting all through their lives; and they also number individuals who, in self-discipline and self-control in matters of food and drink, and in their keen pursuit of justice, have attained a pitch not inferior to that of genuine philosophers.[5]

Galen mentioned Jews in two more passages. In a quotation pre-served in Arabic he compared medical doctors who practiced without scientific training to Moses, who promulgated laws and wrote his books without proofs, simply saying, "God commanded, God spoke!" In his treatise *de usu partium* Galen criticized the Mosaic cosmogony and rejected its reliance on divine miracles.[6] Galen does not make a radical distinction between Jews and Christians in these texts, which is somewhat confusing because by the end of the second century the two movements had completely separated. They both accepted revelation as the foundation of their faith, however, and this is what interested Galen. When he spoke about schools of Jews and Christians he seems to have had in mind the philosophical schools that flourished in considerable numbers in the second century. Thus he takes Judaism and Christianity to be two closely related philosophies that demanded of their followers a certain ethical standard of living. Philosophy during the Antonine age had given up abstract speculation to a large extent, and had turned to the cultivation of a moral life. Abstract speculation was no longer congenial to the spirit of the second century, when the need was for practical guidance amid the vicissitudes of life and the philosopher was expected to be a "physician of souls".[7] Since Christianity was at this time still more a way of life than a set of doctrines, it was natural for Galen to perceive Christians as "acting in the same way" as philosophers, conducting their lives according to the principles of their philosophy.

Galen was far from alone in this perception. Indeed, many Christian intellectuals wished to present Christianity exactly as Galen understood it, namely as a philosophical school. These were the Christian apologists who attempted to explain Christianity to persons of Greco-Roman education and background by making use of the intellectual resources of the Greco-Roman world.[8] They could easily do this because they themselves were wholly immersed in Hellenistic civilization. Such a rapprochement with Greeks and Romans appeared necessary to these Christians because they had realistically resigned themselves to the likelihood that the end of the world and the *parousia* would not occur as soon as the Christians of previous generations had anticipated. Also, after the second Jewish revolt in 135, Christians could not and would not seek protection under the umbrella of Judaism. The fledgling church had to face a hostile world alone. Many Christians—although not all—wanted regulation of the relationship between church and state. For these Christians it appeared that if only they could explain Christianity in contemporary philosophical terms then pagans would understand, and would no longer view the church as a threat to society.

One of the most important of the Christian apologists was Justin Martyr.[9] According to his own account, it was not until after he had joined various philosophical schools, such as the Peripatetics, Stoics, Pythagoreans, and Platonists, and had become disillusioned with all of them, that Justin was introduced to Christianity and accepted it as the true philosophy. Thus it was a quest for philosophical truth that led Justin to Christianity, and he understood Christianity to be a philosophical system comparable and superior to other contemporary philosophies.[10] This was a bold claim, considering the many eloquent and wonderful minds that Stoicism, Platonism, and the other systems produced. Justin supported his claim by opening his own philosophical school in Rome, where he taught Christianity as other philosophers taught their own systems, and by writing many competent works in its defense. In the end his philosophy was put to the supreme test; when ordered to sacrifice to the gods of the state, he steadfastly refused and so became one of Christianity's earliest martyrs. Another apologist, Athenagoras, in his plea for fair treatment of Christians, written around 177, also urged that they be judged by the standards applied to any group of philosophers.[11] Yet another, Melito, the bishop of Sardis, addressed an *Apology* to Marcus Aurelius in which he touched on essentially the same theme. Tracing the development of Christianity, he asserted: "Our philosophy formerly flourished among the barbarians; but having sprung up among the nations under thy rule, during the great reign of thy ancestor Augustus, it became to thine empire especially a blessing of auspicious omen. . . ." Therefore, he concluded, if the emperor wished to continue to rule successfully he must guard the Christian philosophy, "that philosophy which thy ancestors also honored along with the other religions."[12] The list of apologists could be extended, but the point is already clear: these Christians wished the church to be regarded in the same light as any other philosophical movement.

Galen did regard the church in this light, thus marking a major change in the pagan attitude toward Christianity. For Galen, Christians were neither dangerous conspirators nor abominable cannibals, but they were rather adherents of a philosophical school. As a result, Galen (although not the general public) accorded Christianity a certain amount of respectability, and Christians became socially acceptable. But Galen was not happy with the Christian philosophy. It appeared to him to lack a rational basis, even though Christians adhered to a mode of living peculiar to them. For the scientist and scholar, used to demonstrating truth and rejecting hearsay evidence, this acceptance of everything on faith seemed childish and primitive. Lucian expressed this same bias when he sneered that Christians received their doctrines "without any definite evidence," as did Marcus Aurelius when he contrasted the "reasoned and dignified decision" of a Stoic with the "obstinate opposition" of a Christian.[13] Celsus also held the same bias, evident in his comment that Christians "Do not ask questions, only believe!"[14]

Nevertheless, despite this criticism Galen was a sympathetic observer of Christianity. Although he criticized the Christians' lack of philosophical training, he appreciated their moral virtues. He praised their contempt of death, their acceptance of physical deprivation, and their continual pursuit of justice. According to Galen, in spite of their shortcomings Christians acted like philosophers. How did Galen come by his opinion of Christians? We do not know. It is possible that in his later years he had opportunities to observe Christians living their faith. In 161 he moved to Rome where he built a successful medical practice and soon became the personal physician of Marcus Aurelius. In 165 Justin suffered martyrdom in Rome. Did Galen hear about it? Perhaps. In 166 Galen briefly returned to Pergamum, but in 169 he again returned to Rome. In 177 a violent persecution of Christians broke out in southern Gaul.[15] Did Galen hear about this? Again, we cannot be sure. What does seem clear is that in some way or another he must have had access to reliable information to have been able to write so factually about the Christians.

Galen died some time before the end of the second century. His fame survived him, however, and because it did, Galen played an indirect role in the subsequent development of Christianity. It appears that some Christians, heeding Galen's objections, undertook the formulation of a "scientific" theology.[16] During the episcopate of Victor (189-198), a Christian called Theodotus came from Byzantium to Rome and began to teach that Christ was a mere man who only received the Holy Spirit at the moment of his baptism. Although he was excommunicated by Victor, Theodotus had numerous followers, and with them he founded a schismatic sect.[17] *The Little Labyrinth*, a book written against the Theodotians[18] by an anonymous author, from which a few sentences were preserved by Eusebius, sheds some light on them. One section in particular is illuminating:

"They [the Theodotians] have treated the Divine Scriptures reck-
lessly and without fear. They have set aside the rule of ancient faith;
and Christ they have not known. They do not endeavor to learn what
the Divine Scriptures declare, but strive laboriously after any form of
syllogism which may be devised to sustain their impiety. And if
anyone brings before them a passage of Divine Scripture, they see
whether a conjunctive or disjunctive form of syllogism can be made
from it. And, as being of the earth and speaking of the earth, and as
ignorant of him who cometh from above, they forsake the holy writings of God to devote themselves to geometry. Euclid is laboriously
measured by some of them; and Aristotle and Theophrastus are
admired; and Galen, perhaps, by some, is even worshipped . . . they
have laid their hands boldly upon the divine Scriptures, alleging that
they have corrected them . . . either they do not believe that the
Divine Scriptures were spoken by the Holy Spirit, and thus are unbe-
lievers, or else they think themselves wiser than the Holy Spirit, and
in that case what else are they than demoniacs? . . . For they did not
receive such Scriptures from their instructors, nor can they produce
any copies from which they were transcribed. But some of them have
not thought it worthwhile to corrupt them, but simply deny the law
and the prophets, and thus through their lawless and impious
teaching under pretense of grace, have sunk to the lowest depth of
perdition.[19]

As we see, these heretics preferred the dialectic method of theology, promoted an adoptionist Christology, applied textual criticism
to the scriptures, and based their exegesis and interpretation on
philosophical concepts. A modern Christian, to whom all of this is
likely to seem perfectly proper, may well ask why these heretics were
considered to be so very bad. The answer is that they were generations ahead of their time. The reconciliation between theology and
philosophy would be long in coming. Around the year 200, a few
years after the excommunication of Theodotus, the vigorous Carthaginian lawyer Tertullian (160-ca. 220) wrote his treatise *On the
Prescription of Heretics*. In launching this attack on heresy, Tertullian had mostly Gnostics in mind but, it is not difficult to apply some
of his arguments to the Theodotians too. Tertullian believed that
only the original tenets of Christianity were true, and that innovations were heresies.[20] According to him, Christians should avoid
philosophy, because it led nowhere, and should rely instead on faith.
"What has Jerusalem to do with Athens, the Church with the
Academy, the Christian with the Heretic. Our principles come from
the Porch of Solomon, who had himself taught that the Lord is to be
sought in simplicity of heart. I have no use for a Stoic or a Platonic or a

dialectic Christianity. After Jesus Christ we have no need of speculation, after the Gospel no need of research. When we come to believe
we have no desire to believe anything else; for we begin by believing
that there is nothing else which we have to believe." Tertullian did
not support idle philosophical speculations.[21] It was because of such
"ever restless speculation" that Bishop Eleutherus (the successor of
Victor) excommunicated Marcion and Valentinus.

So Tertullian fulminated against heretics. No doubt many of the
Christians whom he castigated would be considered church members in good standing today, but Tertullian sensed that the church
was seeking a peaceful coexistence with, and a place in, Greco-
Roman society. For him this meant an abandonment of primitive
Christian values. He began to look toward the faction in which the
memory of early Christianity was most assiduously cultivated,
namely Montanism. More and more in his writings Tertullian advocated and approved of Montanist principles, he extolled martyrdom
as the highest and most glorious deed, he urged Christians to abstain
from taking part in the secular life and instead to wait for "the fast
approaching advent of our Lord," the second coming.[22] By 207 he was
openly a Montanist, repudiating military service and attacking the
laxity of the church and the evolution of new practices. Tertullian
was convinced that his fight was for the truth; indeed the word
veritas appears time after time in his polemics against heretics and
pagans, people who in his judgment did not possess the truth. But
Tertullian's *veritas* was also judged heresy by the church, and his
stubborn refusal to adjust his faith to the demands of the times was a
rather annoying anachronism. During Tertullian's lifetime Clement
(died ca. 215) used and adopted Greek philosophy in the pursuit of
theology, and when his successor, Origen (died ca. 253-4), took over
the Catechetical School not even the best educated pagan could call
Christian philosophy substandard.

Celsus

Celsus, our other pagan critic, launched a systematic attack on
Christianity in a book called *True Word*, written around 177-180.
Although this book has since been lost, we have a reply to it entitled
Against Celsus, written some seventy years later by Origen. Origen
attempted to refute the charges made by Celsus point by point. In the
process he copied so many quotations from *True Word* that we can

reconstruct a substantial part of the book. And in fact, we even get a good idea about the character and personality of Celsus. He was a man who relied not on rumors and hearsay evidence but on personal observation and careful study. Because he had read both the Old and the New Testaments and was familiar with Jewish and Christian literature, he knew the difference between Gnostic and orthodox theologies,[23] and his book is on the whole free of mistakes and misconceptions, excepting those that reflect the generally held superstitions of the second century. It contains none of the popular pagan antagonism against Christians and makes no unsubstantiated charges. Moreover, it does not reject everything that Christianity teaches. Celsus accepted the Logos doctrine, for example, and on occasion he even had a word of praise for the Christians, especially when he talked about their ethics. But the Christian religion as a whole was nonsense to him. Celsus was first and foremost a Roman patriot who was worried that Christians represented a disruptive force in Roman society. Therefore, he staunchly defended the traditional values of Rome against the encroaching innovations of Christianity.[24]

In general, Celsus characterized Christianity as an inadequate philosophical-theological system, and Christians as a community of intellectually inferior people. He often broadened his attack on Christians to include Jews, and in the first part of his book he used the character of a Jew to criticize Christians and those Jews whom Jesus deluded into giving up their old laws.[25] Celsus believed that the Jews were Egyptians and runaway slaves who had escaped from Egypt and never did anything important.[26] He could not understand why they worshipped heaven and the angels in it, but rejected the sun, the moon, and the stars, which he saw as the most sacred and powerful parts of heaven. How could the whole be divine and not its parts? Celsus also attacked the Christian notion of the devil because it implied a division of the kingdom of God into two opposing camps.[27] He argued that Jews were addicted to sorcery, taught to them by Moses, but at least they had some tradition. Jews were deceived by the sorcery of Moses, and Christianity came from Judaism, and yet, Celsus maintained, Jews and Christians quarreled with one another over the shadow of an ass.[28]

The Old Testament, in Celsus's opinion, was full of very stupid fables. He rejected its accounts of the creation of the world and the origin of man, and he characterized its cosmogony as silly. Celsus thought the story about the creation and the Garden of Eden portrayed God as a weakling. He maintained that the portrayal of God in the Old Testament was blasphemously anthropomorphic; especially when the book of Genesis went so far as to say that, like a worn-out workman, God needed rest on the seventh day. God does not have human characteristics, Celsus declared, and thus, God could not make man after his image. Celsus acknowledged that many reasonable Jews and Christians , unable to accept the notion that man was fashioned by the hand of God, tried somehow to allegorize the biblical story. But he contended that the Bible was incapable of being interpreted allegorically.[29]

Furthermore he found some of the Old Testament stories blatantly offensive. He thought the story about Lot and his daughters, for instance, a greater abomination than the Thyestian sins. Scarcely more edifying was the hatred of Esau and Jacob, brothers selling their brother, the story of a deceived father, or the begetting of children by very old people.[30] Celsus also contended that the inconsistencies in the Old Testament posed insoluable problems. How could God create, and then find fault with his creation? Why could he not even gain the obedience of the man to whom he had given form and life? How could he allow evil in the world?[31] To cap his criticism of the Old Testament, Celsus indignantly contended that some of its themes were borrowed from Greek philosophers, who, incidentally, had expressed them better. For example, the story of the ark and the flood was a version of the story of Deukalion, the story of Sodom and Gomorrha was taken by Moses from the story of Phaethon, and Moses also corrupted the story of the sons of Aloeus when he wrote the account of the tower of Babel.[32]

As we would expect, the New Testament also received Celsus's unsparing scrutiny. He was especially harsh in his treatment of the life and teachings of Jesus. To begin with, he asserted that the Jewish prophets did not explicitly foretell the coming of Jesus, and Celsus believed thousands of other Jews had attained greater success at prophesying than had Jesus.[33] Furthermore, Celsus pointed out that the origins of Jesus remained uncertain; the story of the virgin birth was fabricated, Celsus claimed, by Jesus; in fact, he came from a poor country, and his mother earned her living by spinning. He hired himself out as far as Egypt and learned magic there. After his return to Palestine he gave himself out as a god. How could one believe the story of the virgin birth? Celsus asked; did God have intercourse with

Mary because she was so beautiful? This was unlikely, because no divine power helped her when the carpenter sent her away.[34]

Celsus argued that the other claims for the divinity of Jesus was equally unsubstantiated. He believed that these claims were disproved by the fact that Jesus had not been helped by his Father, nor was he able to help himself. Furthermore, if the story of Herod and the killing of the babies was true, why then did Jesus not become king when he grew up? Why did he have to be taken to Egypt to escape Herod? God could have saved him.[35] According to the Gospel accounts Jesus had a distinguished genealogy, but if this was true, then why was he nothing more than a lowly carpenter? It was more likely, Celsus wrote, that he was the son of the Egyptian magician, Panthera.[36] In any case, Jesus had nothing of the divine about him. He was born with a mortal body and was a mere man. Nor was he a very good man. In fact, Celsus claimed "of such a character as the truth itself makes obvious and as reason shows," a "pestilent fellow" who told great lies and was guilty of other profane acts, which are left unspecified in Origen's account. At the beginning of his ministry Jesus collected around him a group of tax collectors and boatmen, wicked men, from the lowest level of society. With his dubious followers Jesus went from place to place, hiding and making a living as best he could.[37]

Celsus carried his attack even further; he accused Jesus of being a wicked sorcerer.[38] It is known, he said, that Jesus performed miracles, and although some of these miracles—for example, a few of the cures, the resurrections, and the feeding of many people—may have been genuine, most were illusions of the kind commonly concocted by other Egyptian magicians and sorcerers. In his sermons Jesus frequently resorted to wailings, abuses, and empty threats such as "Woe unto you. . . ." Yet as long as he lived he was unable to win anyone over to his beliefs, and when he was to be punished, like a true coward he ran away and hid most disgracefully. Ultimately he was betrayed by his own disciples and condemned to death by the Jews as an insulting offender.[39] When he was crucified, his "Father" did not help him nor could he help himself. Then his disciples, wishing to perpetuate after his death the deception that he had practiced during his lifetime, invented the story that he had known of his fate beforehand and had foretold every event that would befall him. Even if the story were true, Celsus argued, it would prove nothing. After all, what robber and murderer could not predict the punishment that awaits him if he is caught? And were the prediction of such a criminal to be fulfilled, would it make any sense to declare him a god? Celsus argued further that if Jesus really did have divine power, he should have demonstrated it to those who had treated him spitefully, by suddenly disappearing from the cross, for example. But he did not do this, and instead he died as a mortal man. The body that was broken on the cross was not the body of a god, and the blood that flowed from its side was not the blood of a god.[40]

The story of the Resurrection of Jesus was another cruel lie, Celsus claimed. Only a hysterical female saw this event, and perhaps one other person, and he believed they had either dreamt it, had an hallucination, or had simply tried to impress others.[41] After the Resurrection, instead of presenting himself to the multitude, Jesus withdrew into concealment, he made only occasional and fleeting appearances in the guise of some weird phantom and produced only a mental impression of his wounds. It was impossible for Jesus to have risen from the dead for God would not have received back a spirit that had been stained by contact with the body. To Celsus it was clear that death for Jesus had been final. And he could not understand why the Christians worshipped a dead man as immortal.[42]

The elements of Christian faith for which Celsus reserved his sharpest criticism were the doctrines of Incarnation and the Resurrection. He understood the Incarnation to mean that God or the Son of God had come down to earth, but he could not see the purpose of such a descent. Perhaps God wanted to learn what was going on among men, or, if he already knew, planned in some way to correct them. But, why was it only after so many years that God decided to involve himself in human affairs? Had he not cared about men before? In Celsus's opinion, Christians insulted God when they asserted that through Incarnation he took on human attributes. For God this would have meant a change from good to evil, from beauty to shame, from happiness to misfortune. How could he possibly have undergone such a change? Demons might come down to earth, but God and his Son would not.[43]

Celsus argued further that even if we assumed that Jesus was some sort of angel, we would still encounter several difficulties. At his conception his mother had to be defended by an angel, and at his Resurrection angels moved the stone from his tomb; in short, the Son of God needed help![44] Then, too, God breathed his spirit into Mary's womb, even though he already knew how to make men, and he could easily have furnished a body for Jesus. Furthermore, if Jesus was a divine spirit, his body should have been beautiful, instead he was small and ugly.[45] Thus, Celsus rejected the whole idea of Incarnation. He did not understand why, if God had wanted to save the human race from evil, he did not send his spirit over the entire world, rather than to an out-of-the-way spot to be received by, of all people, the Jews. Moreover, Celsus believed the doctrine of Incarnation to be blasphemous, as it implied that the things that had happened to Jesus had happened to God. Christians called Jesus the Son of God, Celsus argued, in order to exalt Jesus and not to pay special reverence to God.[46]

Celsus dismissed the doctrine of the Resurrection as a misunderstanding about reincarnation.[47] Christians saw the Last Judgment as a sort of universal conflagration, when God, like a cook, would roast all of mankind except the Christians, who would be saved. Those who happened to be dead at this time would be raised and would receive the body that they had before. This doctrine repulsed Celsus, and he pointed out that there was even opposition to it among Jews and Christians. Bodies once decayed could never return to their original condition, and Celsus thought that the Christian explanation that "anything is possible to God" was a lame one. God would never want to do such an unreasonable thing; the soul may have everlasting life but corpses, as Heraclitus said, "ought to be thrown away as worse than dung." Furthermore, Celsus charged Christians with being inconsistent. On the one hand, they hoped for the Resurrection, as if there were nothing more precious than the body, yet on the other hand they believed in the eternal punishment of the body as if it had no value. Surely, Celsus concluded, people who believed such things were destitute of reason.[48]

It did not surprise Celsus, therefore, that Christianity appealed mainly to the uneducated. He argued that intelligent persons were driven away by it, and only the stupid and common folk were attracted to it. Furthermore the Christians were narrowminded; they rejected the advice of educated, wise, or sensible people, and even considered such persons as evil. "Wisdom in this life is evil, but foolishness is good" was a Christian principle, he wrote. They substituted faith for wisdom, and they offered no rational arguments to support their claim that Jesus was the Son of God. Jesus had been arrested, disgraced, and punished; yet the Christians merely cited these things as all the more reason to believe in him. These arguments failed to impress intelligent persons, and so the Christians sought out the sinner, the derelict, and the child.[49] But would God send his son to sinners and not to those without sin? Why did Christians invite cheaters, thieves, burglars, poisoners, and grave robbers to their services when all other mystery religions invited only those who had purified themselves?[50] Celsus maintained that, in their ignorance, Christians misunderstood the truth expounded by philosophers, such as Plato, and they "vulgarly discuss fundamental principles and make arrogant pronouncements about matters of which they know nothing."[51] When they wished to display their learning they dared not go into the company of intelligent men, but instead they showed off by going to market places, into crowds of slaves, and amongst companies of fools.[52] Celsus even accused Christians of trying to destroy families and upset the social structure by pitting children against their parents and teachers. He wrote:

> We see, indeed, in private houses workers in wool and leather, and fullers, and persons of the most uninstructed and rustic character, not venturing to utter a word in the presence of their elders and wiser masters; but when they get hold of the children privately, and certain women as ignorant as themselves, they pour forth wonderful statements, to the effect that they ought not give heed to their father and to their teachers, but should obey them; that the former are foolish and stupid, and neither know nor can perform anything that is really good, being preoccupied with empty trifles; that they alone know how men ought to live, and that, if the children obey them, they will both be happy themselves, and will make their homes happy also and while thus speaking, if they see one of the instructors of youth approaching, or one of the more intelligent class, or even the father himself, the more timid among them become afraid, while the more forward incite the children to throw off the yoke, whispering that in the presence of father and teachers they neither will nor can explain to them any good thing, seeing they turn away with aversion from the silliness and stupidity of such persons as being altogether corrupt, and far advanced in wickedness, and such as would inflict punishment upon them; but that if they wish to avail themselves of their aid they must leave their fathers and their instructors, and go with the women and their playfellows to the women's apartments, or to the leather shop, or to the fuller's shop, that they may attain to perfection;—and by words like these they gain them over.[53]

How did Christians persuade people to join them? Celsus charged that their methods of persuasion included inventing terrors and babbling about God in an impious and impure way in an attempt to excite the amazement of uneducated people. Some of the wandering false prophets of Christianity proclaimed doom and salvation; Celsus claimed to have heard their wild stories himself and upon examination to have found them to be lies. These prophets also practiced sorcery, and he had even seen Christian elders with books containing barbaric names of demons and magical formulas, which also had a powerful effect on the uneducated. Celsus recognized that Christians had a certain mystical power, but he claimed they gained this power by pronouncing the names of certain demons and by reciting magical incantations.[54] Celsus likened Christian teachers to quacks who turn their patients away from expert physicians because they fear that competent medical treatment would expose their own inadequacy. These teachers led wicked men away and persuaded them to despise and shun good men, on the grounds that by so doing they would improve themselves.[55]

Celsus found many failings in Christianity, and so he was understandably outraged at the criticism that Christians voiced against pagan religion, and complained bitterly about the inconsistencies in these criticisms. Although they ridiculed the worship of Zeus because his tomb was displayed in Crete, they themselves worshipped one who had supposedly risen from the dead. They honored the prophets of the Old Testament, but despised other prophets, like the priestesses of Dodona or Apollo. They objected to the pagans' worship of other gods, while they themselves worshipped a man who lived only recently, and they then considered this to be consistent with monotheism.[56] Celsus suggested other more likely candidates for them to choose from if they insisted on worshipping a man, such as Daniel or Jonah from the Old Testament, and Epictetus or Orpheus from ancient Greece.[57]

Christians claimed that pagan gods, such as Zeus and Apollo, could take no vengeance when they blasphemed against them or even hit their statues. Celsus countered that the gods did indeed take vengeance upon the Christians, and he pointed to the persecutions as evidence of this. The gods whom the Christians despised continued to crucify them while their Son of God made no effort to help them. The Christians replied to this accusation with the words: "This is the will of God." But Celsus wrote that the persecutions could also be the will of the pagan gods, and he once again noted the apparent powerlessness of the Christian God. This God had not helped the

Jews, who had even lost their homeland, and neither had he helped the Christians, who were being condemned to death.[58] Celsus next turned to the Christian refusal to believe in temples, altars, or images because such objects were fashioned out of wood, bronze, or gold and, therefore, could not be gods. Celsus maintained that this was an absurd argument, since everyone realized that such works were simply votive offerings and images of gods. Furthermore, if the Christians said that these were false likenesses of God, then, Celsus argued, they will have contradicted themselves, as they had already said that God made man in his own image. Celsus thought there was no reason for Christians to refuse to sacrifice to idols if, as they maintained, such idols had no powers. But, he went on, if the idols were demons of some sort then their sacrifice would also be justified, since demons belonged to God. Christians refused to take part in public festivals because they did not wish to feast with demons; but, Celsus wrote, they should then also abstain from the food of all animals, because all food, wine, fruit, water, and even the air we breathe is under the administration of some demon.[59]

Celsus found other faults of a more general nature in Christianity. As a new religion, he said, it lacked the approval of antiquity. Thus, Christians had no authority for their doctrines.[60] Furthermore, they corrupted ancient tradition by taking from it certain ideas and misinterpreting them.[61] He was appalled by the Christians' lack of unity; the multitude of quarrelsome sects, which slandered each other, refused to make concessions to one another, and more often than not detested each other.[62] Together with the Jews, they were like "a cluster of bats or ants coming out of a nest, as frogs holding council around a marsh or worms assembling in some filthy corner, disagreeing with one another about which of them are the worse sinners."[63] The Christians had exaggerated ideas about themselves, and they acted as if God had abandoned the heavens and the world for their sake, and would only communicate with them. In point of fact, Celsus thought they were a secret society that even held its meetings in secret for fear of penalty.[64] "They wall themselves off and break away from the rest of mankind";[65] and they refused to set up temples, images, and altars; a sure sign, for Celsus, of an obscure and secret society. He thought them "boorish and unclean people, destitute of reason and suffering from the disease of sedition." They had no love for life and insisted on offering their bodies for torture and crucifixion. Celsus wished they would all commit suicide, making sure not to leave any of their descendants behind them, thus eradicating their race from the face of the earth.[66]

Finally Celsus called on Christians to abandon some of their more radical views and to return to useful membership in the society of which they were a part. He asked them to give due reverence to "demons, rulers and emperors"; to avoid provoking the anger of the emperor, which always resulted in their suffering and death; to take an oath to be loyal to the emperor; and to swear to his genius. Celsus said that it was only through the emperor that they would receive anything good in this life. Whereas, if everybody followed the Christian example of opposition to the emperor, anarchy would ensue and everything would be destroyed, Christianity included. Celsus tried to persuade Christians to accept public office in their country, to help preserve its laws and piety, to give the emperor their full support and, if need be, even to become soldiers.[67]

Such, then, were the main thrusts of the attack by Celsus on Christianity. Origen may have deleted the most damaging parts, but even in its mutilated form *True Word* is an excellent source on the attitude of educated pagans toward the Christian phenomenon.[68] Not everything appeared to be wrong with Christianity. Celsus even praised the Christians' view of the Logos as the Son of God, and he only mildly concealed his approval of the Christian teaching that God is spirit.[69] Like Galen, he paid unwilling tribute to the Christians' constancy in danger, even in the face of death.[70] On the whole, however, Christianity seemed to him an inferior philosophy, something that was borrowed by them from the Greeks and corrupted in the process. For him the old doctrine of the ancients was the "true doctrine," and the Christians were merely a deterioration and degeneration from it. Their teachings were thus corrupt and their social behavior bad. Consequently, Celsus saw the whole movement as a destructive force. Carl Andresen has argued that the statement by Celsus that "If all men wanted to be Christians, the Christians would no longer want them," shows that Celsus considered Christianity a disease slowly eating away the body without which it could not exist.[71] In the last analysis Christianity represented a political threat for the Roman empire, and it is this concern for his country that dominates the last pages of Celsus's attack.

It is perhaps for this reason that Celsus wasted very little space on the charges of immorality, promiscuous behavior, or cannibalism.

This is all the more remarkable because Fronto's diatribes against the Christians appeared only a few years before *True Word*, and *Octavius* by Minucius Felix only a few years later. Unless Origen omitted the sections dealing with such charges, we must assume that Celsus refused to stoop to the level of cheap criticism. He may have thought that, regardless of how faulty their theology, Christians were still Romans, whose cooperation with the empire was essential and desirable.

Some of the charges made by Celsus, such as that Christians were afraid of educated classes, were no longer valid when Origen wrote his reply. Indeed this particular charge may not have been completely true even in the time of Celsus either. Celsus talked about "the more reasonable Jews and Christians" who were ashamed of the simpler minds among them. He also knew some "Christians who have made some progress in education" and at the beginning of his book he charged that only some among the Christians "do not want to give or to receive a reason for what they believe."[72] This may mean that Celsus was familar with the Christian apologist movement. This question has been often examined but no conclusive answer has appeared yet.[73] Origen, who was more than a match for Celsus, could easily refute many of the latter's theological charges.[74] Often, however, Origen was at a complete loss for an effective riposte. To the contention by Celsus that Christians took children away from their parents, for example, Origen could only respond that Christians did not lure children away from better things or incite them to worse things.[75] This was a lame argument, one that could hardly have appeased a pagan who cherished his family life and worked hard to give his children a good education and a place in society. In this case, Origen's near admission of guilt may only have confirmed many suspicions held by many pagans that Christianity was by and large a disruptive force.[76]

One criticism, which Celsus repeats several times over, is also strongly emphasized in Galen's writings, namely that Christians relied on faith without proof. This was indeed the case. The uneducated were attracted in great numbers to the church, and they were assured that "the foolishness of God is wiser than men."[77] This proud assertion by Paul would not have impressed a fine Platonist like Celsus. Even had Celsus read Irenaeus and Tertullian, which he had not, and learned that both these theologians emphasized the idea of "truth," he would still have remained skeptical. Irenaeus and Tertul-

lian relied totally on the Scriptures, which Celsus regarded as woe-
fully inadequate guides to employ in the search for truth. Like Galen,
Celsus struck a sensitive point, and Christian intellectuals were set
on edge. This, at least, appears to be the conclusion that we must
draw from the fact that, two generations after the publication of *True
Word*, it aroused Origen enough to make him write a detailed reply to
it. It may also say something about the success of Celsus's book
among the reading public. He was a formidable enemy of the church,
and later copies of *True Word* were painstakingly removed from
circulation.

The end of the second century was a period of serious clashes
between paganism and Christianity. It was during this period that
pagan suspicions about Christians surfaced and found expression in
savage attacks and sarcastic remarks. But at the same time, on a
different plateau, a meeting of the minds began to occur. Justin
Martyr and the Apologists, on the Christian side, made the first steps
in this direction. Galen and Celsus, on the pagan side, accepted the
challenge. Christianity may owe much to these two pagans because
they helped to clarify many issues, and they prompted educated
Christians to redefine their position and arguments. Christian reaction was often negative, as *The Little Labyrinth* and the outbursts by
Tertullian amply demonstrate. But in Alexandria the cool and serene
figure of Clement began to radiate a new light. Greek philosophy, he
wrote, is a training for the soul to receive faith, and thus scholarly
study for Christian teachers is not sinful but desirable.[78] These were
strong words for Christians who suspected Gnosticism under the
guise of philosophy, and Clement had to carefully clarify his position.
But a new era for Christian theology had started, and Christians
began to seem themselves in a new light.[79] Pagans based their criticisms of Christianity on actual situations, prevailing perhaps not
universally but certainly at times in at least a few places, and so they
made it possible for Christians to take positive corrective measures.
It is more than problematic, however, whether this response would
have been formulated in the absence of the challenge.

NOTES

1. Rev. 2:12-13.

2. The association of the serpent with the healing arts may have come from the fact that every year the serpent sheds its skin; because of this characteristic the serpent became a symbol of rejuvenation. Even today the caduceus, the wand with two serpents twined around it, is a favorite emblem of the medical profession.

3. For a good summary of Greek medicine see Guido Majno, *The Healing Hand: Man and Wound in the Ancient World* (Cambridge: Harvard University Press, 1975), pp. 141-206, and 395-422. Other literature is cited here.

4. Majno, *The Healing Hand*, p. 406.

5. Quoted in R. Walzer, *Galen on Jews and Christians* (London: Oxford University Press, 1949), pp. 14–15.

6. R. Walzer, "Galenos," *Reallexikon für Antike und Christentum* 8 (1972) 776-86.

7. Samuel Dill, *Roman Society from Nero to Marcus Aurelius* (London: Macmillan, 1920), p. 294.

8. See Adolf Harnack, *History of Dogma*, vol. 2, E.T. (New York: Dover, 1961). Also, Reinhold Seeberg, *Lehrbuch der Dogmengeschichte*, 4th ed. (Graz: Akademie Druck und Verlag Anstalt, 1953), 1:334ff.

9. Harnack, *History of Dogma*, 2:179ff.; C. C. Richardson, ed., *Early Christian Fathers* (Philadelphia: Westminster Press, 1953), pp. 225ff.

10. He said: "Our doctrines, then, appear to be greater than all human teaching. . . ." *Apol.* 2.10.1; Carl Andresen, *Logos und Nomos, Die Polemik des Kelsos wider das Christentum* (Berlin: Walter de Gruyter, 1955), pp. 308-92, proposed that the work of Justin served as a basis for the attack by Celsus on Christianity.

11. *Legatio* 2.

12. This fragment is found in Eusebius *Church History* 4.26.7f. in *NPNF* Series 2, 1:205.

13. *De morte Peregrini* 13; *Meditations* 11.3.

14. Origen *Contra Celsum* 1.9, 1.12, 1.26, 3.44, 6.10f. Also see Justin *Apol.* 1.52.

15. Eusebius *Church History* 5.1.1ff.

16. See Lynn Thorndike, *A History of Magic*, pp. 137ff; also by R. Walzer, *Galen on Jews and Christians*, pp. 75ff.; Robert L. Wilken, "Collegia, Philosophical Schools, and Theology," in *The Catacombs and the Colosseum*, ed. S. Benko and J. J. O'Rourke (Philadelphia: Westminster Press, 1971), pp. 268-91.

17. On Theodotus and his followers (including Artemon) see A. von Harnack, *Geschichte der altchristlichen Literatur bis Eusebius* (reprint, Leipzig: J. C. Hinrichs Verlag, 1958), 1:592; 2:201. See also *NPNF* 2d series, 1:246-47; and Adolf Hilgenfeld, *Die Ketzergeschichte des Urchristentums* (Leipzig: Fues, 1884), pp. 609-15.

18. It was specifically aimed against Artemon, who taught a doctrine similar to that of Theodotus in Rome during the early third century. See Harnack, *History of Dogma*, 2:202, 603, 625. The book is dated around 230-240. Cf. Hilgenfeld, *Die Ketzergeschichte des Urchristentums*, p. 16, fn. 20.

19. Eusebius *Church History* 5.28, 13-19.

20. Harnack, *History of Dogma*, 3:20-34.

21. Ibid., 3:7, 8, 11, 14; E.T., *Library of Christian Classics* vol. 5 p. 36.

22. *On the Shows* 30.

23. 5.2. Celsus knew the difference between orthodox and gnostic concepts concerning the incarnation; some Christians believed, he said, in the same God as the Jews, others said that there was another God from whom Jesus came; Origen *Contra Celsum* 5.61. As long as the laws of Moses and Jesus agreed, Christians said that they believed in the same God as the Jews, but when Jesus contradicted Moses, Christians tried to find another God, ibid, 6.29; 7.18. He also mentioned the sects of the Simonians, Helena, Monarchians, "Harpocratians" (Carpocratians), Marcian, and the Ophites, ibid., 5.62, 6.28. It is to be noted, however, that Origen did not think he distinguished between orthodox and Gnostic Christians, see for example, ibid., 6.28, 30, 53. Celsus also pointed out the similarities between Christianity and the Mithraic mysteries in ibid., 6.24–25. The best modern English translation is by Henry Chadwick, *Origen: Contra Celsum* (Cambridge: Cambridge University Press, 1953); an earlier translation is by F. Crombie and W. H. Cairns, in *ANF*, vol. 4.

24. Celsus is discussed by Henry Chadwick, *Origen: Contra Celsum*, pp. xxivff. His introductory notes and the bibliography are also valuable. The literature on *Contra Celsum* is very large, and most of it is listed in Chadwick.

25. Origen *Contra Celsum* 2.1, 3, 4.

26. Ibid., 3.1; 4.31.

27. Ibid., 5.6; 6.42, 45, 8.11.

28. Ibid., 1.26, 5.25, 41, 1.21, 23, 24, 5.33, 3.1

29. Ibid., 4.36, 38, 48, 49, 50, 6.49, 50, 58, 61, 62, 63.

30. Ibid., 4.45, 47, 43.

31. Ibid., 6.53, 54, 57, 4.40.

32. Ibid., 6.1, 4.41, 21; see also the *Iliad* 5.385ff.

33. Origen *Contra Celsum* 1.57, 2.8, 28.

34. Ibid., 1.28, 38, 39.

35. Ibid., 1.50, 57, 54, 61, 66.

36. Ibid., 2.32, 1.32.

37. Ibid., 3.41, 42, 2.79, 29, 7, 1.62, 2.46.

38. Ibid., 1.71, 2.32, 2.49, 8.41; also see Morton Smith, *Jesus the Magician*; Eugene V. Gallagher, *Divine Man or Magician? Celsus and Origen on Jesus*, Society of Biblical Literature Dissertation Series, number 64 (Chico, Calif.: Scholars Press, 1982); and Harold E. Remus, *Pagan-Christian Conflict Over Miracles* (Ph.D. dissertation, University of Pennsylvania, 1981), pp. 199-312.

39. Origen *Contra Celsum* 1.6, 68, 2.24, 76, 39, 43, 92, 12, 4-5.

40. Ibid., 1.54, 2.13, 15-19, 44, 63, 67-69, 1.66, 2.36.

41. Ibid., 2.55.

42. Ibid., 2.70, 3.22, 2.61, 6.72, 2.16.

43. Ibid., 4.2, 3, 6, 7, 14, 18, 3.78, 79.

44. Ibid., 5.52.

45. Ibid., 6.73, 75.

46. Ibid., 6.78, 7.14, 8.14-15.

47. Ibid., 7.32.

48. Ibid., 5.14-15; see also 7.32, 34, and 8.48-49. In his rejection of the idea of bodily resurrection, Celsus expressed the general pagan attitude. It is expressed also by Pliny *Naturalis Historia* 7.55. 190, "What is this mad idea that life is renewed by death?"

49. Origen *Contra Celsum* 1.27, 3.18, 44, 1.13, 9, 6.10-11, 3.73, 59.

50. Ibid., 3.62, 64, 59.

51. Ibid., 3.68, 1.27, 3.44, 50, 55, 59, 74-75, 6.11-14, 6.7ff., 65, 7.42, 45; see Andresen's comment on the word ἰδιώτης in *Logos und Nomos*, p. 169.

52. Origen *Contra Celsum* 3.50; 52.

53. Ibid., 3.55; cf. Tatian *Oratio* 33: "You . . . say that we talk nonsense among women and boys, among maidens and old women, and scoff at us for not being with you."

54. Origen *Contra Celsum* 3.16, 4.10, 7.11, 6.14, 40-41, 1.6.

55. Ibid., 3.75-78.

56. Ibid., 3.43, 7.3, 9, 8.12. The argument that Christianity was a new religion recurs also in 1.26, 2.4, 6.10. See also 5.25: Jews at least could look back to a long tradition.

57. Ibid., 7.68, 36, 53.

58. Ibid., 7.36, 68, 8.38-39, 41, 54, 69, 5.41.

59. Ibid., 7.62, 8.21-24, 28, 33.

60. Ibid., 3.14, 5.33, 65.

61. See for example, ibid., 6.18ff; 6.21; 6.24f; 7.58; 7.62.

62. Ibid., 3.10, 12, 14, 5.63.

63. Ibid., 4.23.

64. Ibid., 4.23, 1.1, 3.

65. Ibid., 8.2.

66. Ibid., 8.17, 49, 55.

67. Ibid., 8.65-69, 73, 75.

68. Andresen, *Logos und Nomos*, pp. 22 and 232.

69. "Now if the Logos in your view is the Son of God, we too approve of that," Origen *Contra Celsum* 2.31; see also 6.71, 69.

70. He wrote. "And I do not mean that a man who embraces a good doctrine, if he is about to run into danger from men because of it, ought to renounce the doctrine, or pretend that he had renounced it, or come to deny it," ibid., 1.8; "If you happen to be a worshipper of God and someone commands you either to act blasphemously or to say some other disgraceful thing, you ought not to put any confidence in him at all. Rather than this you must remain firm in face of all tortures and endure any death rather than say or even think anything profane about God," ibid., 8.66. On the pagan idea of martyrdom and the Christian reaction to it see Herbert A. Musurillo, *The Acts of the Pagan Martyrs* (Oxford: Oxford University Press, 1954), pp. 236-46.

71. Andresen, *Logos und Nomos*, pp. 146, 219. The statement by Celsus can be found in Origen *Contra Celsum* 3.9. Tacitus also compared Christianity to a disease; *Annales* 15.44; and Pliny, *Ep.* 10.96, referred to it as a "contagious" superstition; Celsus said that the Christians "suffer from the disease of sedition," Origen *Contra Celsum* 8.49.

72. Origen *Contra Celsum* 5.65, see also 1.27: There are "some moderate, reasonable and intelligent people" among Christians, and 1.9.

73. See Andresen, *Logos und Nomos*, pp. 185f. for references.

74. "In the range of his learning [Origen] towers above his pagan adversary, handling the traditional arguments of Academy and Stoa with masterly ease and fluency." Chadwick, *Origen*, p. xii.

75. Origen *Contra Celsum* 3.55.

76. We can well understand pagan sentiments on this issue today, since we often hear about children who have been brainwashed by various religions

and semireligious groups. The sorrow visited upon parents by the spectacle of their children giving up education, family ties, friends, property, and jobs must have been just as deep and real in the time of Celsus as it is in ours.

77. I *Cor.* 1.21-25; A. Harnack, *The Mission and Expansion of Christianity* (Gloucester, Mass.: Peter Smith, 1972), pp. 219ff., 87.

78. *Strom.* 7.20, 1.18; 6.80, 89. For a brief survey see J. E. L. Oulton and H. Chadwick, eds., *Alexandrian Christianity* (Philadelphia: Westminster Press, 1954), pp. 17ff., bibliography on pp. 456-57.

79. See E. P. Sanders, ed. *Jewish and Christian Self-Definition*, vol. 1, *The Shaping of Christianity in the Second and Third Centuries* (New York: SCM Press, 1981), In particular see the article in this book by Robert L. Wilken, "The Christians as the Romans (and Greeks) Saw Them," pp. 100-125.

SUMMARY

Our investigations have shown that in their objections to Christianity the pagans were not gullible fools, but instead were often right. Sometimes they generalized too quickly and that is always a mistake, but at other times they hit on sensible nerves. In particular, we saw that it was not without reason that the name "Christian" evoked a negative reaction. The uneven career of Peregrinus Proteus, who ended life as a cynic, may have been duplicated many times; at any rate, cynics were often obnoxious people and an association with them did not help to create sympathy for Christians. We also saw that there was indeed a libertine strain in early Christianity, and the charges of occasional immoral behavior were well founded. The charges of cannibalism were not so clear, although even that occurred among some fringe groups who bore the Christian name. On the other hand, Christians were deeply influenced by Greco-Roman magic and in fact practiced a Christian type of magic. The scholarly criticism of Christian theology and the daily behavior of Christians was in many instances right on target, and some of the points raised by Galen and Celsus are valid today.

What does all this prove? "Homo sum: humani nihil a me alienum puto." (Terentius, *The Self-Tormentor*) Nothing that is human was strange to the early Christians either; they were children of their milieu. They thought in the categories of their times, and they were part of the society in which they lived. Only within this framework can their history be understood. To deny them this part in the history of humanity with all its pitfalls and errors is to fall into the heresy of Docetism.

BIBLIOGRAPHY

Original Sources

The following pagan authors made references to Christians and Christianity during the second century.

Pliny the Younger (61/62-113) : *Ep.* 10.96, 97
Tacitus (55-117) : *Annales* 15.44
Suetonius (70-160) : *Nero* 16.2 (*Claudius* 5.25)
Epictetus (50-130) : *Discourses* 4.7.1-6, 2.9.19-22
Hadrian (117-138) : Rescript to Minucius Fundanus (Eusebius *HE*.4.9.1-3)

Hadrian (117-138) : (Letter to *Servianus* in Vopiscus, *Saturninus* 7-8 in the *Historia Augusta* is spurious)

Fronto (100-166) = Minucius : *Octavius* 8, 9
Felix (200-240)
Apuleius (123-?) : *Metamorphoses* 9.14 (*Apologia* 90?)
Marcus Aurelius (161-180) : *Meditations* 11.3 (Letter to the Assembly of Asia, Eusebius, *HE* 4.13.1-7 is spurious)

Lucian of Samosata (115-200) : *De morte Peregrini, Alexander the False Prophet*
Aelius Aristides (129-181) : ῾Υπχίρ τῶν τεττάρων. 2:394ff.
Galen (129-199) : See R. Walzer, *Galen on Jews and Christians* (London: Oxford University Press, 1949) pp. 14-15.
Celsus (fl. 177-180) : ᾽Αληθὴσ λόγοσ.

Convenient collections and treatments of these sources can be found in the following works:

1) den Boer, W. *Scriptorum paganorum I-IV Saec. de Christianis testimonia.* Leiden, 1965.
2) de Labriolle, P. *La Réaction Paienne. Étude sur la polémique Antichretienne du Ier au VIe siècle.* Paris, 1934.
3) Stephen Benko, "Pagan Criticism of Christianity During the First Two Centuries." *Aufstieg und Niedergang der römischen* Welt. II, 23/2. pp. 1055-118.

General Titles

The literature of the persecution of Christians is very large. The following is a selection of some useful titles.

Aland, K. "Das Verhältnis von Kirche und Staat in der Frühzeit." *ANRW* 23/1 (1979): 60-246.

Benko, Stephen. "Pagan Criticism of Christianity During the First Two Centuries a.d." *Aufstieg u. Niedergang der Römischen Welt 23/2* (1980):1055-118.

Le Blant, E. *Les persécuteurs et les martyrs aux premiers siècles de notre ère.* Paris: E. Leroux, 1893.

Canfield, L. H. *The Early Persecution of the Christians.* New York: Columbia University Press, 1913.

Chroust, A. H. "A Note on the Persecutions of the Christians in the Early Roman Empire." *Class. et Mediaev.* 28 (1969/70):321-29.

Conrat, M. *Die Christenverfolgungen im römischen Reich vom Standpunkt des Juristen.* Leipzig: J. C. Hinrats, 1897.

Contreras, C. A. "Christian Views of Paganism." *ANRW* 23/2 (1980):974-1022.

Dieu, L. "La persécution au 2ᵉ siècle." *Revue D'Histoire Ecclesiastique* 38 (1942):5-30.

Frend, W. H. C. *Martyrdom and Persecution in the Early Church.* New York: Doubleday, 1967.

Grant, F. C. "Religio Licita." *Studia Patristica* 4 (Texte und Untersuchungen 79), Leipzig: Akademie Verlag, 1961.

Grégoire, H. *Les persécutions dan l'empire Romain,* (Académie royale de Belgique, Classe des Lettres et das Sciences morales et politiques, Mémoires 2,46.1.) Brussels: Palais des académies, 1950.

Guterman, S. L. *Religious Toleration and Persecution in Ancient Rome.* London: Aiglon Press, 1951.

Hanson, R. P. C. "The Christian Attitude to Pagan Religions up to the Time of Constantine the Great." *ANRW* 23/2 (1980):910-73.

Judge, E. A. *The Social Patterns of the Christian Groups in the First Century.* London: Tyndale Press, 1959.

Keresztes, P. "The Imperial Roman Government and the Christian Church." *ANRW* 23/1 (1979) 247-315.

Labriolle, P. De. *La réaction paienne. Étude sur la polémique antichrètienne du Ier au VIe siècle.* Paris: L'artisan du livre 1934.

Last, H. "The Study of the Persecutions." *Journal of Roman Studies* 27 (1937):80.

Last, H. "Christenverfolgungen (Juristisch)." *Reallexikon für Antike und Christentum* 2 (1954):1208-28.

Linsenmayer, A. *Die Bekämpfung des Christentums durch den römischen Staat bis zum Tode des Kaisers Julian (363).* Munich: J. J. Lentner, 1905.

Markus, R. A. *Christianity in the Roman World.* New York: Scribners, 1974.

Molthagen, J. *Der römische Staat und die Christen im zweiten und dritten Jahrhundert.* (Hypomnemata 28). Göttingen: Vandenhoeck and Reprecht, 1970.

Momigliano, A. "The Persecution of the Christians." *Cambridge Ancient History,* edited by S. A. Cook, F. E. Adcock, and M. P. Charlesworth, vol. 10, pp. 887-88. Cambridge: Cambridge University Press, 1934.

Moreau, J. *Die Christenverfolgung im römischen Reich.* Aus der Welt der Religion, N.F. 2. Berlin: Walter de Gruyter, 1971.

Nestle, W. "Die Haupteinwände des antiken Denkens gegen das Christentum." *Archiv für Religionswissenschaft* 37 (1941): 51-100.

Rahner, H. *Kirche und Staat im frühen Christentum.* Dokumente aus acht Jahrhunderten und ihre Deutung. Munich: Kosel-Verlag, 1961.

Sherwin-White, A. N. "The Early Persecutions and Roman Law Again." *Journal of Theological Studies* 3 (1952): 199-213.

Sherwin-White, A. N. "Why Were the Early Christians Persecuted? An Amendment." *Past and Present* 27 (1964): 23-33.

Speigl, J. *Der römische Staat und die Christen: Staat und Kirche von Domitian bis Commodus.* Amsterdam: Hakkert, 1970.

De Ste Croix, G. E. "Why Were the Early Christians Persecuted?" *Past and Present* 26 (1963): 6-38, 27 (1964): 28-33.

Vogt, J. "Christenverfolgung (historisch)," *Reallexikon für Antike und Christentum* 2 (1954): 1159-1208.

Vogt, J. *Zur Religiosität der Christenverfolger im Römischen Reich.* Sitzungsberichte der Heidelberger Akademie. Heidelberg: C. Winter, 1962.

Wilcken, U. "Zu den Kaiserreskripten." *Hermes* 55 (1920): 1-42.

Wlosok, A. "Die Rechtsgrundlagen der Christenverfolgungen der ersten zwei Jahrhunderte." *Gymnasium* 66 (1959): 14-32.

Wlosok, A. *Rom und die Christen. Zur Auseinandersetzung zwischen Christentum und römischem Staat.* Der Altsprachliche Unterricht 13,1. Stuttgart: Klett, 1970.

Workman, Herbert B. *Persecution in the Early Church.* London: C. H. Kelly, 1906.

Pliny and Trajan

Babel, H. "Der Briefwechsel zwischen Plinius und Trajan über die Christen in strafrechtlicher Sicht." Ph. D. dissertation, University of Erlangen, 1961.

Bickerman, E. T. "Trajan, Hadrian, and the Christians." *Rivista di Filologia* 96 (1968): 290-315.

Freudenberger, R. *Das Verhalten der römischen Behörden gegen die Christen im 2. Jahrhundert. Dargestellt am Brief des Plinius an Trajan und den Reskripten Trajans und Hadrians.* Münchener Breiträge zur Papyrusforschung und Antiken Rechtsgeschichte 12. 2d ed. Munich: C. H. Beck, 1969.

Grant, R. M. "Pliny and the Christians." *Harvard Theological Review* 41 (1948): 273-74.

Korte, A. "Zu Plinius' Brief über die Christen." *Hermes* 63 (1928): 481-84.

Kraemer, C. J. "Pliny and the Early Christian Service." *Classical Philology* 29 (1934): 290-300.

Kurfess, A. "Plinius der Jüngere über die Bithynischen Christen." *Mnemosyne* 7 (1939): 237-40.

Mayer-Maly, T. "Der rechtsgeschichtliche Gehalt der Christenbriefe von Plinius und Trajan." *Studia et Documenta Historiae et Iuris* 22 (1956): 311-28.

Merrill, E. T. "Tertullian on Pliny's Persecution of the Christians." *American Journal of Theology* 22 (1918): 124-35.

Nock, A. D. "The Christian Sacramentum in Pliny." *Classical Review* 38 (1924): 58-59.

Reichel, H. J. *Der Römische Staat und die Christen im 1. und 2. Jahrhundert."* Ph.D. dissertation, University of Hamburg, 1962.

Schmid, W. "Ein verkannter Ausdruck der Opfersprache in Plinius' Christenbrief." *Vigiliae Christianae* 7 (1953): 75-78.

Sherwin-White, A. N. "Trajan's Replies to Pliny." *Journal of Roman Studies* 52 (1960): 114–25.

Sherwin-White, A. N. *The Letters of Pliny.* Oxford, Clarendon Press, 1966.

Weber, W. "Nec nostri saeculi est. Bemerkungen zum Briefwechsel des Plinius und Trajan über die Christen." In *Festgabe Karl Müller zum 70. Geburtstag dargebracht,* pp. 24-45. Tübingen: J. C. Mohr 1922.

Wickert, L. "Zum Christenbrief des Plinius." *Rheinisches Museum* 100 (1957): 100.

Tacitus

Barnes, T. D. "Legislation Against the Christians." *Journal of Roman Studies* 58 (1968): 32-50.

Bauer, J. B. "Tacitus und die Christen." *Gymnasium* 64 (1957): 497-513.

Büchner, K. "Tacitus über die Christen." *Aegyptus* 33 (1953): 181-92.

Clayton, F. W. "Tacitus and Nero's Persecution of the Christians." *Classical Quarterly* 41 (1947): 81-85.

Dibelius, M. "Nero und die Christen." *Forschungen und Fortschritte* 18 (1942): 189-90.

Fraenkel, E. "Senatus consultum de Bacchanalibus." *Hermes* 67 (1932): 369-96.

Fuchs, H. "Tacitus über die Christen." *Vigiliae Christianae* 4 (1950): 65-93.

Gelzer, M. "Die Unterdrückung der Bacchanalien bei Livius." *Hermes* 71 (1936): 275-87.

Getty, Robert J. "Nero's Indictment of the Christians." In *The Classical Tradition: Literary and Historical Studies in Honor of Harry Caplan,* edited by Luitpold Wallach. Ithaca, N.Y.: Cornell University Press, 1966.

Hermann, L. "Les Juifs et la persécution des Chrétiens par Néron." *Latomus* 20 (1961): 817-20.

Hitchcock, M. "The Charges Against the Christians in Tacitus." *The Church Quarterly Review* 109 (1930): 300-16.

Hospers-Jansen, A. M. A. *Tacitus over de Joden Hist. 5.2-13.* Groningen: J. B. Wolter, 1949.

Keil, J. "Das sogenannte senatusconsultum de Bacchanalibus." *Hermes* 68 (1933): 306-12.

Kurfess, A. "Der Brand und die Christenverfolgung im Jahre 64 n. Chr." *Mnemosyne* 6 (1938): 261-72.

Kurfess, A. "Tacitus über die Christen." *Vigiliae Christianae* 5 (1951): 148–49.

Michelfeit, J. "Das Christenkapitel des Tacitus." *Gymnasium* 73 (1966): 514-40.

Nestle, W. "Odium generis humani." *Klio* 21 (1927): 91-93.

Roos, A. G. Nero and the Christians." in *Symbola van Oven,* pp. 297-306. Leiden: E. J. Brill, 1946.

Sherwin-White, A. N. "The Early Persecutions and Roman Law Again."
   Journal of Theological Studies 3 (1952): 199-213.

Seutonius

Bammel, E. "Judenverfolgung und Naherwartung." *Zeitschrift f. Theol. u.
   Kirche* 56 (1959): 295-97.
Benko, S. "The Edict of Claudius of A.D. 49." *Theologische Zeitschrift* 25
   (1969): 406-18.
Bruce, F. F. "Christianity under Claudius." *Bulletin of the John Rylands
   Library* 44 (1962): 309-26.
Charlesworth, M. P. *Documents Illustrating the Reigns of Claudius and
   Nero.* Cambridge: Cambridge University Press, 1951.
Janne, H. "Impulsore Chresto." *Annuaire de l'Institut de Philos. et d'Hist.
   Orientales* 2 (1934): 531-53.
May, G. "La politique religieuse de l'empereur Claude." *Nouvelle revue
   histoire de droit francais et étranger* 17 (1938): 37-45.
Momigliano, A. *Claudius: the Emperor and his Achievement.* New York:
   Barnes and Noble, 1961.
Scramuzza, V. M. *The Emperor Claudius.* Harvard Historical Studies, 44.
   Cambridge, Harvard University Press, 1940.
Urch, E. J. "Early Roman Understanding of Christianity." *Classical Journal*
   27 (1932): 255-62.

Peregrinus Proteus

Bagnani, G. "Peregrinus Proteus and the Christians." *Historia* 4 (1955):
   107-112.
Betz, H. D. "Lukian von Samosata und das Christentum." *Novum Tes-
   tamentum* 3 (1958): 226-237.
Betz, H. D. *Lukian von Samosata und das Neue Testament.* Berlin: Akademie
   Verlag, 1961.
Caster, M. *Lucien et la pensée Religieuse de son temps.* Paris: Société d'édi-
   tion "Les Belles Lettres," 1937.
Curti, Carmelo. "Luciano e i Cristiani." *Miscellanea di studi di litteratura
   cristiana antica* 40 (1954): 86-109.
Daumer, V. *Lucien de Samosate et la secte chrétienne.* Cahiers du Cercle E.
   Renan. Paris: Cercle Ernest Renan, 1957.
Fritz, K. V. "Peregrinus (Proteus)." In *Realencyclopädie* edited by Pauly-
   Wissowa-Kroll. 37.656–63.
Glover, T. R. *The Conflict of Religions in the Early Roman Empire.* Boston:
   Beacon Press, 1960.
Jebb, R. C. *Essays and Addresses.* Cambridge: Cambridge University Press,
   1907.
Pack, Roger. "The 'volatilization' of Peregrinus Proteus." *American Journal
   of Philosophy* 67 (1946): 334-345.

Cynicism

Bernays, Jakob. *Lucian und die Kyniker.* Berlin: W. Hertz, 1879.
Bigelmair, A. "Armut". *Reallexikon für Antike und Christentum,* edited by
   Theodor Klauser, vol. 1, pp. 706-9. Stuttgart: Anton Hiersemann, 1972.

Bultmann, R., *Der Stil der paulinischen Predigt und die Kynisch-stoische Diatribe.* Göttingen: Vandenhoeck and Ruprecht, 1910.

Dudley, D. R. *A History of Cynicism.* London: Methuen and Co., 1938.

Höistad, Regnar. *Cynic Hero and Cynic King. Studies in the Cynic Conception of Man.* Uppsala: C. Blom, 1948.

Hornsby, Hazel M. "The Cynicism of Peregrinus Proteus." *Hermathena* 48 (1933): 65-84.

Lecky, William E. H. *History of European Morals From Augustus to Charlemagne.* New York: G. Braziller, 1955.

Sayre, Farrand. *The Greek Cynics.* Baltimore: J. H. Furst and Co., 1948.

Schneider, Carl. *Geistesgeschichte der Christlichen Antike.* 2d. ed. Munich: Beck, 1954.

Strathmann, H. "Askese." *Reallexikon für Antike und Christentum,* edited by Theodor Klauser, vol. 1, pp. 749ff. Stuttgart: Anton Hiersemann, 1972.

Marcus Aurelius

Birley, A. R. *Marcus Aurelius.* London: Eyre and Spottiswoode, 1966.

Coleman-Norton, P. R. *Roman State and Christian Church.* Vol. 1. London: SPCK, 1966.

Haines, P. R. *The Communings with Himself of Marcus Aurelius Antoninus.* London: W. Heinenann, 1916.

Keresztes, P. "Marcus Aurelius a Persecutor?" *Harvard Theological Review* 61 (1968): 321-41.

Martinazzoli, F. *Parataxeis, Le testimonianze stoiche sul Christianesimo.* Florence: Nuova Italia, 1953.

Phipps, C. B. "Persecution under Marcus Aurelius." *Hermathena* 47 (1932):167-201.

Schmid, W. "The Christian Re-interpretation of the Rescript of Hadrian." *Maia* 7 (1955): 10-13.

Sordi, M. "I nuovi decreti di Marco Aurelio contro i cristiani." *Studi Romani* 9 (1962): 365–78.

Stanton, G. R. "Marcus Aurelius, Lucius Verus and Commodus." *ANRW* 2/2 (1975) 478-548.

Wagenvoort, H. *"Marcus Aurelius en zijn verhouding tot het Christendom."* In *Christendom en Historie,* pp. 46-66. Amsterdam, Uitgeversmaatschappi, 1925.

Epictetus

Bonhöffer, A. *Epiktet und das Neue Testament.* Giessen: A. Töpelmann, 1911.

Mörth, Fr. "Epiktet und sein Verhältnus zum Christentum." In *Festschrift, 50 Vers. Klass. Philol.,* pp. 179-94. Graz; 1909.

Sevenster, J. N. *Paul and Seneca.* Leiden: E. J. Brill, 1961.

Sharp, D. S. *Epictetus and the New Testament.* London: C. H. Kelly, 1914.

Simpson, Adelaide O. "Epicureans, Christians, Atheists in the Second Century." *Transactions and Proceedings of the American Philological Association* 72 (1941): 372-381.

Spanneut, M. "Epiktet." *RAC* 5 (1962): 599-682.

Stegemann, Viktor. "Christentum und Stoizismus im Kampf um die geistigen Lebenswerte im 2. Jahrh. n. Chr." *Die Welt als Geschichte* 7 (1941): 295-330.

Xenaxis, J. *Epictetus.* The Hague: Martinus Nijhoff, 1969.

Zahn, Th., *Der Stoiker Epiktet und sein Verhältnis zum Christentum.* Erlangen: E. T. Jacob, 1894.

Charges of Immorality and Cannibalism

Benko, S. "The Libertine Gnostic Sect of the Phibionites according to Epiphanius." *Vigiliae Christianae* 21 (1967): 103-19.

Bickerman, E. "Ritualmord und Eselskult." *Monatsschrift für Geschichte und Wissenschaft des Judentums* 71 (1927): 171-87.

Büchner, K. "Drei Beobachtungen zu Minucius Felix." *Hermes* 82 (1954): 231-45.

Clarke, G. W. "Four Passages in Minucius Felix." In *Kyriakon. Festschrift Johannes Quasten.* Vol. 2. Munich: 1970.

Clarke, G. W. *The Octavius of Minucius Felix.* New York: Newman Press, 1974.

DeVaux, R. *Ancient Israel. Its Life and Institutions.* New York: McGraw-Hill, 1961.

DeVaux, R. *Studies in Old Testament Sacrifice.* Cardiff: University of Wales Press, 1964.

Dölger, F. J. "Sacramentum Infanticidii." *Antike und Christentum* 4 (1934): 188-228.

Dummer, J. "Die Angaben über die Gnostische Literatur bei Ephiphanius, Pan. Haer. 26." *Koptologische Studien in der DDR,* pp. 191-219. Halle-Wittenberg: Martin Luther Universität, Sonderheft, 1965.

Fendt, L. *Gnostische Mysterien.* Munich: Kaiser Verlag, 1922.

Foerster, W. *Die Gnosis,* 1, Zürich: Artemis Verlag, E.T., Gnosis. Oxford: Oxford University Press, 1974.

Freudenberger, R. "Der Vorwurf ritueller Verbrechen." *Theologische Zeitschrift* 23 (1967): 97-107.

Grant, R. M. "Charges of 'Immorality' Against Various Religious Groups in Antiquity." In *Studies in Gnosticism and Hellenistic Religions,* Presented to Gilles Quispel on the Occasion of his 65th Birthday, edited by R. van den Broek and M. J. Vermaseren. Leiden; E. J. Brill, 1981.

Henrichs, A. "Pagan Ritual and the Alleged Crimes of the Early Christians." In *Kyriakon. Festschrift Johannes Quasten,* pp. 18-35. Vol. 1. Munich: 1970.

Henrichs, A. *Die Phoinikika des Lollianos.* Bonn: Rudolf Habelt Verlag, 1972.

Hilgenfeld, A. *Die Ketzergeschichet des Urchristentums.* Reprint, 1884, Hildesheim: G. Olms, 1966.

Leisegang, H. *Die Gnosis.* Leipzig: A. Kröner, 1924.

Mosca, P. G. *Child Sacrifice in Canaanite and Israelite Religion.* Ph.D. dissertation, Harvard University, 1975.

Schwenn, F. *Die Menschenopfer bei den Griechen und Römern.* Giessen: A. Töpelmann, 1915.

Smith, M. *Clement of Alexandria and a Secret Gospel of Mark.* Cambridge: Harvard University Press, 1973.

Speyer, W. "Zu den Vorwürfen der Heiden gegen die Christen." *Jahrbuch für Antike und Christentum* 6 (1963): 129ff.

Stager, L. E. "The Rite of Child Sacrifice at Carthage." In *New Light on Ancient Carthage*, edited by J. F. Pedley. Ann Arbor: University of Michigan Press, 1980.

Wagenvoort, H. "Minuciana." In *Mélanges offerts à Mme Christine Mohrmann*, pp. 66-72. Utrecht: Spectrum, 1963.

Waltzing, J. "P. Minucius Felix." *Musée Belge* 14 (1910): 61-64.

Waltzing, J. "Le crime rituel reproché aux chrétiens du IIe siècle." *Acad. Royale de Belgique, Bull. de la classe des Lettres* 2 (1925); 205-239.

The Holy Kiss

Burnet, John. *Early Greek Philosophy*. New York: Macmillian, 1892.

Crawley, A. E. "Kissing" *Encyclopaedia of Religion and Ethics*. edited by J. Hastings, 7:739. New York: Scribners, 1926.

Deck, John N. *Nature, Comtemplation and the One*. Toronto: University of Toronto Press, 1967.

Dover, K. J. *Greek Homosexuality*. New York: Random House, 1980.

Flacelière, Robert. *Love in Ancient Greece*. London: F. Muller, 1962.

Frankfort, Henri. *Kingship and the Gods*. Chicago: University of Chicago Press, 1948.

Frazer, James G. *The Golden Bough*. Vol. 2. New York: Macmillan, 1935.

Früchtel, Edgar. *Weltentwurf und Logos*. Frankfurt Am Main: Klostermann, 1970.

Grant, Michael. *The Climax of Rome*. New York: New American Library, 1965.

Havelock, Ellis H. "The Origins of the Kiss." In *Sexual Selection in Man*. Philadelphia: F. A. Davis Co., 1905.

Hofmann, K. M. *Philema Hagion*. Ph.D. dissertation, University of Erlangen, 1938.

Hopfner, Theodor. *Das Sexualleben der Griechen und Römer*. Prague: J. G. Calve, 1938.

James, E. O. *The Ancient Gods*. New York: Putnam, 1960.

Jolly, Robert. *Le Vocabulaire Chrétien de L'amour est-il original? φιλεῖν et ἀγαπᾶν dans le grec antique*. Brussels: Presses Universitaires de Bruxelles, 1968.

Katz, Joseph. *Plotinus' Search for the Good*. New York: Columbia University Press, Kings Crown Press, 1950.

Kerényi, C. *Dionysos*. Bollingen Series. Princeton: Princeton University Press, 1976.

Licht, Hans. *Sexual Life in Ancient Greece*. 10th ed. London: The Abbey Library, 1971.

Nygren, Anders. *Agape and Eros*. Philadelphia: Westminster, 1953.

Nyrop, C. *The Kiss and Its History*. E.T., W. F. Harvey. London: Sands, 1901.

Perella, Nicolas James. *The Kiss Sacred and Profane*. Berkeley and Los Angeles: University of California Press, 1969.

Quispel, G. "God is Eros." In *Early Christian Literature and the Classical Intellectual Tradition in Honorem Robert M. Grant*, edited by W. R. Schoedel and R. L. Wilken, pp. 189–205. Paris: Beauchesne, 1979.

Rist, J. M. *Plotinus: The Road to Reality*. Cambridge: Cambridge University Press, 1967.

Stokes, Michael C. *One and Many in Presocratic Philosophy*. Cambridge: Harvard University Press, 1971.

Thraede, Klaus. "Ursprünge und Formen des 'Heiligen Kusses.'" *Jahrbach für Antike und Christentum* 11/12 (1968-1969): 124-80.
DeVogel, Cornelia J. "Greek Cosmic Love and the Christian Love of God. Boethius, Dionysus the Areopagite and the Author of the Fourth Gospel." *Vigiliae Christianae* 35 (1981): 57-81.
Wallis, R. T. *Neoplatonism.* New York: Scribner's, 1972.
Wilbur, J. B. and Allen, H. J., eds. *The Worlds of the Early Greek Philosophers.* Buffalo, N.Y.: Prometheus Books, 1979.
Zinserling, Nerena. *Women in Greece and Rome.* New York: Abner Schram, 1972.

Lucius Apuleius

Abt, A. *Die Apologie des Apuleius von Madaura und die antike Zauberei.* Religionsgeschichtliche Versuche und Vorarbeiten 4, 2. Giessen: A. Töpelmann, 1908.
Glover, T. R. *The Conflict of Religions in the Early Roman Empire.* Boston: Beacon Press, 1960.
Haight, E. H. *Apuleius and His Influence: Our Debt to Greece and Rome.* New York: Longmans, Green, and Co., 1927.
Helm, R. "Apuleius v. Madaura." *RAC* 1 (1950): 573-74.
Labriolle, P. De. *La réaction paienne.* Étude sur la polèmique antichrétienne du Iev au VIe Siècle. Paris: L'Artisan du livre, 1934.
Marchesi, C. *Apuleio Di Madaura Della Magia.* Bologna: N. Zanichelli, 1957.
Nock, A. D. *Conversion. The Old and the New in Religion from Alexander the Great to Augustine of Hippo.* London: Oxford University Press, 1933.
Vallette, P. *L'apologie d'Apulee.* Ph.D. dissertation, University of Paris, 1908.

Alexander of Abonuteichos

Babelon, E. "Le Faux-Prophète Alexandre." *Revue Numismatique* (ser. 4) 4 (1900): 1-30.
Caster, M. *Études sur Alexandre ou le faux prophète de Lucien.* Paris: Société d'édition "Les Belles Lettres," 1938.
Cumont, F. *Alexandre d'Abonoteichos: Un Épisode De L'Histoire Du Paganism Au IIe Siècle De Notre Ère.* Mémoires Couronnées de L'Académie Royal de Belgique 40. Brussels: Academie Royal, 1887.
Cumont, F. "Alexandre D'Abonotichos Et Le Néo-Pyhagorisme." *Revue De L'Histoire Des Religions* 86 (1922): 202-10.
Nock, A. D. "Alexander of Abonuteichos." *Classical Quarterly* 22 (1928): 160-62.
Stein, A. "Zu Lukians Alexandros." In *Strena Buliciana: Commentationes Graulatoriae Francisco Bulic,* pp. 257-66. Zagreb: Stampala Zaklada Tiskare Narodnih Novina, 1924.
Weinrich, O. "Alexandros Der Lügenprophet und Seine Stellung in der Religiosität des II. Jahrhunderts N.Chr." *Neue Jahrbücher für das Klassische Altertum* 24 (1921): 129-51.

Magic

Aune, David E. "Magic in Early Christianity." *ANRW* 23/2 (1980): 1507-57.
Barb, A. "The Survival of Magic Arts." In *The Conflict Between Paganism*

and Christianity in the Fourth Century, edited by A. Momigliano. Oxford: Oxford University Press, 1963.

Bousset, Wilhelm. "Zur Demonologie der späten Antike." *Archiv für Religionswissenschaft* 18 (1915): 134-72.

Brown, Peter, "Sorcery, Demons and the Rise of Christianity from Late Antiquity into the Middle Ages." In *Witchcraft Confessions and Accusations,* edited by Mary Douglas, pp. 17–46. London: Tavistock Publications, 1970.

Casey, Robert P. "Simon Magus." In *The Beginnings of Christianity,* edited by F. J. Foakes-Jackson and Kirsopp Lake, part I., vol. 5, pp. 151-63. London: Macmillan, 1933.

Dobschütz, E. von. "Charms and Amulets (Christian)" *Encyclopedia of Religion and Ethics,* edited by James Hastings, 3.413-30. New York: Scribners, 1962.

Dölger, Franz Joseph. "Beitrage zur Geschichte des Kreuzzeichens VI." *Jahrbuch für Antike und Christentum* 6 (1963): 7-34.

Fridrichsen, A. *The Problem of Miracle in Early Christianity.* Translated by R. Harrisville and J. Hanson. Minneapolis: Augsburg Publishing House, 1972.

Heitmüller, W. *"In Namen Jesu": Eine sprach-und religionsgeschichtliche untersuchung zum Neuen Testament, speziell zur christlichen taufe.* Göttingen: Vandenhoeck and Ruprecht, 1903.

Hopfner, T. *Griechisch-Ägyptischer Offenbarungszauber.* 2 vols. Studien zur Palaeographie und Papyruskunde, 21 and 23. Leipzig: H. Haessel, 1921-24.

Hopfner, T. "Mageia." *Realencyclopädie Der Classischen Altertumswissenschaft.* edited by August F. Pauly, Georg Wissowa, and Wilhelm Kroll, vol. 28, pp. 301-94. Stuttgart: Druckenmüller Verlag, 1928.

Hull, John M. *Hellenistic Magic and Synoptic Tradition.* Naperville, Ill.: A. R. Allenson, 1974.

Hoyt, Charles Alva. *Witchcraft.* Carbondale: Southern Illinois University Press, 1981.

Jacob, B. *Im Namen Gottes.* Berlin: S. Calvary, 1903.

Kolenkow, A. B. "A Problem of Power: How Miracle Workers Counter Charges of Magic in the Hellenistic World." *SBL Seminar Papers,* vol. 1, pp. 105-10. Chico, Calif.: Scholars Press, 1976.

Kolenkow, A. B. "Relationship Between Miracle and Prophecy in the Greco-Roman World and Early Christianity." *ANRW* 23/2 (1980): 1470-1506.

Lea, Henry Charles. *Materials Toward a History of Witchcraft.* edited by Arthur C. Howland, 3 vols. New York: T. Yoseloff, 1957.

Luck, Georg. *Hexen und Zauberei in der Römischen Dichtung.* Zürich: Artemis Verlag, 1962.

MacMullen, R., *Enemies of the Roman Order.* Cambridge: Harvard University Press, 1966.

Nock, A. D. "Paul and the Magus." In *The Beginnings of Christianity,* edited by F. J. Foakes-Jackson and Kirsopp Lake, part I. vol. 5, pp. 164-85. London: Macmillan, 1933.

Preisendanz, K. and A. Abt. *Papyri Graecae Magical.* 2 vols. 2nd rev. edited by A. Henrichs. Stuttgart: Teubner, 1973-1974.

Remus, H. *Pagan-Christian Conflict Over Miracle in the Second Century.* Ph. D. dissertation, University of Pennsylvania, 1979.

Schoeps, Han Joachim. *Aus Frühchristlicher Zeit.* Tübingen: Mohr, 1950.

Segal, Alan F. "Hellenistic Magic: Some Questions of Definition." In *Studies*

in *Gnosticism and Hellenistic Religions*, edited by R. van den Broek and
    M. J. Vermaseren, pp. 349-75. Leiden: E. J. Brill, 1981.
Smith, K. F. "Greek and Roman Magic." *Encyclopedia of Religion and Ethics.*
    edited by James Hastings, 8. 269-89. New York: Scribners, 1962.
Smith, Morton. *Jesus the Magician;.* New York: Harper & Row, 1978.
Smith, Morton, "Pauline Worship as Seen by Pagans." *Harvard Theological
    Review* 73 (1980): 241-49.
Texidor, Javier. *The Pagan God: Popular Religion in the Greco-Roman Near
    East.* Princeton: Princeton University Press, 1977.
Thomas, Keith. *Religion and the Decline of Magic.* New York: Scribners,
    1971.
Thorndike, Lynn. *A History of Magic and Experimental Science During the
    First Thirteen Centuries of Our Era.* 2 vols. New York: Macmillan, 1929.
Zöckler, O. *Das Kreuz Christi.* Gütersloh: C. Bertelsmann, 1875.

Galen

Bowersock, G. W. *The Sophists in the Roman Empire.* Oxford: Oxford Uni-
    versity Press, 1969.
Dill, Samuel. *Roman Society from Nero to Marcus Aurelius.* London: Mac-
    millan, 1920.
Ellspermann, G. L. *The Attitude of Early Christian Latin Writers Towards
    Pagan Literature and Learning.* Washington: Catholic University of
    America Press, 1949.
Hardy, E. R. "The First Apology of Justin, the Martyr." In *Early Christian
    Fathers*, edited by C. C. Richardson, pp. 225ff. Philadelphia: Westmin-
    ster Press, 1953.
Harnack, Adolf von. *Geschichte der altchristlichen Literatur bis Eusebius.*
    Reprint, Leipzig: 1958.
Harnack, Adolf von. *History of Dogma.* Reprint, New York: Dover, 1961.
Hilgenfeld, Adolf. *Die Ketzergeschichte des Urchristentums.* Leipzig: Fues,
    1884.
Labriolle, P. De. *La réaction paienne: Étude sur la polémique antichrétienne
    du Ier au VIe siècle.* Pp. 94-97. Paris: L'Artisan du Livre, 1934.
Majno, Guido. *The Healing Hand: Man and Wound in the Ancient World,*
    Cambridge: Harvard University Press, 1975.
Sarton, G. *Galen of Pergamon.* Lawrence: University of Kansas Press, 1954.
Schöne, H. "Ein Einbruch der antiken Logik und Textkritik in die alt-
    christliche Theologie. Eusebius KG 5.28.13/19 in neuer Übertragung
    erläutert." In *Pisciculi; Studien zur Religion und Kultur des Altertums.*
    Munich: Aschendorf, 1939.
Seeberg, Reinhold. *Lehrbuch der Dogmengeschichte.* Graz: Akademische
    Druck-und Verlangsanstalt, 1953.
Walzer, R. *Galen on Jews and Christians.* London: Oxford University Press,
    1949.
Walzer, R. "Galenos." *Reallexikon für Antike und Christentum* 8 (1972):
    777-86.
Wilken, R. L. "Collegia, Philosophical Schools and Theology." In *The Cata-
    combs and the Colosseum*, edited by S. Benko and J. J. O'Rourke, pp.
    268-91. Philadelphia: Westminster Press, 1971.

Celsus

Andresen, C. *Logos und Nomos, Die Polemik des Kelsos wider das Christentum.* Arbeiten zur Kirchengeschichte 30. Berlin: Walter de Gruyter, 1955.

Bader, R. *Der Ἀληθὴς Λδγος des Kelsos.* Tübinger Beiträge zur Altertumswissenschaft 33. Stuttgart: 1940.

Barnikol, E. *Celsus und Origenes.* Texte und Untersuchungen 77. Berlin: 1961.

Benko, S. "Pagan Criticism of Christianity." In *Aufstieg und Niedergang der römischen Welt,* II/23/2, pp. 1055-118. Berlin: De Gruyter, 1980.

Den Boer, W. "Gynaeconitis: A Centre of Christian Propaganda." *Vigiliae Christianae* 4 (1950): 61-64.

Cataudella, Q. "Celso e gli Apologeti Christiani." *Nuovo Didaskaleion* 1 (1947): 28-34.

Chadwick, H. "Origen, Celsus and the Stoa." *Journal of Theological Studies* 48 (1947): 34-49.

Chadwick, H. "Origen, Celsus and the Resurrection of the Body." *Harvard Theological Review* 41 (1948): 83-102.

Chadwick, H. *Origen, Contra Celsum. Translated with an introduction and notes.* Cambridge: Cambridge University Press, 1953.

Chadwick, H. *Alexandrian Christianity.* Philadelphia: Westminster Press, 1954.

Dörrie, Heinrich. *Die Platonische Theologie des Kelsos in Ihrer Auseinandersetzung mit der Christlichen Theologie auf Grund von Origens C. Celsum.* Göttingen: Vanderhoeck and Ruprecht, 1967.

Gallagher, Eugene V. *Divine Man or Magician? Celsus and Origen on Jesus.* Chico, Calif.: Scholars Press, 1982.

Glöckner, O. *Celsi Alethes Logos.* Kleine Texte 151. Bonn: A. Marcus und A. Weber, 1924.

Harnack, Adolf von. *The Mission and Expansion of Christianity.* Reprint, Gloucester, Mass.: Peter Smith, 1972.

Jordan, H. "Celsus, die älteste umfassende Kritik des Christentums." In *Moderne Irrtümer im Spiegel der Geschichte,* edited by W. Laible. Leipzig: Dorfling und Franke, 1912.

Koch, Hal. "Origenes." *Realencyklopaedie der Classischen Altertumswissenschaft.* 18,1 (1939): 1036-59.

Labriolle, P. De. *La réaction paienne: Étude sur la polémique antichrétienne du Ier au VI siècle.* Paris: L'Artisan du Livre, 1934.

Lods, M. "Étude sur les sources juives de la polémique de Celse contre les chrétiens." *Revue d'histoire et de philosophie religieuses* 21 (1941): 1-31.

Meredith, Anthony. "Porphry and Julian Against the Christians." In *Aufstieg und Niedergang der römischen Welt,* II/23/2, pp. 1119-49. Berlin: Walter de Gruyter, 1980.

Merlan, Ph. "Celsus." *Reallexikon für Antike und Christentum* 2 (1954): 954-65.

Miura-Stange, A. *Celsus und Origenes* Zeitschrift für die neutest. Wissenschaft, Beih. 4. Giessen: Töpelman, 1926.

Muth, J. F. S. *Der Kampf des heidnischen Philosophen Celsus gegen das Christentum.* Mainz: Johannes F. S.-Kirchheim, 1899.

Pichler, Karl. *Streit um das Christentum: Der Angriff des Kelsos und die Antwort des Origens.* Regensburger Studien zur Theologie, 23. Frankfurt am Main: Peter D. Lang, 1980.

Rougier, L. *Celse ou le conflit de la civilisation antique et du Christianisme primitif.* Maitres de la Pensée antichrétienne 1. Paris: Louis-éditions du Siècle, 1925.

Whale, J. S. "Great Attacks on Christianity: Celsus." *Expository Times* 42 (1930/31): 119-24.

Wifstrand, A. "Die Wahre Lehre des Kelso." In *Bulletin de la Societe royale des lettres de Lund.* 5 (1942): 391-431.

Wilken, Robert L. "The Christians as the Romans (and Greeks) Saw Them." In *Jewish and Christian Self-Definition*, edited by E. P. Sanders, vol. 1, pp. 100-125. New York: SMC Press, 1981.

INDEX

Abonuteichos, 109, 110, 111
Abstinents, 46
Acts of the Apostles, 8, 18
Address to the Greeks (Tatian), 2
Ad nationes (Tertullian), 3
Adventures of Leucippe and Cleitophon (Achilles Tatius), 61
Aemilianus, 105
Against Celsus (Origen), 147
Agathobolus, 32
Agrippa I, 19
Alexander of Abonuteichos, 113, 117, 126; as magician, 108–13 *passim*; castigates Christians and Epicureans, 111–12
Alexander the False Prophet (Lucian), 103, 108
Alexander the Great, 36
Alexandria, 19, 23, 68, 69, 72
Aloeus, 149
Andresen, Carl, 156
Annals (Tacitus), 15
Anthesteria, festival of, 93
Anthony, Saint, 49–50
Antigone (Sophocles), 94
Antioch, 17, 65
Antiquities (Josephus), 19
Antisthenes, 38
Antoninus Pius, 1, 2, 34
Antonius, Arrius, 40
Apollinaris, 42
Apollo, 38, 109, 141, 154
Apollonius of Tyana, 108, 112, 114; accused of murder, 61; and magic, 106, 107, 125–26
Apologeticum (Tertullian), 3
Apologia (Apuleius), 104–5, 108
Apology (Melito), 144
Apostolic Constitution, 86
Apostolic Tradition (Hippolytus), 85
Apuleius, 114, 121, 130; on Eastern sects, 22–23; career of, 104; and magic, 104–6, 107–8, 126, 138n125
Aquila, 18
Archon Basileus, 93
Aristides, Aelius, 46
Aristophanes, 92, 93
Arson, 15, 16, 17, 27n33
Artemis, temple of, 37
Asceticism, 44–45, 48
Askesis. *See* Asceticism
Asklepieion, 141
Asklepios, 109, 111, 141
Athenagoras, 42; on punishment of Christians, 2–3; on Peregrinus, 37; defends Christians, 70; on holy kiss, 84; on Christianity as a philosophy, 144
Athens, 104
Atinous, 61
Attic Nights (Aulus Gellius), 35
Augustine, 91; on falsity of pagan religion, 59; on holy kiss, 83, 99n13; on salvation, 89; on magic, 106, 121, 122–23; on Eucharist, 123
Augustus, 5, 15

Bacchanalia, 11–12, 63
Baruch, 23
Bible. *See* New Testament; Old Testament; individual books
Birds, The (Aristophanes), 92
Bithynia-and-Pontus, 4, 5–7, 8
Bossuet, J. B., 97
Brahmans, 35, 38, 43
Britain, 61
Bukolion, 93
Bukoloi, 61
Bultmann, Rudolf, 94

Caecilius Natalis, Q., 54–60 *passim*, 66, 105
Calanus, 35–36, 43
Canidia, 61
Cannibalism, 56, 60, 70–71
Carpocrates, 64
Carpocratians, 64
Carthage, 62, 104
Cataline, 11
Celsus, 41, 108, 140; attacks Christianity, 46, 47, 58, 112, 145, 147–48; accuses Christians of magic, 114; on glossolalia, 117; on secrecy in Christianity, 127; on faith without proof, 157–58; distinguishes between orthodox and Gnostic Christians, 160n23
Chadwick, H., 64
Chrēstos ("good"), and identification with Christians, 2, 3, 18
Christians: punishment of, for admitting their faith, 1–4; in Bithynia-and-Pontus, 5–7; Pliny alarmed by, 10–11; parallels with Bacchanalia, 11, 12; confused with Jews, 20; Roman judgment of, 21, 22; apologists for, and Roman persecution, 24; absence of fear among, 40; parallels with Cynics, 46–49; steadfastness of, 50n2; accused of cannibalism, 70-71; question Alexander of Abonuteichos's credibility, 111–12; accused of magic, 113–14; on existence of

Christians *(cont.)*
    demons, 119–20; Galen on, 142; on
    Christianity as philosophical move-
    ment, 143–44; attacked by Celsus,
    147–56; uneducated among members,
    152–53; reassess their theology, 158
Chrysostom, 83–84
Church History (Eusebius), 42
Cicero, 11, 22
Claudius, 9, 18
Clemens, Favius, 16
Clement of Alexandria, 64, 71, 84–85,
    147, 158
Code of Justinian, 129
Codex Theodosianus, 129
Commodus, 61, 70
Conspiracy, 10–11
Constantine the Great, 32, 129
Constantinople, 48, 85
Corinthians, 9, 73, 89
Cornelian Law, 128, 130, 131
Crates, 38
Crescens, 46
Cross, sign of the, 118–19, 122
Cynics, 33–34, 36, 37, 38–39, 43, 45, 47
Cyprian, 11, 83, 120, 125
Cyril of Jerusalem, 83, 119

Damascus, 86
Daniel, 154
De Baptismo (Tertullian), 124
De civitate dei (Augustine), 121, 122
De Divinatione Daemonum (Augustine),
    121
Demetrius, 8
Demetrius (bishop of Alexandria), 72
Demetrius (proconsul of Africa), 120
Demetrius the Cynic, 33–34
Demosthenes, 105
De principiis (Origen), 89–90
De Vera Religione (Augustine), 59
De Virginiate, 116
Dialogue on Love (Plutarch), 95
Dialogue with Trypho the Jew (Justin), 70
Didache, 39, 45, 112, 117
Digest (Justinian), 128–29
Dio, Cassius, 18, 33–34
Diogenes, 34
Diogenes of Sinope, 33, 38
Dionysius, 113
Dodona, 154
Dominicans, 48–49
Domitian, 14, 16
Domitilla, 16
Druidism, 9, 61
Dudley, D. R., 48
Dumuzi, 93

Ecclesiastical History (Eusebius), 113
Egypt, 23, 93, 150
Elagabalus, 61, 62
Eleusinian rites, 112
Empedocles of Acragas, 36, 41, 43, 87–88
Encratites, 46
Ephesians, 65, 69, 88, 91
Epictetus, 154
Epictetus (Stoic philosopher), 40

Epicureans, 111
Epiphanes, 64
Epiphanius, 65–67, 68, 69
Epode 5 (Horace), 61
Eros, 92, 94
Esdras, 23
Eucharist: misinterpreted by Fronto, 60,
    62; in Phibionite practices, 69–70; in
    Christian worship, 70; holy kiss in, 86,
    97, 98; uninitiated excluded from, 112;
    magical power in, 123–24
Eusebius, 145; reports persecution of
    Christians, 42; on sacrificial practices
    of emperors, 61; on Gnostic practices,
    63–64, 71; reports promiscuity in
    churches, 86; on pagan ceremonies,
    113, 114
Eve, 69
Exorcism, 115–17

Fire of Rome, 15, 16, 28n50. *See also*
    Arson
First Apology (Justin Martyr), 2
Francis of Assisi, Saint, 48
Fronto, Marcus Cornelius, 52n44, 54, 58,
    64, 67, 72, 157; anti-Christian rhetoric,
    11; on Christian services, 60, 62; on
    libertinism among Christians, 62, 63;
    misunderstands Phibionites, 68

Galen, 146, 156, 157; on Christian faith,
    40, 144–45; early life, 140–41; medical
    research of, 141–42; on Jews and
    Christians, 142–43
Gallio, 8, 9
Gaul, 9, 42, 61, 145
Gellius, Aulius, 35
Genesis, 80, 149
Glossolalia, 117–18
Glycon, 110, 111, 112
Gnostics: libertinism among, 63–70; on
    location of divine power, 68; prac-
    tices of, imputed to Christians, 70–71;
    beliefs of, 72
Golden Ass, 22–23, 103. *See also Meta-
    morphoses*
"Gospel of the Egyptians," 72
"Gospel of the Hebrews," 72
Gratian, 59
Greece, 93

Hades, 94
Hadrian, 61, 114
Hebrew Goddess (Patai), 93
Heraclitus of Ephesus, 87, 152
Heros, 150
Herostratus, 37
Hesiod, 92, 93
Hesperius, 123
Hippolytus: condemns Tatian, 46; safe-
    guards holy kiss, 85; on magicians, 110;
    on Carpocratians, 115; on power of the
    cross, 119; on Eucharist, 123; and *disci-
    plina arcani*, 127
Historia Augusta, 61
Holy Communion. *See* Eucharist
Holy Spirit, 82–83, 98, 124

Horace, 61

Ignatius of Antioch, 45, 123
Inanna, 93
Incarnation, 151–52
Irenaeus, 91, 157; on superiority of Christianity, 59; on Gnostic libertinism, 63; on Carpocratians, 64, 115; distinguishes Christians from heretics, 71; on universal salvation, 89; on Christian miracles, 115–16; on Eucharist, 123

Jerusalem, 19
Jesus, 108; teachings of, interpreted by Phibionites, 68–70; conception of, 83; kiss of, and Holy Spirit, 83; unification through, 88, 89; power in name of, 118, 121–22, 135n59; Celsus criticizes, 149–52
Jews: hostility toward Christians, 8, 20, 71; and arson, 17; expulsions from Rome, 17–18; and Christ as Messiah, 18; clashes among, 19; struggles against Rome, 19, 23; worship one god, 56; accusations by pagans against, 60; sacred marriage in lore of, 93–94; Galen on, 142–43; Celsus attacks, 148
John, 69, 96
Josephus, 18, 19
Judas of Galilee, 19
Jude, 73
Judea, 19–20
Julius Caesar, 14
Justin Martyr, 42, 145, 158; on punishment of Christians, 1, 2; combines Christianity and philosophy, 46, 144; on Jews, 60; on the Gnostics, 63; defends Christians, 67; distinguishes Christians from heretics, 70, 71; on kiss in Eucharist, 81; on Christian exorcism, 115; on power of the cross, 118; and *disciplina arcani*, 127
Justinian, Code of, 129
Juvenal, 11, 21

Kiss, holy, 81–82, 86, 97–98

Lactantius, 106, 113, 114, 119, 121
Law, Roman, magic in, 128–30
Libertinism, 63–70
Licinius, 32, 86
Little Labyrinth, The, 145–46, 158
Livy, 11, 62
Lollianos, 61
Love, in Christian theology, 95–97
Lucian of Samosata, 30, 45, 103; criticizes Peregrinus, 37–39; criticizes Christians, 39; beliefs of, 43–44; on Cynics, 47; on Indian self-immolation, 51n25; on Alexander of Abonuteichos, 108–11; on exorcism, 113
Luke, 82–83
Lyons, 42, 70
Lysimachus, 36

MacMullen, Ramsey, 106, 107

Magic: Apuleius accused of practicing, 104–6; allegedly practiced by Christians, 113–14; role of, in Christian practices, 127–28, 131–32; in Roman law, 128–30
Manichaeans, 59
Marcianus, 129
Marcus Aurelius, 54, 70, 144, 145; attitude toward Christians, 41–43; advised by Alexander of Abonuteichos, 110; contrasts Stoics and Christians, 145
Mark, 113
Mary, 69, 83
Matthew, 47
Maxentius, 61
Maximus, 48
Meal, common, at Christian gatherings, 12, 13
Meditations (Marcus Aurelius), 41
Melito, 42, 144
Mesopotamia, 93
Metamorphoses (Apuleius), 103–4, 107
Mezentius, 105
Miltiades, 42
Minucius Felix, 11, 54–58, 157
Monasticism, 48
Montanism, 147
Moses, 88, 108, 148, 149
Mucianus, 33–34
Murder, ritual, 56, 60, 61–62

Neo-Platonism, 91
Nero, 9, 15, 17, 20, 112, 130
New Testament, 65, 72, 130; Christian ideal in, 44–45; condemns licentiousness, 73; holy kiss in, 81, 82–83; criticized by Celsus, 149–52
Nicolaitans, 65, 68–69, 140
Nicopolis, 40
Night meetings, of Christians, 10, 12
Nygren, Anders, 91

Oath (*sacramentum*), 12–13
Octavian Augustus. *See* Augustus
Octavius (Minucius Felix), 104, 157
Octavius Januarius, 54, 58, 105
Old Testament, 65, 69, 148–49
Olympia, 35, 36, 37, 38
Olympic games, 35, 36–37
Olympus, 35, 37
On the Death of Peregrinus (Lucian), 37
On the Prescription of Heretics (Tertullian), 146–47
Origen, 147, 156, 158; on Christian suffering, 41; castration of, 47; accuses Jews of false rumors, 71; on unification with God, 89–90; on glossolalia, 117; on exorcism, 118; on magic, 122; on secrecy in Christianity, 127; reply to Celsus, 157
Orpheus, 95, 154

Paedagogus (Clement), 84–85
Pagan, definition of, 25n9
Panarion (Epiphanius), 65–66
Parium, 30, 32, 37
Patai, Raphael, 93

Paul, 10, 40, 67, 69, 91, 157; as apostle, 8, 45; admonishes Jewish troublemakers, 19; chastises Gnostics, 73; on holy kiss, 79, 81; on unification through God, 88–89; on love, 95; opposes destructive magic, 130–31

Peregrinus Proteus, 107, 108; life of, 30; exiled and embraces Christianity, 30–31; imprisoned, 31; excommunicated by church, 32; in Rome, 34; in Greece, 34–36; suicide, 36–37, 43; as a Christian ascetic, 44, 45, 49

Perella, J. J., 97

Pergamum, 140–41, 145

Peter, 67, 73, 79, 81

Phibionites: practices described by Epiphanius, 65–67, 68; condemned by other Gnostics, 67–68; theology, 68–70; as typical Gnostics, 72

Philip, 45, 69

Philostratus, 107, 125–26

Phoinikika (Lollianos), 61

Plato, 88, 120

Platonism, 91, 144

Plea for the Christians (Athenagoras), 70

Pliny the Elder, 4, 9

Pliny the Younger, 14, 20, 21, 23, 24, 63, 125; career, 4–5; on Christians in Bithynia-and-Pontus, 5–10 *passim*; alarmed by Christian meetings, 12; leniency toward Christians, 13; associates Christians with magic, 127

Plotinus, 90–91

Plutarch, 11, 95, 125

Polycarp, 4, 10, 43

Pontus, 112

Poppaea, 20

Porsenna, 41

Priscilla, 18

Psalms, 69, 97

Ps. Clementine Epistle on Virginity, 85

Pseudo-Clementine Homilies, 120

Pythagoras, 106, 107

Pythagoreans, 144

Qabbalah, 93–94

Refutation on All Heresies (Hippolytus), 110

Resurrection, 151, 152

Romans, 89

Rome, 104; Bacchanalia in, 11–12; fire of, 15; confuses Jews and Christians, 20; religion in, 21–22; views Christianity as a superstition, 22–23; suspicious of Christianity because of Jewish origin, 23; persecution of Christians because of their name, 24; religious liberty in, 59; Galen in, 145

Runaways, The (Lucian), 38, 47

Sallust, 11

Scaevola, Gaius Mucius, 41

Second Apology (Justin Martyr), 1

Senate, 12, 61

Sentences of Paulus, 128, 130

Shema, 88

Simon (Gnostic), 63–64

Smith, Morton, 21, 113, 117, 127

Socrates, 58, 105, 120

Song of Songs, 96, 97, 102n72

Sophocles, 94, 95

Speaking in tongues. *See* Glossolalia

Stoics, 144, 145

Stromateis (Clement), 64

Suetonius, 23, 63; career and works of, 14; on Claudius's expulsion of the Jews, 18; on Christianity, 20–21; on exclusions from Eleusinian rites, 112

Suicide, 36–37

Sulla, laws of, 128–29

Symmachus, 59

Syria, 62, 85, 93

Tacitus, 20, 22, 23, 63, 130; career, 14; encounters Christianity in Asia, 15; on Jews and Christians, 16; associates Christians with magic, 127

Talmud, 94

Tatian, 2; on Cynics, 34; on Peregrinus, 37; founds Christian sect, 46; defends Christians, 70; on demons, 120

Tatius, Achilles, 61

Tertullian, 9, 40, 42, 157, 158; on punishment of Christians, 3–4; on Jewish hostility toward Christians, 20; on Christian concern for prisoners, 31–32; on Peregrinus, 37; on Christian contempt of death, 41; on Christian occupations, 47; on superiority of Christianity, 59; on ritual murder, 61, 62; on charges against Christians, 70–71; on heretics, 85; on kiss among pagans, 84; on Christian exorcism, 116, 119–20; on sign of the cross, 118, 119; on baptism, 124–25; on pagan suspicions about Christians, 126–27; attacks heresy, 146–47

Theagenes, 35

Theodotus, 145–46

Tiberius, 16, 18

Tiberius Alexander, 19

Timothy, 73

Titus, 14, 34

Tolstoy, Leo, 49

Trajan, 5, 23, 31; treatment of Christians, 7, 13

True Word (Celsus), 58, 108, 147, 156, 157, 158

Twelve Tables, 11, 12, 128

Universalism, 86–90

Valentinian II, 59

Valerian, 61, 113

Verus, Lucius, 54

Vespasian, 14, 33–34

Victor, 145

Vienne, 42

Xenophanes, 86–87

Zeus, 38–39, 154

Zohar, 94